BODILY HARM

BODILY HARM

The Breakthrough Treatment Program for Self-Injurers

KAREN CONTERIO AND

WENDY LADER, PH.D.,

with Jennifer Kingson Bloom

HYPERION

New York

This book represents a set of general principles and a philosophy; it should be considered as a reference source only and is not intended to substitute for an individual's medical and/or psychological treatment. It is not the equivalent of, nor is it intended as a replacement for, any professionally supervised treatment. All matters regarding your health require medical supervision. Consult your physician before adopting the suggestions in this book. The authors, S.A.F.E. Alternatives, and the publisher disclaim any liability arising directly or indirectly from the use of this book.

All names and identifying characteristics of patients have been changed.

Copyright © 1998 Karen Conterio, Wendy Lader, and
Jennifer Kingson Bloom

S.A.F.E. Alternatives is a trademark of S.A.F.E. Alternatives L.L.C.

Library of Congress Cataloging-in-Publication Data
Conterio, Karen
   Bodily harm : the breakthrough healing program for self-injurers / Karen Conterio and Wendy Lader, with Jennifer Kingson Bloom.
      p.   cm.
   Includes bibliographical references and index.
   1. Self-mutilation.   I. Lader, Wendy.   II. Bloom, Jennifer Kingson.   III. Title.
RC552.S4C66   1998
616.85'82—dc21

98-38171
CIP

FIRST EDITION

10 9 8 7 6 5 4 3 2 1

CONTENTS

Part One   BODILY HARM

Part Two   THE S.A.F.E.
ALTERNATIVES®
PROGRAM

A MESSAGE FOR SELF-INJURERS: YOU ARE NOT ALONE

This book is for everyone who is concerned with the phenomenon of self-injury: family members, therapists, medical professionals, policy makers. But it is primarily for you, the self-injuring reader.

You are likely to feel hopeless and desperate, like your problem is yours alone, something nobody else shares or understands. You may feel you walk around every day with an embarrassing secret too painful to discuss with anybody, one that will never go away. We want to show you that there is a different path, a more meaningful and productive life, that you can pursue.

Getting from here to there won't be easy. You are in for some very hard work. Breaking a deeply ingrained and highly comforting pattern of behavior can be one of life's greatest challenges, but it is no greater than many of the other challenges we face as we mature to adulthood.

Wouldn't it be easy if someone else could just take responsibility for you, take charge of your life, keep you safe from yourself? Wouldn't it be nice if someone just could take *care* of you, to show you how much they care *about* you? Unfortunately, that isn't a realistic option for an adult or growing teenager. Most people who let others take over in this way wind up feeling resentful at being coddled like a child. There is nobody on earth who can, or will, save you from yourself. You are going to have to do it for yourself—but not by yourself. There is a wealth of resources available to you, and many people who want to help if you will let them.

Remember, getting "help" doesn't mean finding a savior. It means finding people and resources—like this book—who can show you how to attain a healthier way of life. Your job is to let them in.

"I couldn't find anyone anymore to take responsibility for me, so I came to the S.A.F.E. program," writes Rosa G., one of our former patients. "Today, I take with me a new beginning. I have direction. I have a list of alternatives to use instead of self-injury. I have a desire to want to use those alternatives. Sometimes this 'feeling' stuff is awful, but I'm more alive than I ever was."

Right now, hurting yourself probably feels very soothing to you. We sometimes call self-injury the "wounding embrace," because people use it to harm and comfort themselves at the same time. The razor blade takes the place of a hug, a compliment, a mother's kiss. Something so nurturing and so powerful may seem impossible to give up.

You *can* give it up, but you must agree to work diligently, and you must be willing to admit your secret to select outsiders: a journal, a therapist, a friend. You must reach out. As Rosa put it, "Reach out even if every fiber yells at you not to." The bottom line is that self-injury is a *choice*, and you can *choose* not to injure just the same way that you choose to injure. You never have to put another scar on your body if you don't want to.

We will talk to you about the options you face, the emotions you feel, and the prospects in front of you. Our patients—those in the process of recovery and those who have seen the better life that comes from abandoning self-injury—will talk to you too. We hope to show you that you can do it, and the rewards are worth it.

How will you know I'm hurting
If you cannot see my pain?
To wear it on my body
Tells what words cannot explain.
— C. Blount

BODILY HARM

INTRODUCTION

In 1985 we founded the first treatment program in the nation specifically for people who physically harm themselves. Our program is called S.A.F.E. Alternatives, and our acronym—"Self Abuse Finally Ends"—has proven true for hundreds of patients we have treated.

Over the years, we have seen an alarming rise in the number of people who feel compelled to handle life's frustrations by wounding their bodies. They use razor blades, fire, knives, and countless other items—usually household tools turned into weapons. The creativity our patients show in finding ways to hurt and deform their bodies is astounding, but more important is the poignant way in which they are all alike: they are struggling with inner conflicts that seem too vast to cope with.

Our many years of experience with this little-understood population has led us to develop a comprehensive program to help self-injurers stop their behavior and learn more successful coping strategies. It is this program, unique among those we know, which we will describe in this book. Our hope is to uncloak the mystery that surrounds self-injury so patients, their families, their therapists, and others in the medical community feel less frightened and threatened by the behavior. We want self-injurers—also called self-mutilators, or even, in slang, "cutters"—to use this book as the centerpiece of their treatment, and for their doctors and families to use it to aid them in their recovery. We strive to teach everyone concerned with this growing problem all the knowledge we have gained and how to apply it. We also want to impart a strong message of hope.

One of us began our counseling career in the addictions field, and one is a psychologist who specializes in women's issues. (Though self-injury is not exclusively a women's issue, at least 90 percent of S.A.F.E. patients are women.) When we began working with self-injurers in the early 1980s, people wondered if we would find enough patients to fill our program. Today, the problem has exploded, turned mainstream, and self-injury is being called "the new anorexia." As sad as we are to see how many people struggle with this syndrome, we celebrate the fact that the public is growing increasingly aware of it, with the hope that public education leads to greater understanding of the behavior and less of a stigma. We also hope that people will come to view self-injury as we do, as a maladaptive coping strategy that can be replaced with healthier ones. Just as drugs, alcohol, and other harmful habits can be halted by people with courage and commitment, so can self-injury be overcome by people who get the right therapeutic help and learn more effective ways of handling stress.

Healing isn't easy. It requires continuous self-reflection and self-examination. The reasons people self-mutilate are often the same as the reasons people binge on food, starve themselves, or drink or take drugs excessively: they are sad, lonely, depressed, angry, frightened, isolated, or any combination of these.

As with any compulsion, overcoming self-injury takes a great deal of work, and deep delving into the sufferer's psychological motivations. We strongly recommend that self-injurers who are using this book employ a psychotherapist as part of treatment, and we will explain how to find one who can offer the most help. For therapists, the book will also recommend intervention techniques that we have found useful.

When patients first come to us, they consider their problem a shameful secret, one that would make anybody recoil in horror. Using the various therapeutic tools we will describe, we aim to show sufferers that self-injury is a serious psychological problem, but not an indictment of the person who has it. Just as we are empathic to our patients and the reasons for their suffering, so do we hope to show self-injurers how they can have compassion for themselves.

To people unfamiliar with self-injury, the behavior may seem too bizarre, upsetting, or freakish to comprehend. We will attempt to prove otherwise. We could not go into work every day and interact with dozens of self-injurers if we did not know that they could get better, that their lives could be radically improved, and that we could be part of the solution. Self-injurers can and do recover—though usually not under the auspices of the traditional medical system.

Though the media and the medical community appear to have just "discovered" self-injury, the phenomenon has been documented as early as biblical times. Mark 5:5 refers to a demon-possessed man who "always, night and day, was crying and cutting himself with stones." In the Middle Ages a religious sect known as the "flagellants" wandered through Europe, lashing themselves with cats-o'-nine-tails, attempting to atone for society's sins and to lift the great plague ravaging the continent. Manifestations of self-injury—as ritual, rite of passage, or to appease angry gods—have existed in virtually every culture and every era.

Just as our national preoccupation with thinness and fitness appeared to give rise to anorexia and bulimia over the last two decades, so have a complex mélange of cultural and social factors helped bring on the rising tide of self-injury. The syndrome has taken the late 1990s by storm: its grip on schools, college campuses, jails, and other sectors of society continues to tighten, and appears to be leaving a lasting impression.

In Hollywood, celebrities like Roseanne and Johnny Depp have said in interviews that they struggled with the problem. Princess Diana of Wales, before her premature death, said in a television interview that she had cut herself deliberately several times. A new biography of Alfred Kinsey, the sex researcher, reveals that he too engaged in self-injurious activities, including an attempt to circumcise himself.

Thirteen years ago when we founded S.A.F.E., self-injury was virtually unheard of. Back then our patients would have routinely been categorized as suicidal, psychotic, or manic-depressive. Today our phones ring off the hook with people who are concerned about their behavior, and we could not possibly begin to admit even a fraction of the patients who want to enroll in our program. The demand is there, but supply of treatment programs is frighteningly limited.

How did such a seemingly curious behavior grow so quickly over such a short period of time? Clearly, we believe, contagion must have played some role. Media exposure of the problem—while fantastically helpful in getting self-injurers the care they need—may also inadvertently give people ideas they may not have had before. Music groups are now expressing themes of self-injury, and even popular television shows like *Beverly Hills, 90210* and *Seventh Heaven* are giving exposure to the problem. More significantly, people tend to take their cues from one another—particularly teens, who are desperate to fit in with their contemporaries—and we hear more and more reports of self-injurers who picked up the behavior from a classmate, a sibling, or someone else they know. We must add, however, that it is not the typical, well-adjusted adolescent or adult who is likely to run with the role model of self-harm. Rather, it is the psychologically vulnerable person who may seize on something she views as a fad, and fashion it into a strategy to deal with preexisting agonies.

THE RISE OF YOUTHFUL SELF-INJURERS

Being "tough" and rebellious have always been hallmarks of the adolescent years, when youths latch on to cultural trends they think will annoy their stodgy parents. The 1960s and 1970s had the rumpled "hippie" look, which seemed threatening at the time, but in retrospect seems to have conveyed a benign message of peace and harmony. Heavy drug use was the downside. The 1980s featured a number of different "looks," most notably the sexed-up paradigms of the Valley Girl and the Material Girl. While those ideals appalled traditionalists by emphasizing the sex appeal of young girls, the trends did place value on taking care of one's body and appearance. Indeed, girls used to spend hours finding just the right outfit, jewelry, hairstyle, and makeup to go to a Madonna concert.

The 1990s have brought us grunge. We believe one reason self-injury has taken such an insidious hold among teenagers is the disheveled look that our youth culture reveres: the super-baggy pants, ripped T-shirts, messy hair, and tattooed and pierced skin that seems to tell the world, "I don't feel good about myself."

When teenagers cultivate this "look" and attitude, it seems less of a stretch for them to begin injuring themselves. They are already accustomed to using external appearance to communicate their identity struggles; indeed, the body and its adornments seem to have become the repository for all their dilemmas about life and relationships. At S.A.F.E. we often see teenagers who have carved actual words into their bodies, vulgarities or disparaging remarks about themselves and their bodies. *Fat* and *ugly* are the two most common.

Grunge does not disappear after people work their way through adolescence. Instead, it transmutes into what we have labeled the "culture of ugly," in which people in their late teens and early twenties deliberately festoon themselves in ways that not only repel their seniors but also many contemporaries. Look at any college campus or community of young, normal women, and what do you see? Women dyeing their hair pink or green, wearing head-to-toe black with clunky shoes, nose rings, and belly button rings. The droopy clothes mask their figures and sexuality; the makeup and accessories are meant to shock, to repulse. We see this "uglification" trend as part of the large-scale anxiety and backlash against the sexual pressures placed on our youth.

Advertising, television, movies, even the playful comments of adults, all seem to push children to behave sexually at an earlier age. Not necessarily to have sex—even though puberty seems to come on younger and younger with each generation—but to understand the sexual tension between the genders and to behave accordingly. Uglification, in our view, is an unconscious effort by young people to protect themselves against premature sexuality. Self-injury is a pathological extreme of this.

The task of the adolescent is to leave childhood and begin forging an independent, adult identity. Rites of passage help to define the process and guide the metamorphosis. As the number of structured rites of passage we observe as a society dwindle, some teens are filling the void with self-injury. The behavior becomes a token of independence and symbol of separation.

If self-injury is a rite of passage, it is most certainly one designed to command maximum attention. It is at once a form of cultural affiliation with people who feel disenfranchised and "ugly," and at the same time a firm tweak at anyone who is supposed to care about the child.

Janelle Hart, a staff psychologist at S.A.F.E., often finds that adolescents become more frenzied in their attempts to communicate with their parents, "upping the ante" with more and more visibly self-damaging behavior. Some of them graduate from eating disorders to self-injury, with the twin goals of gaining a response from adults and pushing people away with angry and defiant gestures. Dr. Hart describes the attitude of the rebellious and self-injuring adolescent this way: " 'See my pink hair?' 'How do you like the safety pin in my ear?' It's a further way of being offensive."

Dr. Hart comments wryly that behaviors considered outrageous by the adult world ten years ago don't even produce a blink anymore, and that her adolescent patients are forever in search of something that horrifies. She said, "In the 1960s you could be shocking by wearing long hair and wearing grungy clothes. Today, that doesn't shock."

Our teenage patients often complain that practically nothing they do or say rises to the level of their parents' attention, so what does it matter if they self-injure? Many adult self-injurers have similar feelings about the people in their lives, and the lengths they must go to to capture the interest of others.

ADULT WOMEN

Like the spate of housewives in the 1950s who became alcoholics from the boredom of being stay-at-home moms in suburbia, today's women are turning to self-injury to cope with the mass of pressures facing them.

First, there is the myth of the Superwoman. A woman has to do everything, from working and earning money to tending house and kids. Study after study shows that even after hundreds of millions of women have entered the workplace, men are not picking up the slack in household tasks. By and large, the "privilege" of working has simply added to a woman's burden rather than replacing one set of tasks with another. Moreover, the working woman's psychic grievances are exacerbated by the string of cutely labeled workplace phenomena that hold her back: the "Mommy Track" and the "Glass Ceiling."

Sometimes it seems that women can't win in today's cultural milieu. Despite the progress made by women's lib and other factors, anything female is still denigrated as "less than" male. Despite social and economic changes that have given women more financial independence, emotional and attitudinal changes have lagged. Women are still expected to be responsible for the brunt of domestic duties and are belittled if they cannot do that *as well as* hold a job. Men don't question this arrangement, since child rearing in our culture is seen as women's work. Raising children is viewed as an easy task with low importance. This attitude may be showing itself in the increase in self-destructive behaviors among our children—and among older women, whose voices are stifled even as more is expected of them.

CULTURAL FORCES

We are often asked what it is about our culture that might foster self-injury, and we generally point to several phenomena:

- *Society is becoming increasingly disenfranchised.* The extended community—grandparents, aunts, uncles, neighbors—are seldom available for day-to-day support or to help parents care for children. This is especially true among Caucasians, from which the statistical preponderance of self-injurers emanate. Relatives can live hundreds of miles from one another. People move frequently, making relationships with friends and neighbors more transient.
- *The collapse of the extended family and increasing isolation of the individual has given people—especially children—fewer confidants in times of difficulty.* The modern child may grow up relying very little on words, verbal expression, and the conversational exploration of her thoughts and feelings. She may depend more on "doing" rather than "telling" or "saying." Technology has exacerbated this tendency, sending us all around on our own in our personal motorized driving pods or sitting by ourselves in front of our private liquid crystal display computer screens.
- *Our culture increasingly emphasizes the "quick fix," immediate gratification.* Even fast-food meals are too slow and television commercials too long for us. By extension, any feeling that is experienced as uncomfortable must be attended to instantly, given "voice" through some sort of action or behavior that offers immediate, palpable relief. Anyone who feels anxious or depressed knows to reach for an over-the-counter pill, a drink, or a package of chips.
- *We have become a nation of addicts and "a-holics."* Sexual perversions, kleptomania, incest, compulsive shopping, gambling, and self-injury are all statistically on the rise in the last two decades. Anyone who

watches daytime talk shows might well believe that is has become chic to be considered "dysfunctional" in some way—a word that was scarcely on our radar screens a decade ago.

■ *We live in a relentlessly body-focused culture where appearance and presentation are all-important, and where we are encouraged by cultural imperatives to remain "on the surface of things."* The media saturates us with messages about how we can "feel better about ourselves" by modifying the shape, contours, or appearances of our bodies. We are beckoned to jump on the bandwagon of the "fitness craze": to diet; exercise vigorously; change our faces and bone structure through cosmetic surgery; change our hair color at the salon and skin color in the tanning booth; and use a bewildering array of lotions, creams, and ointments to heighten our beauty. Adornment and decoration of the body are our culture's primary means of self-expression: walk into any roomful of adolescent girls and you will hear the latest on fashion, body art, piercing, and tattooing.

■ *Persistent and debilitating gender biases are driving young women to more severe emotional extremes than ever before.* Self-injury is just one example of the measures girls will take to express their frustration, fear, and anger. Mary Pipher makes this point in her immensely popular bestseller, *Reviving Ophelia*, and blames the predicament on our "girl-harming" culture.

■ *As more parents work outside the home, latchkey children have become the norm, after they outgrow day care, baby-sitters, and nannies.* Children are increasingly being reared by veritable strangers rather than family members, and as they approach adolescence, children are literally raising themselves, looking toward their equally clueless peers for guidance.

These observations are not meant as an indictment of working mothers or child-care arrangements. On the contrary, we more often see self-injurers whose mothers did *not* work. The point here is that families are becoming atomized, each person fending for himself or herself, and that the acceptance and understanding of this is pervading our culture. Community activities and neighborhood spirit are being replaced by microwave meals for one and solitary pastimes like computer games and the Internet.

People who are isolated either physically or mentally tend to turn inward. When those people are fragile to begin with or have led a life of emotional deprivation, solitude can seem too great a burden. It becomes easier to understand why they feel compelled to use their bodies as bulletin boards for the frustrations and feelings that have gone ignored.

THE SIGNIFICANCE OF BREAKING SKIN

As long as human beings have existed, they have used the skin to communicate identity, status, and any number of other things. Many cultures—primitive and modern—have used tribal markings to unite their community and imbue a sense of belonging. For instance, native American tribes developed elaborate rituals of facial decorations, markings, and cuttings; Hindu women denote their faith with a red dot on the forehead; various African peoples are known for their distinctive tattooing, scarification, and face-painting practices.

We see this phenomenon at work today in the United States, where gang members in inner cities boast their affiliation through tattoos, distinctive clothing, body piercings, and other cosmetic means. This culture has spread to the mainstream, with middle-class suburban children trying to emulate the hip look of the ghetto.

Among other segments of society, body art—tattoos, piercings—can advertise anything from one's political leanings to one's sexual orientation, much the way a bumper sticker does on a car. Our patients often say their scars tell their life's history. Each scar represents a particularly important life event that the patient does not want to forget. One of our patients described it to a reporter for the *New York Times* this way: "I've got physical scars. . . . It shows that my life isn't easy. I can look at different scars and think, 'Yeah, I know what happened,' so it tells a story. I'm afraid of them fading."

We are inspired every day by our patients' determination and success. We hope you will take away the same message.

Part One

BODILY HARM

Chapter One

WHAT IS SELF-INJURY?

A shley P. is sixteen. When her father, a chronic alcoholic, screams at her in a drunken rage and her mother stands idly by, she retreats to her bedroom and begins cutting her arms with a razor blade. An accomplished high school student, Ashley calls self-injury "my friend I can turn to at any point in the day." It is easier and more comfortable, she says, to pierce her skin and draw blood than to confront the people and emotions that anguish her.

Donna W. is forty-six. She was twenty years old when her second husband, a police officer, began having extramarital affairs, telling Donna that she no longer appealed to him because she had gained weight and cut her hair. Donna began raking the skin inside her arms with her fingernails; soon she was using a sharpened screwdriver.

Donna, who holds a responsible job as an X-ray technician, calls herself "weak and insecure," and "ugly and fat." Though she has succeeded professionally and raised two children—one of them a college senior—she feels terrible about herself, constantly envious of people who come across as friendly and open. Four years ago she began wounding herself more seriously, using harsher implements and inflicting the jabs on the tops of her thighs. Donna feels numb to the pain, which, she says, lets her blot out her even more searing memories and

emotions. She writes in her journal: "I am afraid to give up this behavior, because I think it somehow keeps me feeling in control."

Donna and Ashley are not freaks. They are ordinary people you and
I encounter every day. They are also representative of an exploding
population—many of them women—who use violence against themselves to handle life's emotions.

Some turn to alcohol, narcotics, or other destructive substances.
Others binge, purge, or starve themselves. For more and more people,
however, comfort comes from the razor blades, knives, scissors, and
other household implements that they use to carve physical expressions
of their anguish on their skin. By most accounts, self-injury is rapidly
displacing eating disorders as the most serious mental and physical
health problem confronting our society.

What is self-injury? We define it as the deliberate mutilation of the
body or a body part, not with the intent to commit suicide but as a
way of managing emotions that seem too painful for words to express.
It can include cutting the skin or burning it, or bruising oneself through
a premeditated accident. It can mean scratching the skin until it
bleeds, or interfering with the healing of wounds. In more extreme
cases, self-injurers break their own bones, amputate their own digits,
eat harmful substances, or inject their bodies with toxins.

Leaving aside the more dramatic examples, there are aspects of the
syndrome that are prevalent among "normal" people and among people
with milder disturbances. Self-injury encompasses a range of behaviors,
some of them not so distant from the stress-busting strategies of the
healthy population. How many people do you know—yourself included—who bite their nails, pick at acne lesions, or scratch mosquito
bites until they bleed? How many people have gone on starvation diets
to fit into a certain pair of pants? Where does one draw the line between the harmless things that people do to their bodies and those
that merit serious attention?

TYPES OF SELF-INJURY

Cutting and burning the skin are the most common forms of self-
injury. Some sufferers scratch or "draw" delicate traceries of weblike
lines in their flesh, using razor blades, knives, shards of glass, or other

sharp instruments—even a pen cap, bottle cap, or credit card will do. Relatives who try to stop self-injurers from harming themselves by taking away sharp objects are often surprised to find how resourceful people are, and how they can turn anything into a weapon in a pinch.

Self-injurers' skin cutting ranges in intensity, from superficial nicks to deep gouges. Some people make rounded punctures in their skin, using sharply pointed objects. Arms and legs are common targets, as are breasts, stomachs, thighs, and genitals. Many self-injurers begin by cutting on parts of their bodies that people are unlikely to see; then find they can no longer control themselves and cut in more obvious places. Sometimes they carve words into the skin—like *fat* and *ugly*—to project their feelings about themselves to the world; they pick at the scabs and reinsert the knife when the skin under these words begins to heal. More often than not, they wear long sleeves and long pants to disguise the carnage.

Many people progress from cutting to burning, finding that they need to wound themselves more severely to get the same relief, the same "high" from the pain. Some people vary their cutting implements—razors, artist's knives, sharp glass, nails—and some rely on a single tool. About 75 percent of injurers use more than one method. Self-injury can include:

- Cutting skin
- Hitting oneself
- Extracting hair to excess
- Head banging
- Scratching to excess
- Biting oneself
- Burning oneself
- Interfering with the healing of wounds
- Breaking bones
- Chewing the lips, tongue, or fingers
- Eye enucleation (removal)
- Amputation of limbs, breasts, digits, genitals
- Facial skinning
- Ingesting sharp or toxic objects

Many injurers develop a set routine or pattern of self-injury that they plan for and engage in regularly. Others perform the acts more randomly, whenever difficult feelings beset them. Self-injurers tell us they hide razor blades in their school lockers, nightstands, and glove compartments so as never to be "without" when the urge strikes; some say they must resort to punching walls and banging their heads on the floor when they do not have instant access to a potential weapon.

We have seen patients commit the most frightening acts against themselves. One woman put fish hooks in her vagina, and another put a knife there—and kept it there—thinking she might stave off rape. One patient, a nurse, injected herself with the HIV virus and later died of AIDS; another patient who had amputated her big toe was eager to show us the stump. One woman you will meet in this book injected urine in her ears and smeared her burns and cuts with her own excrement to infect them. Another woman—also a professional nurse—eats cat feces and smears them on her face and up her nose. She has also soaked her jeans in gasoline and set herself on fire.

Self-injurers hold a variety of views about their behavior. Many agree that it is damaging, but feel unable to stop because of the comfort it provides. Some are proud of their "achievements" and the artistry they believe their injuries demonstrate. The message they think they are sending is, "I can take anything—I'm the toughest person around." They flaunt their wounds as battle scars and symbols of the emotional war they have been fighting with the outside world. The distortions in their thinking are complex and multifaceted; a patient will come to our program with her limb nearly amputated and tell us, "I'm not as bad as the rest." On the other hand, some patients say they are ashamed of their scars and wish they could magically undo the vandalism on their body.

Self-injurers whose behavior rises to the attention of the medical system are given several diagnostic labels: major depression, psychosis, multiple personality disorder, bipolar disorder (manic depression), or borderline personality disorder. The last category is by far the most commonly diagnosed syndrome. "Borderlines" are characterized by their rapid mood swings, difficulty maintaining friendships, emotional sensitivity, and impulse problems. Because they have trouble regulating their emotions, many are compulsive gamblers, shoplifters, or drinkers.

These diagnoses may or may not be accurate, depending on the individual self-injurer. They reflect the medical and psychiatric community's struggle to understand this frightening and mystifying behavior by putting it in a better-understood conceptual context. But what we have come to recognize is that there is a group of self-injurers who have never come to the attention of the medical community, nor sought out mental health intervention. Because they are able to work and live normally, these self-injurers have remained largely hidden within society; any efforts to help them have usually focused narrowly on the medical treatment of specific wounds, and not on the holistic care of the person and his or her psychological problems. Their symptoms are a shade different from the more severely troubled self-injurers: though self-injury may consume their thoughts, the behavior has not taken complete grasp of their everyday existence, and the injuries they sustain are less lethal and grisly. One of our staff psychologists, Janelle Hart, has identified hundreds of these sufferers through outreach on the Internet. While their problems may seem less severe than those of the patients we treat, we believe these people make up the bulk of the silent "epidemic" of self-injury.

"AN ACT OF SELF-HELP"

While some self-injurers come from relatively healthy homes, the vast majority grew up under harrowing circumstances. Many were physically, sexually, or emotionally abused, or had parents who ignored their basic needs. Many are children of alcoholics or mentally ill people who neglected and tormented them. Most grew up in rigid households where expressions of emotion were quashed and religious or military-style thinking ruled the day, or where their every move was scrutinized and criticized by a hovering and intrusive parent. On the other end of the spectrum, some self-injurers grew up in homes where there was little or no parental guidance or emotional involvement.

The "typical" self-injurer, if there is one, would be a white, middle-class woman of above-average intelligence who began cutting herself in adolescence. She has low self-esteem and may suffer from bouts of depression. She has trouble relating to people and forming intimate relationships. Despite her smarts and education, she has an extremely hard time articulating her thoughts and feelings and a seemingly insatiable need for love and acceptance. Because she did not internalize positive nurturing skills from her parents, she does not take very good care of herself and feels that she is too bad a person to "deserve" comforts or luxuries.

Having acquired no truly adaptive, internal abilities to soothe herself or control distress, the self-injurer comes to rely on action—not thoughts, fantasies, or words—to gain relief from any uncomfortable feelings or thoughts. Ironically, her goal is to put an end to the pain and suffering she feels in her head, even if it means her body bears the brunt of an attack. Her emotions reach a fever pitch; she feels she is going to "explode" if she does not release tension; she barely feels her body is connected to herself. The razor pierces the skin and the blood flows out, carrying with it all the poison, rage, and self-loathing that the sufferer feels inside. The sight of the gash and the numb sensation that surrounds it bring comfort and relief; she feels "whole" again, grounded in reality.

Strange as it may sound to the uninitiated, self-injury represents a frantic attempt by someone with low coping skills to "mother herself." Operating without a paradigm of parental care, she feels alone and terrified, with no hope that a soothing presence will come "make it all better." Bodily care has been transformed into bodily harm; the razor blade becomes the wounding caregiver, a cold but available substitute for the embrace, kiss, or loving touch that she truly desires.

"Habitual self-mutilation may best be thought of as a purposeful, if morbid, act of self-help which enables the subject to reestablish contact with the world," writes Armando R. Favazza, a professor and associate chairman of the department of psychiatry at the University of Missouri–Columbia School of Medicine, in the journal *Hospital and Community Psychiatry*. Dr. Favazza, who has collaborated with us in research and who is one of the country's leading experts on self-injury, believes that the "riddle" of why patients self-injure has not fully been solved.

HOW BIG IS THE PROBLEM?

For reasons that are difficult to pinpoint, self-injury has become pervasive in the United States, and all signs indicate it is growing. The syndrome is more prevalent than most people think, and yet it is still grossly underreported and misdiagnosed. The best estimates that we and other experts have been able to make, based on studies and clinical observations, are that 1,400 out of every 100,000 people in the general population have engaged in some form of self-injury. One survey of 245 college students found that 12 percent admitted to having harmed themselves deliberately.

Self-injury is not a new phenomenon—it has been documented in biblical times and in virtually every culture in every era—but it has undoubtedly taken the late 1990s by storm. Its tightening grip on schools, college campuses, jails, and other sectors of society is leaving a lasting impression, yet the number of people with any training or experience in treating the problem is alarmingly small.

Self-injury knows no geographic, cultural, or class boundaries. From the corn-fed public high schools of America's heartland to the polished corridors of New York City's elite private schools, teachers and counselors report an alarming rise in the number of students who come to class with scars. College mental health services are flooded with patients who show these symptoms.

Medical reports of self-injury are rising. Across the country psychiatrists and other doctors have been blindsided by the number of patients—many of them high-functioning adults—who confess to this type of behavior. Even more are injuring in secret, frightened to confess to something considered so disturbing and reviled. While anorexia, alcoholism, and other compulsive problems have come out of the closet, self-injury still seems unspeakable in most circles. Because of the stigma, "so many individuals are harming themselves and not knowing what to do about it," Dr. Favazza said in a television interview. "They're afraid to tell people; they're afraid to come to treatment."

Dr. Favazza writes in *Hospital and Community Psychiatry*: "Despite the prevalence of self-mutilation, attempts to understand it have been hampered by negative social attitudes. Laymen usually perceive self-mutilation to be repulsive and purposeless, while mental health professionals often focus on their own feelings of helplessness and of being 'torn apart' or 'emotionally blackmailed' by patients who deliberately harm themselves. Patients in need of medical attention may 'confess' to a suicide attempt because they have learned that physicians and nurses confronted with self-mutilation may act in an angry and inappropriate manner. For example, sutures may be applied without an anesthetic."

There is a strong correlation between self-injury and other types of addictive behavior: a good percentage of our patients (though not all) abuse drugs or alcohol, and a high number suffer from eating disorders. Few end their lives in suicide, although they may struggle with suicidal thoughts. Almost none has ever harmed anyone but themselves. Dr. Favazza used several studies to come up with the following numbers:

Type of population	Percentage who also practice self-injury
Bulimics	40.5
Anorexics	35.0
Patients with multiple personality disorder	34.0
Prisoners with personality disorders	24.0
Mentally retarded people in institutions	13.6

Nobody knows exactly why self-injurers are a growing part of our society. It's easy to chalk up this newfangled behavior to the increasing social and economic complexities of modern life, but that might not tell the whole story. The growing prevalence of such activities as body piercing and tattooing as legitimate forms of self-expression point to the powerful draw that the body as "palette" seems to have engendered in this decade.

THE TEENAGE YEARS

A particularly alarming aspect of the rising tide of self-injury is that the behavior is making its appearance earlier and earlier in the childhood and adolescent years.

At first, self-injury may appear as harmless "accidents" sustained by a young child or teenager. It may seem like a manifestation of youthful experimentation with body decoration, tattoos, or body piercing. Some teenage self-injurers say they started after they accidentally cut themselves, then were surprised when they were flooded by feelings of relief. Others pierce body parts—ears, eyebrows, nose, navel—at first as a fashion statement, and later on because of the "high" they get from the needle's sharp jab. Another category of young injurers says the urge to self-harm occurred spontaneously—"it just happened"—and quickly spiraled into an intimate ritual.

The phenomenon known as "contagion" is growing. Teens are learning about the behavior from one another, from the press, and from popular culture, and it is giving them ideas. Several popular singers and rock groups—including the Indigo Girls—portray self-injury in their lyrics and album art. Other popular teen heros—like Kerri Strug, the Olympic athlete who performed a vault on a badly sprained ankle— tacitly encourage the behavior as well.

Due to better nutrition and a host of other factors, children are entering puberty earlier today than ever before, plunging into adolescence perhaps before their cognitive and emotional capacities have had a chance to adjust. Their rapidly changing bodies force many issues of identity, maturity, and responsibility to the surface. The onset of menstruation, which is happening earlier and earlier with girls these days, often corresponds with the beginning of self-injury.

The younger the self-injurer, the more time there is for the pattern of self-injury to grow increasingly dangerous and intense. The good news is that younger self-injurers respond well to treatment and intervention, and the sooner the behavior is discovered, the quicker it can be overcome.

THE GENDER GAP

The vast majority of self-injurers are women. In our thirteen years of running S.A.F.E., we have had scarcely more than twenty male patients, compared to thousands of female ones. We seldom have more than one male at a time. Lately, we seem to be getting more male patients and are contacted more frequently by male self-injurers, which is probably a reflection of the overall growth of self-injury as a problem in society.

There are several reasons for the inbalance. Women are more likely than men to seek out psychiatric treatment and to become inpatients in mental health wards. Men are more likely to turn their emotions outward, and many with violent tendencies end up in prison. Men are more likely to use drugs and alcohol to banish unwanted thoughts and emotions.

Historically, academic papers about self-injury have made a distinction between the "delicate self-cutting" that tends to characterize female self-injury—that is, the wounds are sliced with care so as not to hit a vital artery or vein—and the type of dramatic self-injury exhibited by men, which is clinically known as "coarse." These categories took shape in the 1930s, when Karl Menninger did his groundbreaking work on self-injury in America and termed it "focal suicide." At the time most known self-injurers were men, because a lot of the early studies looked only at cases of self-injury that ended up in hospital emergency rooms. Self-injury was probably a lot rarer back then too, since society was so different and the pressures placed on people were not the same as they are today.

We have found "coarse" and "delicate" forms of self-injury among both genders and tend not to make generalizations about which sex injures more severely. One of our patients, Luke C., poured hydrochloric acid on his hands, shot himself in the foot, and purged his system with laxatives for weeks on end. His was clearly a case of "coarse" self-injury. Yet many of the women we treat have shown equally serious symptoms, often creating wounds that require more than one hundred stitches or cause permanent deformities.

To be sure, we see nuanced differences in the conditions of male and female self-injurers. But more striking is that the issues male self-injurers struggle with are similar to the women we see: childhood trauma, difficulty managing emotions and tensions, confusion about identity and sexuality, problems forming and sustaining relationships. (A more detailed discussion of male self-injurers follows in chapter 9.)

Because the preponderance of self-injurers are female, we will rely heavily on the case histories of girls and women in this book and will tend to refer to the self-injurer as "she."

ADDICTION, DISEASE, OR CHOICE?

One of the questions most frequently asked of the S.A.F.E. team is whether self-injury is a disease or an addiction. We believe it is neither.

Self-injury shares certain characteristics with addiction. The sufferer experiences the need to engage in the behavior as uncontrollable, and necessary in larger and larger quantities to achieve the desired effect.

The behavior shares some characteristics with addictive substances in that it seems to provide relief from tension. This calming, or analgesic, phenomenon is probably the most commonly reported consequence of injuring.

Indeed, the self-injurer experiences the urge to mutilate at least as strongly as the chain-smoker feels the tug for a cigarette. "Nicotine urges are *less* powerful than self-injury urges," asserts Victoria R., a former smoker and recovered self-injurer. "I was addicted to several different drugs, and I was an alcoholic. Self-injury felt more powerful than drinking or drugs. It was also a bigger deal, because there was such a stigma and all—among my friends it wasn't a stigma to get drunk. Self-injury gave more of a relief because it was a bigger deal."

Another patient of ours, Donna W., describes a conversation with a boyfriend who was a drug addict. "We were talking about our addictions, his to cocaine and mine to self-injury, and comparing the feelings we each experience when we did them," she said. "He related to me how it felt when he injected the drug, and his description of the feeling was exactly the same feeling I get when I self-injure."

Some research, most notably work conducted by New England psychiatrist Bessel van der Kolk, suggests the act of self-injuring may release certain chemicals in the brain that are similar to addictive opiates. This may be one reason patients have trouble halting the behavior after they start. Even people who scratch their skin to relieve an itch can experience this release of endorphins, which eases the local discomfort and may provide a more general sense of relief. Other scientists are at work trying to establish more concrete links between self-injury and different types of brain activity.

While we applaud any research that sheds light on self-injury, our experience tells us that self-injury is rooted in emotional causes. Though recent findings indicate that addictions like alcoholism may be linked to inherited genetic traits, we don't believe there is such a thing as a "self-injury gene" or chromosome. We acknowledge that there may be an inherited disposition for low frustration tolerance or poor impulse control, but there is still a great deal of learning and life experience that takes place from birth forward. This is an important distinction, because we are always trying to impart the message to self-injurers that their behavior is a matter of choice, not an innate part of their physical makeup. Clearly, there are identifiable physiological phenomena that take place in connection with self injury—changes in brain function and in chemical levels but for the most part they are consequences of the behavior, not motivators of it.

This is why we refer to self-injury as an "addictive-like" behavior rather than an actual addiction. Another way of saying this is that self-injury is an "addictive solution" to emotional distress. Though the sufferer may experience the syndrome as addictive, our recovery program emphasizes our belief that self-injury is volitional, and people who engage in it can learn to make a different choice.

From the sufferer's perspective, it is comforting and helpful to know that you don't have to stand under a label. By calling self-injury a "choice," we indicate our firm belief that self-injury can be overcome. The behavior does not need to be a permanent part of your identity or self-concept.

The classification of self-injury is more than a mere semantic issue. Insurance companies and health maintenance organizations must understand that self-injurers can and do get better, that they are not necessarily chronic or untreatable. If self-injury were miscategorized, it would undercut patients' ability to receive medical treatment and curtail the amount of expenses third parties are willing to reimburse.

Because of our attitude toward self-injury, we do not believe that the traditional "Twelve Step" model for treatment and recovery works for this population. We agree with the Twelve Step approach for problems that truly are addictions, and we encourage self-injurers who are also drug or alcohol abusers to attend Alcoholics Anonymous and Narcotics Anonymous meetings. But we do not think the Twelve Step program's message about addictive substances—"once an alcoholic, always an alcoholic"—holds true for self-injury. The S.A.F.E. Alternatives model imparts that people do not always have to be self-injurers, that they are *not* powerless to control their behavior. The position we take—that this is treatable—makes a significant difference in the approach to, and outcome of, psychiatric intervention.

IS THERE HOPE FOR SELF-INJURERS?

We have seen many self-injurers stop their behavior for good. Even people who injured more than once a day and whose lives were in danger have walked out of our doors never to injure again. Like many ingrained patterns of unhealthy coping, self-injury is a *learned* behavior that can be *unlearned*. We have seen so many people with extremely severe symptoms make full recoveries, and we have had a particularly high success rate with teenagers.

Self-injury is a behavior people rely on to relieve or distract themselves from difficult feelings, or to communicate emotions that they seem unable to speak. Once people learn to express themselves in other ways—verbally or in writing—the impulse subsides. The troublesome feelings may not go away, but the coping mechanism becomes a healthy one.

We have come to learn that the proper treatment structure—along with a belief in the resiliency of the human spirit—can work wonders with a population whom many, if not most, medical professionals have regarded as basically untreatable.

CAN MY DOCTOR HELP?

Unfortunately, many medical professionals are just as uninformed as laypeople about self-injury and how to treat it. While your general practitioner can refer you to a psychotherapist or recommend hospitalization if your symptoms are severe enough, he or she is unlikely to have the knowledge or resources to aid in your recovery.

Your medical doctor can bandage your wounds, stitch your skin, and prescribe antidepressants or other medications. But few doctors—or psychiatrists, for that matter—have experience treating patients who self-injure. Those who haven't seen a case before are likely to offer some misdiagnosis or, worse still, to express distaste for the problem. These reactions can reinforce the patient's feelings that nobody understands her, that people are disgusted by her, and that nobody can help. Even doctors who have seen the behavior before often feel helpless when confronted with it.

Certainly, your doctor should be made aware of your condition, consulted about the injuries themselves, and kept up to date on your progress. But to stop the behavior and to understand the reasons behind it, you need to work with an open-minded, nonjudgmental psychotherapist. The second section of this book, "The S.A.F.E. Alternatives Program," offers suggestions on finding someone suitable and explains how to use the S.A.F.E. treatment program in conjunction with psychotherapy.

Many self-injurers bounce from one psychotherapist to another, never getting any better and never addressing the problem squarely. One reason may be that people who self-injure have difficulty making personal connections with others. Another reason may lie with the naive, unempathic, and pejorative responses that patients tell us they have received from medical professionals.

Amanda B., a thirty-three-year-old elementary school teacher from Kansas, described her picaresque search for professional help. "Most therapists ignored me, and some said they couldn't help me at all," she said. "One therapist told me to take a red marker and draw on my arms. That helped me feel a little better, but it didn't help me understand what was going on with me or why I felt compelled to do this. Finally, I found a therapist who gave me the first explanation for it that I had ever heard. He said self-injury caused endorphins and dopamine to be released in the brain. He was the first person who ever acknowledged to me that it made sense what I was doing, but he told me it wasn't the best coping strategy. He helped me get disability, and he helped me find the S.A.F.E. program."

When doctors, friends, or relatives discover someone is self-injuring, they naturally grow alarmed and frightened. Many medical professionals impose counterproductive measures, like placing patients in arm restraints or having them supervised round-the-clock in mental hospitals. Sometimes doctors order that outpatients be "baby-sat" day and night by home health aides, who cost insurance companies a pretty penny but cannot possibly stop someone who is hell-bent on injuring herself from doing so. Friends and family members often adopt similar "rescue" tactics, like staying up all night with the self-injurer, issuing ultimatums, or taking away all potentially dangerous objects. For reasons we will explore later, these frantic heroics are doomed to fail; they serve only to inject relationships with additional conflict and melodrama.

ARE SELF-INJURERS DANGEROUS TO OTHERS?

We rarely see self-injurers who exhibit a pattern of violence toward others. Aggression is one of the most difficult emotions for self-injurers to face directly, which is why they disguise it and work it out through acts of self-harm.

But certainly self-injurers can strike fear into others. When we first opened S.A.F.E. Alternatives as a unit of a Chicago-area hospital, the support staff was terrified to venture near our wing. They knew what problems our patients had and feared someone would try to harm *them*.

The hospital staff soon came to regard our patients as among the *least* dangerous and threatening. Self-injurers are struggling with tortured feelings, thoughts, and memories about themselves, their own lives, and the people who have harmed them in the past. They take vengeance against *themselves* for the wrongs that have been committed against them, and for their own perceived failings. A relatively small percentage of self-injurers do have difficulty managing rage and may physically harm others or destroy property. However, in more than ten years of working with this population, we have seen that the primary target of their physical aggression has been their own bodies.

SELF-INJURY VERSUS SUICIDE

Self-injury is a distinctly different activity from a suicide attempt, but the boundaries often seem murky, and many self-injurers do indeed have suicidal thoughts or have committed acts aimed at ending their lives. On rare occasions a self-injurer will carry her actions a step too far, inadvertently causing death.

Paradoxically, self-injury is usually a *life-sustaining* act, a mechanism to cope with stress, relieve inexpressible feelings, and gain attention. Most sufferers say it is a mechanism to stave off suicide or more serious forms of emotional disorganization; it is a "life preserver" rather than an exit strategy. Indeed, in many cases the type of superficial cutting and burning patients use is not the type of behavior usually associated with people who kill themselves.

To be sure, a small percentage of self-injurers do end their own lives, either on purpose or as an unplanned side effect of an extreme bout with self-injury. Some patients have told us they've come so close to dying so many times that they don't really believe they *can* die. Others engage in a macabre game of Russian roulette, testing fate to see whether they are meant to live or die.

In our experience, the handful of people who have committed suicide were those who also suffered from a very long-term and profound depression, with sustained feelings of hopelessness. If self-injurers were suicidal as a group, we would be hard pressed to help them to the degree that we have, and we would be far less confident of their prospects for recovery.

In terms of its dangers, self-injury can be compared to anorexia, bulimia, or drug and alcohol abuse. All are potentially lethal problems when carried to an extreme. But people seldom think of anorexics or alcoholics as suicidal; people view them as having a difficult problem that can be overcome through perseverance and treatment. We look at self-injury the same way.

Because we believe suicidal intentions are a separate problem from self-injury, we tend to defer applicants to the S.A.F.E. program who say they have a specific suicide plan. We try to make distinctions between patients who truly want to get better and those who want to end it all.

Most self-injurers get very angry when hospital staffers or hotline crisis workers call them suicidal. Sufferers view their behavior as a heartfelt and genuine gesture, one that expresses their thirst for a better life. Since self-injurers as a group have extreme difficulty articulating their thoughts and getting heard, it is indeed frustrating for them when the action they are using to communicate is misinterpreted.

A lot of adolescent self-injurers have dreamy, distorted, and emotionally immature views about death and dying. They fantasize about who would come to their funeral, how many people would prove how much they care. We try to help them understand the permanence of death and the impact it has on others, as well as the fact that this option offers no hope of reaping the rewards from those relationships. Half the battle in treatment—for teens as well as grown-ups—is to get patients to realize that self-injury is not a solitary act, but one that affects other people profoundly.

Many teenagers are so caught up with what's "cool" and with rebelling against their parents that it's hard for them to step back and recognize the truly important things in their lives. Sometimes the presence of a self-injurer can lead everyone in a family to reflect on their behavior and values. In the happiest cases, the self-injurer recovers and the family's introspection leads to more meaningful and harmonious relationships. This was the experience of Alexis G. and her family, whose story appears in the next chapter.

Chapter Two

DRAWING THE LINE: WHAT IS NORMAL, WHAT IS NOT

For sixteen-year-old Alexis G., it all started when she decided she wanted to pierce her belly button. A high school sophomore in Colorado, Alexis loved the "look" of a navel ring and used to paste pictures of fashion models who had them on her bedroom walls. A few of the popular girls in her class had gotten permission to have it done at the mall, and Alexis wanted to be part of their crowd.

When her mother said "no way" to a belly button ring, Alexis got really angry and depressed. She had already been feeling pretty bad about the way she looked and thought that a navel ring might be an improvement. Moreover, things weren't going well in school—she was failing math—and it suddenly seemed like the piercing was the *only* thing that would make her life worth living.

Still her mother wouldn't budge, so one day Alexis took matters into her own hands. She bought a gold earring stud at the mall, sterilized it, sharpened it, and plunged it through the narrow fold of skin atop her navel. She hadn't counted on the blood that gushed forth and stained her bedspread—or on the instant relief from her feelings of depression and self-hatred.

"It just made me feel so much better when I was done," Alexis recalls. "It hurt, but everything was okay then—I had control."

Alexis hid the piercing from her mother, who usually knew everything that went on with Alexis and her younger brother. Though Alexis described her family as "about as average as you can get," her mother tended to intrude on the children's lives in heavy-handed ways: she read their mail and taped their phone conversations. Alexis had never defied her mother in any big way before, but suddenly, in self-injury, she felt she had hit on something useful.

Alexis, a tall and attractive teenager with dark brown corkscrew curls and a cheerful smile, began purposely cutting herself. At first she stuck to her ankles and stomach, where she thought nobody would see the wounds, and then she moved on to her forearms. "I've used knives or razors, or tacks or safety pins," she says. "I'd go into my bathroom, my bedroom to do it —wherever there's a closed door."

Her habit escalated from once a week to more than once a day, "just whenever I had an emotion," Alexis recalled. Over time she had to make deeper cuts to get the same relief. The more she started to cut, the more she felt controlled by the behavior, and fearful of it. She knew she had to stop but sensed she couldn't. She was too scared to tell her parents and worried about what the reprisal would be.

One day, after another bad grade on a math test, Alexis cut herself in the bathroom at school, and the blood wouldn't stop. She panicked. "It was just like reality hit —this was a big problem," she said. She confided in a teacher, who insisted she tell her parents. First Alexis sought treatment at a local hospital, where her symptoms worsened; then she came to S.A.F.E.

Alexis's mother was bewildered by the entire experience. "When I learned that Alexis was cutting herself, I saw it as manipulative behavior and I wasn't going to succumb to it," she said. "I didn't realize the danger she was in."

For parents, it can be particularly hard to distinguish what constitutes a "normal" teenage experiment with body modification—like a nose ring, a pierced belly button, or a tattoo—and what behaviors fall into a separate category, one whose central purpose is the management of terrible anxieties in a young person. In Alexis's case, one activity seemed to segue seamlessly into the other. In other examples, a teenager's interests are satisfied when she gets what she wants, perhaps a weird-looking eyebrow ring or a flower tattooed on her ankle. While that girl's mother may not like what she has done to her body, the fact that the daughter does not seek to continue it—and does not draw emotional sustenance from the actual skin penetration—signals that she is simply expressing herself.

To the inexperienced, it may be difficult to distinguish a pathological syndrome from youthful rebellion. Since our culture condones activities that once were considered taboo, does it also foster an environment in which children feel they can dabble in other forms of so-called body art? "We've had a few students who we *know* have started cutting themselves," said the head of a private New York City junior high school for girls. "But there are a lot more of them we suspect have been trying it."

Certain situations are clear-cut. If someone is cutting or burning her own skin habitually, she is a self-injurer. The "classic" or most common cases involve people who use knives, razors, scissors, cigarette tips, and cigarette lighters against themselves.

Other circumstances can be ambiguous. Many behaviors may become *defined* as self-injurious for certain people despite the fact that they are not self-injurious for all people. For instance, plenty of people—women and men—get their ears pierced. Even two or three holes in each ear can be considered "normal." But when somebody starts planning her life around getting more holes in her ear, or eagerly anticipating the jolt she will get when the needle jabs her skin, something is going awry.

At S.A.F.E. we frequently get calls from people who say, "My daughter has pierced her ears and various body parts twenty times—is this self-injury?" Or they ask, "I've been picking at my skin repetitively—do I have a problem?" Or, "I've been biting my cuticles until they bleed, and I can't stop."

All of these activities have the potential to do harm to the body, but can be basically harmless under many conditions. In cases that sound borderline, it's important for you to decide, *in your particular situation,* if the activities constitute a pattern of self-injury. Ask yourself the following:

- Do you feel compulsively drawn to engage in the behavior?
- Do you get a "high" from the way the activity feels physically, or are you just trying to make an artistic statement with your body?

- Does the behavior consume your thoughts or interfere with your ability to function normally?
- Realistically, could you stop the behavior today if you wanted to?

All of us fall back on less than ideal physical habits, particularly when we're tense or agitated. We bite our nails, scratch our skin, tug our hair, or pop acne blemishes. For most people these activities are mild and contained enough that they fall well below the level of pathology.

However, in psychiatry even these familiar and seemingly innocuous habits are sometimes used to diagnose certain syndromes and anxiety disorders. When a behavior reaches a certain degree of intensity—for instance, it monopolizes so much energy that it saps time from the sufferer's everyday activity and relationships—then "normal" becomes "abnormal."

This idea, that the difference between healthy and unhealthy behavior is a matter of degree, is an important one as we continue to consider what "qualifies" as self-injury. As with most human behaviors, there is a continuum from the innocuous to the destructive. At some point along the continuum, a behavior that may be benign in one person could qualify as self-injury in another.

Take the example of an adolescent girl who has pierced her ears three times and now wants to pierce her nostril. Elders may recoil at the thought, but within her peer culture a nose ring is considered a sign of artistic sensibility. The girl gets her nose pierced, after bracing for the pain of the procedure, and is pleased with the new image she projects. She may look different, but she is not a self-injurer.

Another girl in her situation, who may have the same amount of piercings, may have additional motivations. Suppose she reveals that she "craves" the "high" that she gets from the piercing procedure, and that she feels depressed or agitated when deprived of the opportunity to "add to her collection." Getting a nose ring merely whets her appetite for further modification. Obviously, the picture is more cloudy in this case, and these two girls are significantly different.

There is also a vast distinction between someone who has undergone ten or fifteen voluntary cosmetic surgeries in a short period of time and the average middle-aged woman who gets her first face-lift. The healthy person may or may not be pleased with the results, but probably does not feel compelled to repeat the experience—or at least, not to engage in a frantic, and possibly dangerous, pursuit of multiple surgeries.

Along the same lines, the athlete who pushes herself to continue despite repeatedly torn ligaments, sprains, or the potential for cardiac arrest is a far cry from the typical "fitness hound" who knows when to call it quits.

The differences are not merely a matter of quantity (three pierce holes or a dozen, two surgeries or ten, one sprain or many) but also of motive. If someone is using a particular behavior to try to gain relief from certain thoughts or emotions, then that person is probably a self-injurer.

COMPULSIVE EXERCISE

Many questionable actitivies are so much a part of our culture that we are distracted from the potentially destructive or pathological impulses that sometimes underlie them. Since we all know, for instance, that exercise is "good for you" and that athletic competition can promote teamwork and sportsmanship, it's easy to lose sight of the fact that exercise, when misused, can be harmful and destructive. Jane Fonda exhorted us to "feel the burn." A recent television commercial for a sports drink used the slogan, "Better to wound your body than your pride."

In our patients and in the population at large, we often hear reports about exercise beyond the point of endurance, or to the point of injury or dehydration. Some newfangled sports actually require competitors to put forth this kind of exertion. There are articles in the newspapers about "super" marathon runners, who train themselves to run races of sixty or eighty miles. Television carries coverage of the "Ironman" competition, in which contenders must swim 2½ miles, bicycle 112 miles, then run a 26-mile marathon. Readers may recall, as we do, watching in horror as competitors stagger deliriously through this race, struggling to stay conscious in order to finish. Fans line the race course to cheer on the athletes who have clearly made themselves ill and have perhaps even harmed themselves irreversibly.

The "Ironman" phenomenon manifests itself in the general population under various socially accepted guises. Consider the wrestler who dehydrates himself to meet a certain weight goal before a competition, or the gymnast who starves herself to remain competitive in her sport. Then there is the teenage girl who exercises compulsively—and may undernourish herself as well—to emulate her favorite athletes or to conform to an unrealistic notion of what her body should look like. We believe these activities are unquestionably cause for alarm.

Our heroes and role models are partly to blame. Baseball legend Cal Ripken Jr. was awarded and applauded for playing so many consecutive games despite the infirmities he suffered along the way. As a nation we worship Michael Jordan, the basketball giant who is famed for his ability to play regardless of illness or injury. Sportscasters rhapsodize about his ability to "block the pain" of a torn ligament or scorching fever. When our patients describe something similar, we call it "dissociation," and we identify it as a harmful behavioral syndrome.

Another sports idol—particularly among our patients—is Kerri Strug, the Olympic gymnast whose most memorable contribution to the 1996 summer games in Atlanta was performing a vault with a severe ankle injury just before Team U.S.A.'s dramatic victory. Strug sustained the injury during her first vault—the score from which would have been enough to clinch the United States' win—but she performed the second vault anyway, in obvious pain and perhaps unsure of her team's standing. Coach Bela Karolyi carried the wounded athlete in his arms to collect her medal, literally holding her up as a hero instead of someone who might have just done something really stupid to herself. Our patients tell us, "If Kerri Strug can take it, so can I." Interesting, isn't it, that we applaud this pain-blocking behavior in popular culture, yet our psychiatric institutions are filled with people for whom it has escalated to a dangerous intensity?

BODY AS BILLBOARD

Not all people who overexercise are paying homage to the shrine of athletics. Many people—especially women—engage in strenuous, frequent exercise regimens in service of their ongoing need to define themselves by appearance. Society idolizes thinness, and everybody wants to look like a supermodel. When someone actually goes so far as to harm herself to realize this goal, she has crossed the line into self-injury.

Author Joan Jacobs Brumberg explores this phenomenon in her book *The Body Project*. Brumberg concludes that certain behaviors are even "more flamboyant and provocative than either dieting or working out." She writes:

"Body piercing, once regarded as characteristic of 'primitive people,' has emerged in the 1990s as the latest form of self-expression among American adolescents. . . . Although multiple ear piercing has been stylish in the United States for more than a decade, the repertoire of pierced body parts has recently expanded to include the eyebrow, nose and navel. There are also some audacious teenagers who pierce their lips, tongues, nipples and genitals."

Certain motives behind the piercing craze seem normal, Brumberg states: the act of piercing embodies rebellion, the struggle for autonomy, the expression of a new and complicated set of sexual mores. Yet she captures the problematic aspects of the trend's extremes, observing that body piercing "follows logically from the pared down, segmented, increasingly exposed, part-by-part orientation toward the female body that has emerged over the course of the twentieth century. In fact, in a culture where everything is 'up close and personal,' it should not surprise us that some young women today regard the entire body, even its most private parts, as a message board."

Brumberg is making a social commentary on practices that may be controversial—especially within families—but that are nevertheless part of the societal mainstream and not pathological per se. Yet many times women who self-injure tell us that their body is their only "message board." The cuts and burns they inflict on themselves bear mute testimony to the thoughts and feelings they cannot find words to express: "See my pain!" their bodies say.

Body modification has become surprisingly common, especially among our youth. An April 1998 *New York Times* poll of 1,048 youths aged thirteen through seventeen found that 6 percent of girls have pierced their bodies in places other than the earlobe, and 25 percent would like to do so. An additional 37 percent would not want such a piercing themselves, but like the "look." Among the same girls, 5 percent have a tattoo, 31 percent would like to get one, and another 31 percent like the way they look.

The numbers for boys were slightly lower but still significant. Three percent of boys in the poll had pierced their bodies, and 11 percent wanted to do so. Five percent had a tattoo, and 34 percent wanted one. In the survey, 30 percent of the teenage boys admired the aesthetic of a body piercing or tattoo, but did not want one for themselves.

Again, only if the activity becomes habitual and compulsive does it mean there may be a more serious problem lurking.

PLASTIC SURGERY

During speaking engagements and interviews, we are often asked whether plastic surgery qualifies as self-injury: are women who obsessively alter their appearances with liposuction, face-lifts, eyelifts, nose jobs, tummy tucks, and face peels carrying on a secret agenda of self-mutilation?

The underside of plastic surgery has recently become a hot topic. Several writers have suggested that modern women's passion for surgical modification suggests a desperate attempt to ward off aging and loss of sexual allure. Tabloid newspapers gobble up every detail about the body-modification program of pop singer Michael Jackson, whose psychological issues we will not attempt to delve into here, but whose surgical efforts seem to have succeeded in erasing most signs of his race, gender, and facial structure.

People magazine and *Vanity Fair* have published pieces about New York socialite Jocelyn Wildenstein, whose relentless pursuit of multiple cosmetic facial surgeries has aroused consternation and alarm. One of Ms. Wildenstein's friends is quoted in *Vanity Fair* as saying she regretted the manner in which Jocelyn has "mutilated herself."

Does this mean anyone who has ventured forth for liposuction and a face-lift is a self-injurer? How many piercings "qualify" as self-mutilation? Does the athlete who "goes for the burn" harbor a secret pathology? How do you know that you have "crossed the line" into self-injury? Obviously, the answers are complex. As these examples reveal, in many contexts a certain degree of self-inflicted pain or harm is tacitly or overtly sanctioned by society. This sanction does not remove the potential for danger, but it does provide a convenient excuse for some people who would like to deny a problem.

To be clear, self-injurious behavior is the willful alteration of body tissue, in disregard for considerations of health and safety, which serves the purpose of restoring or preserving a person's emotional equilibrium. Often, the behavior develops to the point of being the person's primary method of regulating internal tension or distress. As self-injury progresses, the sufferer uses it in a characteristic, repetitive way, like a "ritual" that must be carried out with progressive frequency. When deprived of the behavior, she is likely to become increasingly panicked, disorganized, and distressed.

To clarify some borders that may seem blurry and help people decide if they might indeed have a problem, we have developed a questionnaire that addresses self-injury and the behaviors and circumstances that often accompany it.

QUESTIONNAIRE: COULD YOU BE A SELF-INJURER?

People call us all the time to ask us if their skin picking, hair pulling, pimple squeezing, or body piercings qualify as problems. Many others who have not made a formal inquiry may also wonder if their behavior rises to the level of self-injury. You might be asking yourself, "If I cut or burn myself only occasionally, do I have a serious problem?"

There's no simple yes or no answer to such questions. Zit popping and nail biting might seem like petty concerns that would raise eyebrows only among dermatologists or manicurists, but each situation is different. One of our patients, David H., began picking his face when he was an acne-ridden thirteen-year-old; some forty years later, he was still making deep gouges in his face with fingernails, tweezers, and other implements, despite the thick scar tissue enveloping his cheeks and chin. Karl Menninger describes a patient whose nail biting progressed until she nearly bit her fingers off.

Many people say they "can't stop" and feel "driven" to engage in what might normally be considered socially acceptable—if unattractive—behaviors. The choice of words suggests that the person is struggling with a psychological issue, a compulsion of some sort. Activities such as tattooing, body piercing, plastic surgery, or branding might be considered on the "fringe" of self-injury, but often people who engage in them do so because of peer pressure or aesthetic preference, not to relieve emotional anxiety.

If you hear that someone cuts or burns from time to time, you should assume that the person is a self-injurer. It's important to identify the circumstances surrounding the behavior, to see what the motivations are and what the person thinks about himself or herself. Only then can you assess the symptoms and decide how they should be addressed.

Since the issues surrounding these activities tend to be complex, we try to answer them at S.A.F.E. through an assessment screening, in which we ask a set of questions designed to explore a person's background, behavior, and motivations. The following questionnaire is drawn from our screening process, and answering it should help you gauge the severity of your own self-injurious symptoms. You can get a sense of if you need to seek treatment for self-injury and what level of care is needed: outpatient treatment, inpatient hospitalization, or some combination.

For this book we have modified the questionnaire to target certain key issues that are consistently identified by the self-injurers we have worked with over the years. These categories have also been identified in scientific research to be correlated to self-injury, or to predict it.

However, we must emphasize strongly that the questionnaire is not meant as a formal diagnostic tool. We object to the concept of "checklist diagnosis" and only intend the questions to focus your attention on pertinent issues to consider in deciding to seek help.

Ideally, the questions should be answered as honestly as possible by the person who may have a problem with self-injury. While it's possible for someone close to that person to draw some conclusions from the questionnaire based on his or her knowledge of the situation, nobody but the sufferer will be able to answer all the questions accurately. If you are trying to help someone you suspect has a problem, you might want to ask him or her to take the quiz. If the person is denying a problem, you could point out that answering the questionnaire could confirm that no problem exists and help put the issue to rest.

The questionnaire has four sections, or categories. The first consists of questions regarding specific childhood memories and perceptions. The second involves a self-assessment, and the third category asks for an examination of thoughts regarding potentially self-injurious acts. The fourth section involves specific questions for the person who already identifies himself or herself as a self-injurer, and who may be trying to gain more understanding of the severity of the problem.

Following the questionnaire is an in-depth description of each section and what your responses may suggest about you.

SECTION ONE

1. I was often told as a child to be strong.
   True _✓_ False ___

2. I do not remember much affection being displayed in my family.
   True _✓_ False ___

3. Anger was the feeling most often displayed in my family.
   True _✓_ False ___

4. I rarely felt I could express my feelings to my family.
   True _✓_ False ___

5. As a child I remember my mother and/or father as overly intrusive.
   True _✓_ False ___

6. As a child I remember being sexually abused.
   True _✓_ False ___

7. As a child I remember being physically abused.
   True _✓_ False ___

8. As a child I remember being emotionally abused.
   True _✓_ False ___

9. As a child I remember my mother and/or father being emotionally absent.
   True _✓_ False ___

10. I remember times when I was punished for strong feelings, such as when I was angry or upset and in tears about something.
    True _✓_ False ___

11. When I was upset or frightened, my mother and/or father often ignored me.
    True _✓_ False ___

12. I grew up in a very religious household.
    True _✓_ False ___

13. I had a parent who was unable to raise me due to a physical illness or trauma.
    True ✓ False ___
14. I grew up with a lot of double messages.
    True ✓ False ___

SECTION TWO

15. I often think of myself as a "bad" person.
    True ✓ False ___
16. I often believe that I'm at fault for everything that goes wrong.
    True ✓ False ___
17. I often think that everyone would be happier if I were dead.
    True ✓ False ___
18. I often believe that negative attention is better than no attention.
    True ✓ False ___
19. I hate change.
    True ✓ False ___
20. I seem to have an all-or-nothing attitude.
    True ✓ False ___
21. I usually can't find words that explain how I feel.
    True ✓ False ___
22. I don't have many friends.
    True ✓ False ___
23. I am a perfectionist.
    True ✓ False ___
24. I think I am a burden to others.
    True ✓ False ___
25. I do not want to die; I just want to stop my emotional pain.
    True ___ False ✓   i want to die
26. I get scared when I get close to anyone.
    True ___ False ___
27. I could never intentionally harm anyone else.
    True ___ False ___
28. I do not know how to get attention in positive ways.
    True ___ False ___
29. Some people think I am childlike.
    True ___ False ___

30. I am heterosexual ___ homosexual ___ bisexual ___ unsure ✓

Questions for females only
31. I hate my periods.
    True ✓ False ___
32. I strongly hate having a pelvic exam.
    True ✓ False ___
33. I would be better off without a vagina.
    True ✓ False ___
34. I am jealous of men.
    True ✓ False ___

Questions for males only
35. I hate my genital organs.
    True ✓ False ___
36. I would be better off without my genitals.
    True ✓ False ___
37. I am jealous of women.
    True ✓ False ___
38. I wish I were a woman.
    True ✓ False ___

SECTION THREE

39. I have had elective plastic surgery more than once.
    True ___ False ___
40. I have had plastic surgery against the advice of a doctor.
    True ___ False ___
41. My friends and family have become concerned about my body piercing.
    True ___ False ___
42. I have decided to continue piercing despite the fact that one or more significant others have told me that they are repulsed by it.
    True ___ False ___
43. I find that when I tattoo or pierce, I feel different afterward—I get a rush, or I feel like I'm much calmer than before the session, or I feel sexually aroused.
    True ___ False ___

44. I become anxious when anyone tries to stop me or prevent me from getting a new piercing.
    True ___ False ___
45. I have problems with drugs or alcohol.
    True ___ False ___
46. I have exercised to the point that I have become sick or injured.
    True ___ False ___
47. I have sometimes neglected to seek medical attention for an illness or injury when part of me knows that I should have.
    True ___ False ___
48. I have an eating disorder, or have had one sometime in the past.
    True ___ False ___
49. My doctor has told me I am underweight, but I would still really like to lose a few more pounds.
    True ___ False ___
50. I am secretly delighted when I can avoid eating a meal.
    True ___ False ___
51. I have stolen things.
    True ✓ False ___
52. I have—or have had—a tendency to be promiscuous.
    True ___ False ___
53. I have overdosed on drugs.
    True ___ False ___

SECTION FOUR

54. I often obsess about self-injury.
    True ___ False ___
55. I sometimes can't explain where my injuries come from.
    True ___ False ___
56. I get anxious when my wounds start to heal.
    True ___ False ___
57. I often believe that if I don't self-injure, I'll go "crazy."
    True ___ False ___
58. No one can hurt me more than I can hurt myself.
    True ___ False ___
59. I can't imagine life without self-injury.
    True ___ False ___
60. If I stop self-injuring, my parents win.
    True ___ False ___

61. I often believe that if I don't self-injure, I'll explode.
    True ___ False ___
62. I almost always carry something with me that I can use to self-harm.
    True ___ False ___
63. I often self-injure as a way to punish myself.
    True ___ False ___
64. I often self-injure to show others how bad I feel.
    True ___ False ___
65. Self-injury helps me feel in control.
    True ___ False ___
66. I have carved words or symbols into my flesh.
    True ___ False ___
67. I have used self-injury to control others.
    True ___ False ___
68. The sight of my blood comforts me.
    True ___ False ___
69. Self-injury helps me feel "real" again.
    True ___ False ___
70. Self-injury helps me control my mind when it's racing.
    True ___ False ___
71. Self-injury helps me feel relaxed.
    True ___ False ___
72. Self-injury helps me feel less lonely.
    True ___ False ___
73. Self-injury helps me feel less depressed.
    True ___ False ___
74. Self-injury is my best friend.
    True ___ False ___
75. The first time that I self-injured, I didn't let anyone know.
    True ___ False ___
76. I have self-injured: Only once ___ 2–5 times ___
    6–10 times ___ 11–20 times ___ 21–50 times ___
    More than 50 times ___
77. My decision to self-injure is usually made (check all that apply):
    On the spur of the moment ___ An hour before ___ Several
    hours before ___ A day before ___ A week before ___ More
    than a week before ___

78. I often have a regular routine I follow when I self-injure.
    True ___ False ___
79. Immediately after I self-injure, I usually feel:
    Better ___ No change ___ Worse ___
80. The amount of pain I feel when I self-injure is usually:
    None ___ A little ___ A moderate amount ___ A great deal ___
81. I have lost relationships because of my self-injury.
    True ___ False ___
82. I am unable to hold down a job because of my self-injury.
    True ___ False ___
83. I have at times missed school because of my self-injury.
    True ___ False ___
84. I like the attention I get from people when they find out that I
    have physically harmed myself.
    True ___ False ___
85. List the ways in which you have harmed yourself. List them in
    the order in which you most often harmed youself, e.g., 1. Cut-
    ting, 2. Burning, etc. 1 _____ 2 _____ 3 _____ 4 _____
    5 _____
86. When did you last harm yourself? Within the past week ___
    Past month ___ Past six months ___ Past year ___ More than
    a year ago ___
87. My self-harm helps me atone for my sins.
    True ___ False ___
88. Sometimes my self-harm puts me in closer contact with God.
    True ___ False ___
89. I consider my tendency to self-harm an addiction.
    True ___ False ___
90. Many times I harm myself more out of habit than for any spe-
    cific reason.
    True ___ False ___

ANALYSIS OF RESPONSES

These observations are broad guidelines and are *not* meant as diagnoses
or clinical recommendations. The questionnaire is meant to help you
start thinking about your behavior in an objective and analytical way.

Whether or not your behavior is a problem or even a concern to you, it is never a bad idea to seek professional advice and consultation.

SECTION   ONE

The more questions you answered "true," the more likely that your early experiences were similar to those described by diagnosed self-injurers.

Naturally, a person could answer "true" to all these questions and still not be a self-injurer. The point here is that many self-injurers report similar circumstances in their childhoods, and these conditions seem to play a role in the development of the condition.

This section might be referred to as the "family emotional climate" category. The childhoods of self-injurers were often characterized by grave parental difficulties in dealing with normal human emotions, expressing basic needs, and maintaining appropriate generational boundaries.

The concept of boundaries involves the delegation of rights and responsibilities within the family, as well as respecting the basic bodily boundaries of the child. Our patients often tell us that the roles, rights, and responsibilities in their family systems were confusing and chaotic. As children they may have been expected to parent other siblings in the house or, worse still, to take care of the physical, sexual, or emotional needs of a parent.

Self-injurers often receive the message to "be strong" (question #1) and keep a stiff upper lip, and many interpret that to mean that there is no room for them at all to be a child, with needs and vulnerabilities. When the future self-injurer was told to "be strong," the parent was more often than not expressing his or her inability to tolerate age-appropriate emotional expression. Some self-injurers describe being told, "Big boys don't cry," or "Stop that crying or I'll give you something to cry about." Presenting a strong front was necessary for the family to maintain whatever calmness or equilibrium it had.

Sexual and/or physical abuse (#6, 7) certainly represent the most extreme form of boundary violation, and the abuse victim's role clearly changes from that of a dependent child to an inappropriately precocious adult. The abuse victim also often finds him- or herself "in charge" of maintaining the emotional stability of the abusing caregiver. Our experience—and the experience of all other researchers in the field—confirms that a large proportion of self-injurers have experienced physical or sexual trauma. While the presence of self-injury should not be considered an automatic signal that such abuse has occurred, it often indicates a family environment with serious difficulty.

At another extreme is the emotionally intrusive parenting experience, which impedes the child's ability to gain autonomy. Some of our self-injurers have felt that their feelings and behaviors were actively controlled by a hovering parent, and that they could never learn to "think for themselves." The overly intrusive parent (#5) can cause a child to become overly secretive or withdrawn as he or she tries to salvage a sense of "self" that is separate from the parent. Many of our adolescent patients have called their moms "smothering." They say things like "Sometimes I don't know where my mom ends and where I begin—we've merged." Self-injury represents a symbolic effort to cut the parent loose.

Growing up without direct encouragement or affection (#2) tends to mar the development of a healthy sense of self. The emotionally absent parent (#9) tends to send a message to the child not to be excited about accomplishments and not to expect too much out of life. A child needs praise and encouragement to thrive and develop self-esteem. Moreover, children who grow up in homes where the thinking structure is rigid and the parents have little tolerance for creativity also have a hard time. Many of our patients come from backgrounds that are deeply religious (#12), and their parents used religion as a tool of emotional control and suppression.

In short, the family emotional climate that we most frequently observe in the self-injurer may have any or nearly all of these characteristics. The common ties that bind these experiences are an atmosphere of severe anxiety and the inability of the parents to respond appropriately to the child's emotional needs. The parents' own difficulty in dealing with emotions—which may be due to extreme stress or psychological disturbances—prevents them from being truly available or responsive. Thus, the potential self-injurer grows up with a range of difficulties identifying and managing emotional states.

If you answered most questions "true" in Section One, there is a likelihood that you experience difficulty in maintaining emotional stability. You may have grown to maturity in a family that was fertile ground for self-injurious behavior to develop.

SECTION TWO

The more questions you answered "true" in this section, the more your view of yourself matches the views commonly expressed by self-injurers.

Again, these statements involving manifestations of low self-esteem do not necessarily correlate to self-injury. There may be many other reasons—medical, psychological, and otherwise—why you might view yourself in these ways. But the opinions expressed in this section are held dear by a large majority of self-injurers.

Section Two might be referred to as the "self-concept" category. Self-injurers are often besieged with feelings of "inner badness," worthlessness, and a sense of being "toxic" to others. They tend to take inappropriate degrees of responsibility for what happens to them, sometimes blaming themselves for events outside their control, but sometimes not taking enough responsibility for their own actions and their consequences. This is another possible outcome of family situations in which there is confusion over the roles that children play.

The self-injurer frequently feels sad, ruminates about death and dying (#17), but has difficulty identifying other feelings that might be mixed in (#21). She tends to do and say things in a negative way, believing that no one will give her the time of day unless she is behaving destructively (#18).

The self-injurer views herself as fragile and perceives that she is poorly understood by the people around her. With her all-or-nothing thinking pattern (#20), she cannot accept partial gratification. Thus, she is rapidly and easily disappointed—and enraged—in her relationships. (If you tend to think this way, you may also tend to respond impulsively to these thoughts.)

Because their behavior is typically so regressed, many self-injurers report that others describe them as "childlike" (#29). Self-injurers are quite frequently unsure about their sexuality and sexual orientation; hatred of their body parts, genitalia, and gender roles (#31–38) exacerbate this confusion.

SECTION THREE

If you answered "true" to any one of these questions, it might signal that you have a problem with self-injury.

Section Three deals with "fringe" behaviors that may, for some individuals, be harbingers of self-mutilation. The behavior can sometimes
start behind the mask of a socially acceptable (if controversial) "body
modification" program—piercing, tattooing, or weight control. If you
found yourself answering in the affirmative to any of these questions,
if might be time to consider that your body-modification behaviors have
a serious underlying agenda: you are trying to allay anxiety or cope with
psychological distress through these activities. Medical self-neglect
may also fall into this category.

A "true" answer to some of these questions does not necessarily
mean you are a self-injurer. For example, in question #41, your family
may frown on your piercings or tattoos, while you may view them as a
form of expression. But any response that indicates you are getting an
unusual emotional lift out of these activities is something to be concerned about. Even the rebellious youth with a striped mohawk and
multiple ear and nose studs is not necessarily a self-injurer. The important distinction is how much emotional sustenance is drawn from
the ritual of having one's body modified.

Many self-injurers suffer from a variety of compulsions and unde-
sired behaviors. Naturally, answering "true" to any or all of these questions does not mean you are a self-injurer, but you do have something
in common with a majority of self-injurers.

SECTION FOUR

We suggest that anyone who answered "true" to any one of these questions might benefit from a consultation with a therapist. You can use
this questionnaire as a tool for discussion with the counselor.

Severe self-injurers might answer "true" to all the questions posed
in this section. The more "true" responses you gave, the more likely it
is that you have a serious problem, that self-injury has come to dom-
inate your life as a primary means of "taking care" of yourself.

Section Four covers thoughts and patterns associated with self-
injury. The first eight questions pertain largely to thoughts about self-
injury. If you are constantly thinking about injuring—even if you aren't
doing it—you have a problem.

Self-injurers often report to us that they constantly carry objects
with them to use for injuring (#62). These may include pieces of glass,
razor blades, nails, matches, or other items to "clutch like a security

blanket," or hide in a school locker, glove compartment, pocketbook, or nightstand. Our patients compare these weapons to an insurance policy—"just in case" they need to duck into a quiet place to seek relief through an act of injury. Since this is an addictive-like behavior, self-injurers are as scared to be without a weapon as an alcoholic is without a drink.

Questions 54–61 describe the mind-set of the self-injurer, who becomes more entrenched in her patterns as self-injury takes hold of her everyday life. The self-injurer grows convinced that the automatic response to anxiety must be self-injury. She comes to rely on it more and more and feels she can't function without it. Part of our treatment program involves untangling the distortions involved in this thinking. We ask the patient to question why she can't "survive" anymore without injury, why she has closed off the possibility that everyday tension might be managed differently.

Questions 63–74 deal with the most frequently reported purposes and meanings of self-injurious behavior. You may notice that they tend to fall into three categories: soothing and calming (what we call the "analgesic aim"); thought control and reality orientation; and interpersonal communication. Self-injurers often say that their behavior helps them in more than one of these categories. Depending on the situation and her state of mind, an injurer may carve words as "rageful messages" to someone, and simultaneously find herself calmed by the sight and sensation of her own blood flowing.

The sense of increased control, focus, or calm reported by the self-injurer is often fleeting—a temporary respite that fades quickly when the next stressor comes along. While the self-injurer may believe she is "controlling" another person through her behavior, she often finds that self-injury brings about a loss of relationships, control, and autonomy.

Often the injurer claims that her behavior is a "best friend." It begins to replace human relationships rather than enhance them. In this way injuring becomes a furtive, private act, a clandestine "love affair."

Questions 76–80 assess the "structure" of the habitual self-injurer's behavior pattern. Someone who has self-harmed between two and ten times is considered "prodromal"; she has begun to dabble, but has yet to develop a set pattern, or ritual, of self-injury. If you fall into this category, now is an excellent time to seek outpatient therapy to arrest

the problem. This lets you put into words the distress you have begun to act on.

Frequency is not the only issue to consider, however. A "dabbler" may already be engaged in a coarse and dangerous form of self-injury; for example, cutting herself deeply or close to a vital blood vessel. In such an instance, the imminent risk to her safety would suggest inpatient hospitalization as a better choice. Similarly, self-injurers who report more frequent episodes and who seem to have developed a pattern should certainly consider inpatient treatment. Our rule of thumb at S.A.F.E. is that the earlier the person seeks help, the better.

The two questions that consider premeditation versus "spur of the moment" injury also present interesting issues. A person who premeditates for a lengthy period of time—and who perhaps has an elaborate injury ritual (time, place, "equipment")—may at first seem to be more entrenched in the habit. However, our experience has suggested that the self-injurer who plans ahead—who must go through "steps" toward self-injury—may actually have a greater capacity for self-control and more ability to interrupt the ritual and use other ways of coping. The person who injures suddenly, on the spur of the moment, has a much smaller window of opportunity for stopping the behavior. If you fall into that category, you might need the more structured recovery approach of an inpatient or partial hospitalization program to help you learn better ways of coping.

Again, our questionnaire and our analysis of the responses are meant as guidelines, not diagnoses or prescriptions. We are not trying to pass judgment on anyone or any behavior, merely trying to recommend that people with certain possible trouble spots seek help. We understand and sympathize with the reasons that people resort to self-injury, and we are constantly seeking to explain the valid reasons behind this behavior to others. Those reasons are explored in depth in the next chapter.

Chapter Three

WHY DO PEOPLE CHOOSE SELF-INJURY?

How many times have you—or someone you know—gotten so angry and frustrated that you banged your hand on the table to express your feelings? Have you ever punched a pillow in anger, or struck a wall, or smashed a plate on the floor? Have you ever pinched yourself, or bitten your lip, to hold back tears?

Whether or not you suffer from self-injury, you can probably relate to the occasional temptation to blow off emotional steam through physical means. Some people go to the gym to exercise their anger away. Some people jog, swim, or take yoga, both for health reasons and for the happy physical and emotional sensations. The activity—or the limited act of destruction—releases endorphins, which soothe the nervous system.

The patients we work with have a heightened, often extreme experience of this sensation. They say it is easier to deal with tangible, physical pain than intangible, emotional pain. Their experience and definition of pain is often quite different from other people's.

"DOESN'T IT HURT?"

The most bewildering aspect of self-injury to people who do not engage in it is the question of pain threshold. How could you inflict "obviously" intolerable wounds on yourself? Wouldn't you pass out from the pain at some point?

The explanation is clear, though it does require some intuitive leaps. The self-injurer is very out of touch with the experience of physical pain and may even at times be temporarily unaware of her behavior. Most self-injurers say they feel "numb" or "empty" during the cutting and burning. After the act is complete, the pain can indeed be excruciating, but it also feels oddly calming, soothing—alive.

On the other hand, some self-injurers say they *do* feel pain during the act of injuring, but that it doesn't stop them from proceeding. Seeing with their own eyes the wound they are producing is the object of the exercise, and pain is a small obstacle. Seldom is the pain so unbearable that it compels them to stop. People who mutilate themselves to atone for perceived transgressions or as a form of self-punishment view the physical agony as part and parcel of the discipline. They may even relish the pain as an enhancement to their penance, or view it as a confirmation of their feelings of sinfulness.

In either case, whether pain is present or absent, what takes place during the act of injury itself is something known in psychology as "dissociation." It could be described as an unconscious disconnection between what is going on in a person's mind and what is being experienced by her body. Dissociation can sometimes take the form of an almost dreamlike state, in which the self-injurer pictures herself in the kind of fuzzy, distant way that dreamers do. Usually her mind is so consumed with unmanageable feelings that her body and its needs are of secondary concern.

"When I'm self-injuring, I don't feel anything," says Liz C., thirty-nine. "The pain kicks in sometimes a couple of days later, sometimes not until it starts to heal and it starts itching. Breaking bones or giving myself concussions—usually it's not until the next day that I feel it. Most other times—with cutting or burning—I don't feel it at all."

To understand how this can happen, a healthy person who has never had this experience needs to accept the unusual cognitive twists that can take place in the self-injurer's head. When strong emotions or enraging memories are stirred in self-injurers, they begin to feel overwhelmed. Many patients report the sensation that their senses are "flooded." Then dissociation takes place, in which the mind begins to function separately from the body. Dissociation leaves the sufferer feeling estranged, surreal, and panicked.

At this point, because the body no longer seems to be a valid part of her experience, the self-injurer feels she can damage it freely as an expression of her grief. Cutting the skin becomes no different from daubing paint on a canvas, writing angry words on a piece of paper, or slicing into a wheel of cheese. Some self-injurers even report using their own blood to paint a picture, highlighting the connection they make between bodily violence and artistic voice.

Some patients reach such a state of alienation that they question if they're truly alive. They cut in an attempt to feel the physical sensation of pain, the blood that will prove to their minds they are human.

"Prior to my episodes of self-injury, I am usually experiencing a panic attack and have feelings of desperation and worthlessness," says Leila H., twenty-three. "During the act of self-injury, I feel numb and detached, as if my body wasn't mine. After an episode of self-injury, I feel immensely relieved and also a bit embarrassed by my actions, because I know other people will judge me harshly."

Leila made the following chart of her feelings surrounding self-injury:

Before	During	After
1. Panicked	1. Intense	1. Disappointed
2. Anxious	2. Numb	2. Ashamed
3. Lonely	3. Miserable	3. Embarrassed
4. Exhausted	4. Hysterical	4. Guilty
5. Undecided	5. Concentrating	5. Relieved

A few patients report that they do stop injuring once they start feeling the pain, that it is a signal to them that they have gone far enough. And although some may faint from blood loss, they never faint from the experience of the pain itself. This is in part because self-injury functions for them as a survival tool: they are using it to continue coping in circumstances that seem to them to be oppressive. An analogy can be drawn to the fox with a leg stuck in a hunter's trap that chews off its limb to free itself. Or, as Louise J. Kaplan writes in her 1997 book *Female Perversions*, "As horrifying as self-mutilation might

be, the perverse strategy that empowers the behavior is aiming to prevent worse mayhem—homicide, black depression, utter madness."

At some point all self-injurers do experience pain from the wounds
they inflict. If they didn't, they might never stop injuring. Some are
quite clinical about it, and well versed in anatomy. They'll make such
distinctions as "Well, I can cut my skin this deeply, but I won't sever
a vein or an artery." Often, that's how attentive emergency room per-
sonnel can tell the difference between self-injurers and people who
have attempted suicide. Many self-injurers enter medical professions
out of their fascination with anatomy, and they have an idea exactly
where they can and cannot safely cut.

Self-injurers separate the experience of their bodies from the experience of their minds and thoughts. The divorce typically takes place
very early on in childhood, as we will explore. Because of this psychological schism, self-injurers often talk about their bodies and skin as if
they were another substance: cardboard or granite, for instance. Some
of them compare bouts of mutilation to "cutting into a loaf of bread."
Unlike healthy people, they don't experience their skin or their flesh
as living, breathing matter that is connected to what goes on in the
head.

While "cutters" have an extremely high tolerance for self-inflicted
pain, they tend to have no tolerance at all for any other kind of pain.
Paradoxically, the same cutters who say they can wreak havoc on their
limbs without feeling a thing often howl loudly whenever they get a
headache and demand powerful sedatives. Similarly, when someone
else physically harms a self-injurer, she usually feels intense pain. Self-
injurers remember vividly the pain they have suffered at the hands of
other people, and the hurts that have resulted from sicknesses or injuries that were not self-inflicted. There seems to be a two-point
threshold, one for self-harm and another for every other kind of pain.

This contrast leads to the question of how much of the pain the
self-injurer feels is a matter of personal control. That is, when she
controls the pain with the blade of her knife, it seems not to hurt, but
when it comes from outside, it needs to be quashed instantly.

One patient of ours, Amanda B., had poured chemical oven cleaner
all over her forearms one day when the telephone rang. Amanda answered the call and got so distracted by her conversation that she forgot
about the oven cleaner on her arms and only remembered to rinse it
off when she smelled her flesh burning. "You would think that it would

hurt," Amanda observes. "But it actually feels kind of like a natural high, like a runner's high."

There *are* analogies to be drawn to marathon runners, who "work through" the pain to finish the race or complete the workout. Self-abusive ballet star Gelsey Kirkland would dance on broken legs. Basketball legend Michael Jordan—known for his stoic ability to play when feverish with flu—has said that there is something about the goal that seems to dismiss the pain.

HOW DOES ANYONE THINK OF IT IN THE FIRST PLACE?

Many self-injurers we've treated say the first time they injured it was spontaneous, and they had never heard of anyone doing it before. "It just happened," patients will say. Or sometimes the injury was an accident and the blood release felt surprisingly soothing, so the patient tried it again.

"I can't recall exactly what made me start doing it," says Ceci J., thirty-six, a corporate lawyer. "The first time it happened, when I was in my twenties, I cut up my legs. I told everyone I was running with dogs in barbed wire."

This sudden compulsion to take blade to skin may be hard for healthy people to relate to, but many of us may have experienced something similar. One host of a talk show we appeared on said that when her father was sick and dying, she felt so out of control that she had an impulse to run her car into something. Needless to say, the healthy part of her prevailed, and she didn't cause an accident.

Self-injurers seem prone to getting involved in suspicious-sounding "accidents," which sometimes turn out to be deliberate. A hand or foot injury with a fishy explanation may turn out to have been an experiment in punching or kicking a wall. A headache or blurred vision may be the result of a self-imposed concussion. Another telltale sign is a strafe of gashes on the inner arm, few of which ever seem to subside.

Victoria R. was thirteen when she started self-injuring. At the time, Victoria says, she defined herself as an artist who was preoccupied with suicide, and she was in her room painting a picture of an arm with slashes on the wrist. For no particular reason that Victoria can remember, she sat back for a moment from her easel.

"I took an artist's knife and did it to myself," she says. "Then I spattered my blood on the painting."

ANGER = VIOLENCE

"Anger feels like I'm out of control," says Yvonne K., twenty-eight. "Anger is like a broken dam that held all the water back, and when it couldn't hold much more, it broke like a soda pop bottle when you shake it up and open it—all the pressure came out. My fantasies are that I would like to kill the person I'm angry at, or scream at the person. Self-injury seems to relieve my anger, my rage."

Self-injurers live with the myth that when someone gets mad, somebody has to get hurt. They blur anger and violence into a single category. Usually, this is because they grew up in homes where an adult's rage led to acting out. It is certainly true in Yvonne's case. "My family almost never showed any anger, but when they did, it sure got bad," she says.

"Before I self-injure, I feel an extreme amount of anxiety and confusion," says Yvonne. "Sometimes I'm just bored and don't know what else to do.

"My fantasies are that I want self-injury to the point of death, or just seeing as much blood as I can see, or as far as I can go to the point of death. Sometimes I feel like if I self-injure, maybe someone will notice me."

Under a self-injurer's reasoning, it is better for her to hurt herself than to hurt someone else, or to let someone else hurt her first. Self-harm can seem "safer" or more immediate than lashing out at the person or circumstance that is causing the anger, and it can also serve as an indirect means of retaliation: *"I'll show her!"*

Self-injury is an "action symptom." Sufferers believe every thought and feeling must be purged, that they need to "get it all out" whenever something uncomfortable or difficult comes to mind. This is a model that we call the "Pressure Cooker Theory," and we tell patients that we disagree with it vehemently. We have seen no evidence that there is a limit to the amount of feelings that people can tolerate. We try to show patients how they can simply turn off the heat, avoiding what they view as an inevitable explosion.

This fallacy of catharsis is rooted in the surprisingly strong physical sensations that most injurers feel as a prelude to their actions.

"Getting angry feels like my whole body tightening up, like a spring coiling," says Donna W. "My teeth become clenched, and it feels like my skin is too tight. My heart pounds in my chest, and my thoughts become screams in my head. My hands clench.

"Sometimes when I'm angry, I fantasize about losing control and giving in to the rage by acting destructively," she continues. "I think about throwing and breaking things, overturning furniture, screaming, hitting. These fantasies are frightening because I sometimes feel I will suddenly lose control for real. I do not like people to see me angry, because I don't think I do 'angry' well."

Donna says her anger is usually set off by "feeling unappreciated" and "being in situations I can't control." For Liz C. the "triggers" are similar, and also include "being lied to" and "not being listened to or heard." Liz gets frightened by the physical sensations that accompany these triggers; she believes she *must* respond to them with action.

"It happens whenever I've been treated unfairly, or I feel like I'm not in control of the situation," Liz says. "My muscles tense, my body starts shaking, and I think if I don't get some relief I will explode."

PURPOSES OF SELF-INJURY

One of the most intriguing questions people ask us is why people choose self-injury to soothe themselves rather than alcohol, drugs, an eating disorder, or another coping mechanism.

Actually, these behaviors are in no way mutually exclusive. According to a survey we did in conjunction with Dr. Armando Favazza, 56 percent of self-injurers acknowledge a problem with alcohol, and 30 percent have used street drugs. A whopping 61 percent admit that they have, or have had, an eating disorder.

Both self-injury and eating disorders can serve the purpose of revenge against a real or perceived perpetrator. What better way for a

young child to exert power over an adult than to refuse to ingest food?
Self-injury engenders the same type of helplessness, fear, and anger in
significant others.

The motives behind self-injury are numerous and complex. Some
are similar to more socially acceptable forms of stress management,
like smoking (tension release, head rush), drinking alcohol (anesthetic
effect, drowning out sorrows), and binge eating (physical pleasure,
soothing). Some overlap with other compulsions, like food restriction
(control, "showing" other people), bulimia (purging), and drug addiction (need for a "fix," use of ritual). Self-injury serves many purposes
for its practitioners, from the fulfillment of fantasy to the everyday
management of life's bumps and hardships. Far from being a "crazy"
or random behavior, self-injury plays many vital roles in a patient's
survival.

The purposes of self-injury fall under two broad headings, each with
several subcategories:

- *Analgesic or palliative aims.* These include the physical calming that
  most patients experience when they self-injure, and the connections
  they say the behavior forges between mind and body. Self-injury
  makes people think they are in control, and this feeling temporarily
  boosts their morale. Self-injury also helps people feel "cleansed," as
  if they are ridding themselves of emotional toxins they believe lurk
  inside them.
- *Communicative aims.* People use self-injury to depict their emotional
  state and express wishes, needs, and desires. They use it to communicate with themselves—as self-punishment for perceived sins,
  for example—and with other people. Self-injury can represent an act
  of vengeance, a reenactment of earlier abuse, or a desperate cry for
  help and compassion.

  Though done in private and often kept hidden, self-injury clearly
  has a strong interpersonal agenda. It can be a disguised way of lev-
  eling aggression against others, or a desperate attempt to engage the
  caring responses of others. Ultimately, the patient finds that these
  strategies are counterproductive. In reality, her behavior frightens
  and alienates other people. Since she knows this at some level, her
  acts are also an expression of her ambivalence about letting other
  people get close.

Dr. Armando Favazza reports some additional motives, ones that we encounter infrequently. He interviewed more than three hundred self-mutilators and drew several conclusions, based not only on the interviews but on talks with clinicians and literature about self-injury.

Among patients with "major mutilation," he found several motivations drawn from religious beliefs. Passages in Mark 9:47–48 and Matthew 5:28–29 direct Christians to tear out an offending eye and to cut off an offending hand, since losing part of one's body is better than being cast whole into hell. Some patients Dr. Favazza interviewed said these biblical exhortations led them to pluck out an eye or attempt to saw off a hand. Another passage from Matthew that describes people who have "made themselves eunuchs for the kingdom of heaven's sake" have inspired some men to castrate themselves, the survey found.

Dr. Favazza encountered people who had mutilated themselves to identify with Christ's sufferings; to atone for mortal sins; to obey a "heavenly command"; to rid themselves of demons; or to make a sacrifice to God.

Dr. Favazza also found sexual themes among the major self-injurers. Some transsexuals had attempted castration, as had a man who feared he was a homosexual and wanted to prevent himself from acting on that impulse. Some patients wanted to control their abnormal libidos, or repudiate guilt over sexual parts they viewed as "sinful." Other patients were inexplicably obsessed with amputation.

Among people who injured themselves "moderately," Dr. Favazza found a "broad variety of conditions." Among the reasons supplied by patients for their behavior were: tension release; establishing "control"; feeling secure and unique; returning to "reality"; venting anger; irresistible urges; relief from alienation; and confirming negative self-perceptions.

Our patients—whose injuries fall into both the moderate and severe categories—most often cite the same reasons as the moderate injurers in Dr. Favazza's survey. Though we frequently treat patients who are quite religious, seldom do we encounter anyone who uses the Bible or religious teachings to justify self-injury; indeed, it is usually quite the opposite, with religious patients telling us that God loves them *despite* their problem. In terms of sexuality, we find a number of connections. Self-injury is usually embedded with issues of sexual tension, of avoiding or managing sexual guilt and shame. For a small number of people it can be a disguised form of sexual release. Some self-injurers have reported a sense of eroticized euphoria and sexual arousal connected to the act of harm.

ANALGESIA

The self-injurer experiences pain and distress as never ending. She feels she is "about to explode" or to "fall apart into a million pieces." Feeling anxious or agitated quickly escalates into panic, accompanied by the physical sensations of a severe anxiety attack. Thoughts start to whir, buzz, and race. Her heart pounds; she perspires; she is unable to catch her breath.

"Before I self-injure, I fantasize about the relief I'll get," says Susan L. "I see myself making deep cuts and producing lots of blood. The blood is so soothing. It's warm. While I do it, I go very fast. I feel very much in control. I decide when to stop.

"During the cutting I feel calm, I feel powerful, and I feel focused. After self-injury I feel so much relief. I feel very calm. My inside pain and feelings are gone. I go to the emergency room and can't even tell the doctor why I did it because the feelings are so buried."

If the self-injurer is a child-abuse victim like Susan, she may never have learned with confidence to expect relief, or calm. She is prone to climb quickly into a highly flustered and uncontrollable state of agitation. Yvonne K. likens the pressure to a pot that is about to boil over: the mind roils and seethes with fear and rage until the lid pops and the razor makes its mark.

"During an episode I feel a sense of relief, and the pressure of my anxiety is gone," Yvonne says. "After self-injury I feel guilty, but also, like, 'Oh, my gosh, what have I done to myself!' I panic! But I also wish the cut would be deeper."

Susan L. said the "overwhelmed" feeling that Yvonne described makes her feel she has "nowhere to turn but to my old friend," self-injury. Unlike many people in Susan's life, self-injury has "always been there for me. It's never been disappointed in me—and, most of all, it never leaves me. It never expects anything from me."

After harming herself, the self-injurer usually feels a strange sense of calm, usually tinged with remorse and guilt. Research has suggested that when the self-injurer harms herself, the brain releases chemicals that function as relaxants. Many of our self-injurers' descriptions confirm this analgesic function of self-injury, in which the injuring act— paradoxically—produces a calming, soothing, sensation. The tension and agitation "drains" out, and the patient feels she can control her thoughts and feelings once again. Once the cut is made, the danger has passed.

CONNECTING BODY AND MIND

Self-injurers usually suffer from faulty connections between their physical and emotional selves. Some describe feeling chronically "numbed out," disconnected from their senses and body states. We have talked about the idea of dissociation and the means that some self-injurers have used as children to cope with overwhelming trauma. As adults, however, it is a deeply uncomfortable state of mind; some people say they feel like they are "losing my grip on reality," or "losing my mind." They feel as if they don't exist.

Gerri S. recently told us of a disturbing experience in which she was sitting at home and looked down at her hands. In an instant she felt like they were inanimate, lifeless stumps that didn't belong to her. Similarly, when Jacqueline G. cuts herself, she envisions her body as a cow carcass hanging from a butcher's meathook.

For patients who feel distanced from reality, isolated, or dehumanized, the sight of their own blood can jolt them back to reality. It reassures them that they are alive, intact, and have personal boundaries. Patients like this will say, "I feel real again."

Often, self-injurers talk about their need to channel, focus, contain, or modulate their chaotic inner sensations. They describe self-injury as a means for regulating their mood: once they feel aroused to an intolerable level, they feel a "panicky agitation" that subsides after the act of injury. The injuring serves to halt the unmanageable feelings.

Many injurers feel chronically unaware of physical pain. For them, self-injury serves to jar them back in touch with themselves and their bodies. It is a "focusing" maneuver that seems to serve as a quick antidote to disturbing states of mind. It reassures them that they are alive, intact, and have personal boundaries. Self-injury is the remedy that "brings the skin alive," connecting the physical self to the emotional self.

It may seem somewhat contradictory that self-injury could serve all these purposes. However, if you think of the idea of self-injury as a "regulator valve," it might make more sense. When someone feels choked, flooded, or overwhelmed with tremendous panic, she uses self-injury to "turn down the heat," since it produces the soothing and calming effect she needs. In other situations, when she feels *too* numbed out and detached from the world, she uses self-injury to "turn up the heat," to sharpen and enliven her senses.

CONTROL

A self-injurer's sense of mastery and control over her body is usually quite damaged, especially if she has suffered from sexual or physical abuse. For such people, self-injury seems to permit control over the rupture of skin/environment boundaries.

What the child-abuse victim experienced as passive victimization, the adult self-injurer converts into an active ritual: turning the tables on her childhood, this time *she* dictates the beginning, middle, and end of the physical manipulation. She may reenact the abuse she has suffered, sometimes repeatedly, to do so in a way that lends her command over the previously overwhelming trauma.

In other kinds of family situations, self-injurers may have had different boundary-disturbing experiences. For instance, the child of a severe alcoholic may be saddled with the responsibility of caring for siblings or for sick relatives, clouding her understanding of her role in the family. Kelly B., whose father was an alcoholic and whose mother was disturbed and overwhelmed, was often responsible for the basic care of her baby brother, plus cooking, cleaning, and other chores for the family. In other cases the self-injurer may have been reared in a home where one or another parent gets furious or violent at the slightest sign of the child's increasing independence or separation from the family unit.

For people who struggle with interpersonal boundary issues—"Do I have an independent self?" "Where do I end and others begin?"—breaking the skin is a powerfully symbolic way to give voice to this confusion. Self-injury is sometimes described as a way of forcibly es tablishing a line between the injurer and someone to whom she feels dangerously joined.

CLEANSING

Cutting also serves another fantasized purpose, that of cleansing or purifying. Most self-injurers have a subjective sense of being inherently "bad" or "dirty." They'll say things like "I'm the black spot on a cancerous lung," or "I have a bad soul."

This type of message may have been conveyed to them as a child by abusive or neglectful parents. It may be the opinion the abuse victim holds toward her body and sexual self, which feel damaged and ruined by the abuse. It may—separately or simultaneously—stem from various extremely held religious beliefs, in which the body and, in particular, the sexual organs are viewed as filthy or shameful.

Before the advent of modern medicine, doctors routinely used bloodletting to release what they believed to be poisons, or badness, out of people's bodies, and to cure a panoply of little-understood afflictions. Once a patient was bled, he or she was thought to have been "cleansed." Various religious sects have also viewed the release of blood as a means of exorcising demons from the body. Some S.A.F.E. patients voice the idea that their emotions are like poisonous substances that are forever threatening or needing to "leak out" of them.

In addition to cleansing, self-injury—which often takes the form of flagellation—can act as a self-imposed punishment. Patients say they are trying to atone for their inherently sinful selves or for individual transgressions. However, whenever we ask our patients what heinous things they have done to deserve these punishments, they are usually at a loss for words.

"WORDS CANNOT EXPRESS MY PAIN"

Self-injurers usually have grave difficulties identifying and communicating emotional states, wishes, and needs. Some say they never were able to develop the "language" of feeling, or that they lost their ability to use it. They cannot find the words, symbols, and metaphors for what is going on inside them, or what they want from others. The self-injurer might hang her hat on one emotion—like anger—and use it to describe almost any state of being "worked up."

Psychologist Lisa Cross described her work with a patient with a known IQ of 145 who began every single therapy session answering questions about her state of mind by saying, "I don't know, I don't know." Another patient, also a highly intelligent professional, likened her razor cuts to a "bright red scream"; the wounds expressed anguish she could not articulate.

How could such smart people be at such a loss for words? We already know that most self-injurers grew up feeling neglected, "unheard," and misunderstood. These feelings led to a hopelessness about the prospects of using words to get her needs met. The only language she ever learned was the language of action, in which every sign of inner tension had to be discharged physically. Since taking a blade to the skin and requiring an emergency room visit and stitches gets a much quicker response, why bother learning to speak your thoughts?

Self-injurers say that their harmful acts show how much pain they're suffering, in a way that language cannot. This belief, in which impulse immediately leads to action, is a response usually associated with young children who lack the facility to behave differently. Most self-injurers have not advanced beyond this regressed way of communicating.

Self-injurers use their behavior to communicate feelings not only to themselves but to others. As a communicative tool the behavior clearly has an interpersonal agenda. Jared T. called self-injury "the tangible face to my intangible pain—see my pain!"

GETTING A RISE OUT OF OTHER PEOPLE

Leila H. is up-front about it: she cuts, burns, and overdoses to test people's limits and force them to react to her. "One pattern in my life that I'd like to change is my need to 'poke' at people in order to see how much I can trust them and whether or not they'll leave me," she says.

"Other people often react to me with shock or disapproval, while some react with sympathy or pity," says Leila. "Some of my friends and relatives act guilty, because they assume they are somewhat responsible for my self-injury. When people in the general public find out about my self-injury, the most common reaction is fear. It's as if being around me when I'm self-injuring will cause them to self-injure—as if it were a terrible, contagious disease."

Self-injurers report a variety of strong, visceral reactions from others, from deep concern and sympathy to utter revulsion and disdain. Perhaps most frustrating are the people who show no reaction at all, who self-injurers say are surprisingly common.

"I feel that my friends feel helpless and frustrated when I self-injure," says Yvonne K. "They don't know how to respond to me. They get concerned and worry. But my parents don't feel any concern or show any emotion when they hear I've self-injured."

Some parents accuse their children of using self-injury as an attention-getting stunt. While the charge may well be true, it is certainly not something that is routinely acknowledged by the self-injurer, who feels that the statement belittles her turmoil. Jared T., a rare exception, terms self-injury "a completely selfish action."

He tells us: "I've thought, 'I'll show them just how worthless I am, and how much I hurt.' But the feeling I elicit from others, though not intended, is horror. 'Oh, my goodness—why would he do that?' they say. Some people think it's a suicide attempt, which it really is *not*. Some people feel anger at me and think I'm an attention seeker. Some people might sneer and think, 'He deserves it.'"

As mentioned earlier, many self-injurers learn to love the "negative" attention they get for their wounds: attention from doctors, nurses, and psychotherapists, as well as family, teachers, friends, and coworkers. In the sufferer's mind, the injuries send a message of being "tough" and "different" and "strong enough to take it." Conversely, she may be attempting to convey, "Can't you see how much I hurt? Can't you see how badly I need you?"

"I have self-injured only twice in front of others," Donna W. says. "Both were boyfriends. The first incident occurred when my boyfriend and I were both drinking, and we got drunk and started to argue. I began self-injuring hoping he would be shocked and would realize how much I needed him to love me.

"The second time I was sober and with another boyfriend, but I was acting out in a rage. I had broken a mirror and some figurines in my apartment during an argument, and I self-injured with some broken pieces, hoping he would also be shocked and would try to calm me down by holding me. When I knew someone would be seeing the cuts, I was hoping they would feel compassion and want to help me. It didn't turn out that way. Nobody really even noticed."

THE RESCUE FANTASY

When self-injury is not being used to level aggression against others, it most often represents a desperate attempt to engage people's caring responses. The fantasy is that if the other person *truly cared* enough, he or she would keep the self-injurer from her habit, prevent the wound, knock the instrument of torture from her eager grasp.

Susan L. describes self-injury in terms of the "feelings I've wanted to create in others, of wanting them to help me." But the actual feelings Susan encounters are usually quite different. "I elicit attention, worry, fear," she says. "Feelings of pity, feelings of frustration and helplessness."

Since anything less than a dramatic gesture goes ignored, the injurer feels that both she and her pain are invisible, and her feelings must rise to the surface of her skin to be seen by anyone. When significant people in the self-injurer's life abandon her or respond in harsh or uncaring ways, this confirms her belief that the world is an unsafe place with unsympathetic people. Without therapy, she fails to realize that it is her own behavior that brings about the understandable fear, anger, and helplessness in others. Ultimately, the patient finds that her strategies are counterproductive: in reality, her self-injurious behavior frightens and alienates others.

As the problem progresses, self-injury begins to replace relationships. Self-injurers describe their scars and the weapons they use against themselves as "friends." Eventually, they must come to realize that these are not true friends, since they serve to destroy all that the sufferer truly loves and values.

The only person who can ultimately save her from herself is the patient. However, self-injurers tend to look to medical professionals to provide the nurturing that their parents did not, and that their intimate friends cannot. In reality, neither round-the-clock monitoring nor other sorts of heroic intervention can stop the injurer from taking up arms against herself.

Just as the act of self-injury becomes a ritual, so does the need to gain sympathy through frequent medical attention. Susan L. expresses it well. "I will miss getting stitches," she wrote toward the end of her stay at the S.A.F.E. program. "Chatting with the doctor as he sews me up. The feeling of the needle going through my numb skin. Taking off the bandage when I get home and recounting the stitches. The good nights they bring. Touching them. Looking at them. Watching them heal. Picking at the scabs when they are removed."

As patients get better, they replace the desire to be rescued with the instinct to take care of themselves. Susan, for instance, learned to derive pleasure from her activities and hobbies—her church group, sewing, and singing—and no longer felt the need to distract others through desperate acts on her body.

VENGEANCE

Many self-injurers want to exact vengeance on the people who have caused them pain, though they may not know how to go about it. Often, the opportunity for legal or protective action has long since passed. The self-injurer may worry about the consequences of broaching the topic with the person who caused the torment—who is often a parent or close relative—for fear of retribution, or for fear that the person will refuse to own up to the acts of wrongdoing. Many self-injurers take it as a foregone conclusion that their hurts will be ignored or dismissed, the crimes committed against them brushed under the rug like dirt.

Since sufferers are frequently unable to put into words their feelings of anger and maltreatment, their rage takes a diffuse form; it simmers internally as an inchoate mass of noxious, painful feelings. Self-injury becomes a concrete outlet for the expression of this confusion.

One of the writing assignments we give at S.A.F.E. asks patients to identify the people who have wronged them, create a "fantasy" of revenge, and then imagine what actual apologies, punishments, or retribution might reasonably occur. Needless to say, it's a popular assignment, though it does tend to stir many strong and difficult feelings, as people recall the abuse they have suffered at the hands of people whom they love and who were often responsible for their primary care.

"I feel that my mom hurt me as a child by ignoring my needs and focusing on my brother's needs," wrote Yvonne K. "She heard my brother's cries but not mine. My dad abused me emotionally and sexually. I felt belittled by him and shamed for having feelings.

"I don't feel that any of my mom's actions have been acknowledged. She says that she treated my brother and me the same. We have fought over whom she loved more, and the different treatment she showed us. I still feel that she loves me, but I still have problems believing that she loved me as a child.

"About my dad, I confronted him two years ago on the sexual abuse, and he denied it. My mom doesn't recognize my abuse at all. I would like to see my dad go to jail for the crimes he did to me when I was a child. I would also like to see a confession from him, but that won't happen. I guess a confession from both of my parents would make me feel better."

As these categories suggest, self-injury is a complex and highly symbolic behavior, one with multiple functions and aims for the self-injurer. The sufferer comes to rely on it as her primary means of gratification and tension release. She uses it to remind herself that she is alive, that she is a human being distinct from all others. Perhaps most of all, she uses it to communicate unspeakable thoughts and feelings to herself and others.

We encourage each self-injurer who embarks on a healing journey to give some time and consideration to figuring out the "hidden agendas" behind her self-harm. The more she can discover about the messages she is sending, the more likely she will gain a true sense of control and mastery by facing her needs and feelings in a direct, nondestructive manner.

Chapter Four

THE LINK TO CHILD ABUSE
AND EARLY TRAUMA

Susan L.'s childhood memories are so upsetting that they sear in the memory of anyone who learns of them.

"My mother kept me clean and fed," Susan recalls. "She beat me and my sister, Beth, what seemed to be daily. When I was four, she took all my and Beth's toys into the backyard and burned them."

Life at home was unrelenting for Susan and Beth, who was fifteen months older: their mother beat them, threw objects at them, bloodied their noses. "My mother would make us take off all our clothes and lie over a stool, and then she'd whip us with a belt," Susan says. "She had a wooden paddle she would hit me with. 'No more, Mama, no more,' I'd beg. She would tell me I was a filthy slut, stupid, dumb, and useless. 'You can't do anything right, you never will!' she'd scream. My father ignored the abuse."

No children were allowed to come over and play at Susan's house, which was a strict Mormon home where the rules of the church were followed to the letter. Though Susan was permitted to play at other homes in the neighborhood, she soon learned that her house was not the only place where she was unsafe.

A next-door neighbor, the father of one of her playmates, began sexually abusing Susan when she was four. "He used to make me put his penis in my mouth and play with his penis," she says. "When I was seven, he raped me. The raping continued until I was eleven."

Susan told her sister Beth about the neighbor's abuse, and Beth told their mother, but their mother accused Susan of being a liar. Susan's mother used to take her to the neighbor's to have the man baby-sit while she and the man's wife went shopping.

"The first time I remember self-abusing is when I was four years old," Susan recalls. "It was after my mother went out with the man's wife, and I was left alone with him. He took out his penis and shoved my mouth down on it. I threw up. He was very angry. He grabbed me by the hair and threw me back against the couch. He cleaned himself up. When my mom and his wife returned, Mom asked, 'What's wrong with Susan?' He said, 'Oh, um, she just got sick.'"

After that Susan's mother took her home, gave her a bath, and boiled water for Jell-O. "When she took the pan off the stove, I put my hand on [the stove]," Susan says. "This was the first time I remember doing anything like that."

Susan's self-injury continued in private throughout her childhood. "I reacted to my mother's beatings and neighbor's sexual abuse by cutting, burning, and scraping," she wrote in her diary at S.A.F.E. "I feel, and felt, that I must be a very bad girl to have had such a life."

At first she would rub her skin off with sandpaper, pot scrubbers, or pencil erasers. She would burn herself on pancake griddles, light-bulbs, stove burners, and with hot water. She beat herself with a hammer regularly, and cut her skin with myriad implements. All in private.

"As I got older, in my twenties, I got creative," says Susan, who is now thirty-seven. "I would inject urine in my ears and under my skin. I would rub my skin off and infect it with fecal matter. Once I put liquid Drano on my face, and I've also put it on my hands. I've also chemically burned with other things. No one ever knew I was doing it."

Bulimia was also a part of Susan's self-abuse. At age fifteen she began throwing up breakfast and dinner, angry at herself for being slightly overweight. By the time she got to S.A.F.E., Susan said that her weight problem had contributed toward her feelings of being unlovable for all of her adult life. As a result, she had never had a sex life, and her emotional problems had helped break up a relationship with the one man with whom she had had a caring and loving relationship.

INFANCY AND EARLY CHILDHOOD

While some self-injurers come from normal, stable households, most of them are like Susan: they come from very stormy, dysfunctional families and had extremely traumatic early lives. Many self-injurers were abused by their parents emotionally, sexually, physically, or through neglect. Some parents suffered from emotional problems of their own, which prevented them from nurturing their children in a normal way. One recurring theme in the very early lives of most patients is a sense of something profoundly missing in the bond between themselves and their early caregivers.

Some patients say their mothers were very depressed at the time of their birth or shortly afterward. Others have told of surviving infancy and early childhood amid chaotic family events like a divorce, a dramatic geographic move, or the death or life-threatening illness of a relative. For example, one patient told of the birth of her twin sister, who was severely mentally retarded and absorbed all the attention and concern of her emotionally fragile parents.

The distinction—that the parents were emotionally fragile—is important. Plenty of babies and young children live through divorces, moves, and other big changes and come out emotionally unscathed. With self-injurers there is usually some supplemental factor that made the situation impossible to deal with, like a parent who did not shield her from the upheaval.

At the most severe end of the spectrum, self-injurers tell of profoundly damaging neglect and abuse at the hands of extremely disturbed caregivers. One patient, Kelly B., had a mother who used to brag to neighbors that she could "feed the baby without touching her," and insisted that her infant "did not like being touched." When Kelly got older, she believed—with good reason—that her mother despised her and and wished her dead from the moment she was born. Her mother would neglect to give her dinner, ignore her when she was sick, and overlook the sadistic sexual abuse that Kelly's stepfather perpetrated. Moreover, Kelly seems to have been singled out for her mother's hatred; she remembers her mother saying, "I wish I could crumple up my first child and throw her away—I made all my mistakes on her."

We take for granted that a child's early caregivers will give freely of their touch, comfort, affection, and willingness to respond to the infant's cries. No parent is perfect—all inevitably have crises and "bad moments"—but most do a good enough job responding to their children's needs. Many self-injurers never even got this good enough experience that we know to be the cornerstone of emotional health and sanity.

Babies first learn about their bodies through touch, both their own (fingers in the mouth, etc.) and their mother's (through holding, cleaning, feeding, etc.). These tactile sensations help them begin to differentiate themselves from other people. Through the early experience of someone "coming when I cry," the growing child learns to expect that distress is temporary, and that care, concern, and relief from tension are just around the corner. The caressing touch of a loving adult "brings the skin to life," giving a young child a sense that her body is part of her, part of emotional life, loved and valued. Eventually, a child also learns that painful states have names, language to describe them. This is taught when a caregiver comes to the child's aid and says out loud, "You must be hungry," or wet, or tired, or cranky, etc.

This is the way we eventually learn to "parent ourselves," or take care of our own needs. These early experiences become part of our personality, and we learn the language of feeling that helps us communicate our needs. We also learn that our bodies are an important part of the developing self, and that our thoughts, feelings, and physical selves function as a synthesized whole.

At first we are entirely dependent on the care of adults, who must recognize, respect, and respond to our bodily needs. In keeping the child safe from harm, the caregiver helps form a vital boundary between the child and the outside environment. Many self-injurers report that their absent or emotionally unavailable caregivers made them feel continuously endangered and profoundly vulnerable.

While these feelings may develop for many reasons, the abused child is a prime example of a failure of caregiving that may give rise to self-injury. Child abuse is in many ways the most readily understandable explanation for a person's decision to resort to self-injury: the child's skin boundaries were not respected, so her recognition or appreciation of those boundaries could not develop normally.

The problem of abuse or incest by a caregiver is often compounded by the presence of another caregiver who permits the crimes to take place—an "enabler," in psychology lingo. For example, the second parent may be too sick (physically or emotionally) or powerless to intervene on the child's behalf, or may be absent altogether. Self-

injurers who have survived incest or chronic abuse talk about the feeling that there are no discernible limits between themselves and others,
and that they feel chronically endangered, easily "penetrated" or victimized.

The significance of the body is that it is an "object," both desired
and despised by the abuser, and viewed with loathing by the victim as
the "betrayer." The body is a vital piece of her identity, but it is also
the cause of her pain and suffering. Carrie G., age thirty-five, who was
sexually abused by her father, talks about wishing she were "dead from
the neck down." Many child-abuse victims have learned to cope by
dissociating or "numbing out." This might have been the only way to
survive the abuse they were suffering. To actually be in touch with the
physical pain and the emotional intensity of the abuse experience
might have resulted in suicidal despair or madness.

Dissociation may be a vital strategy for the traumatized child, but
when the child reaches adolescence and adulthood, it poses tremendous problems. Many self-injurers with abuse histories say they continue to feel separated from their bodies even when they don't
consciously desire to feel that way. They have difficulty recognizing
when they are tired, sick, or hungry. They often cannot enjoy pleasur-
able experiences, such as sexual arousal or lovemaking, though some
of them do say they enjoy nonsexual hugs. While they crave physical
affection and caresses, some adult abuse survivors say that when they
receive it, it leaves them feeling empty, numb, or unsatisfied—or even
frightened and mistrustful.

Our patients routinely tell us they came from parents in which roles,
rights, and responsibilities were delineated poorly, and they often felt
the roles of parents and children were reversed. Some say they had to
"mother" the other siblings in the house and cater to the physical,
sexual, or narcissistic needs of one or both parents. Parental illness or
early loss are also common themes, as is the presence of another child
in the family whose illness or death renders the parents unable to take
care of the other people in the house.

In our clinical observations of the families of self-injurers, we have
seen another pronounced trend. Many families enforced strict and rigid
codes of morality and behavior, codes that usually allowed little room
for the expression of normal human emotions. Many families were
deeply religious and judged one another's actions by their conformity
to church rules or their interpretations of what God would want. In

all, we have noticed a variety of dogmatic perspectives on human behavior.

These rigidities often conceal the parents' deep-seated anxieties. Children raised in these kinds of environments often say their parents were intolerant of their emotions and needs, or hypocritical about the ways they imposed rules of morality. They felt they were not allowed to find a place for their feelings, since they were never "permitted" to feel sad, angry, vulnerable, or otherwise "childlike." They were encouraged to be precociously adult in thought and behavior, amid threats and an absence of empathy. A lot of self-injurers tell us their parents would say, "Stop crying or I'll give you something to cry about."

They also report that their parents had bizarre reactions to ordinary childhood injuries, illnesses, or vulnerabilities of any kind. Some self-injurers suffered gross and malevolent neglect of their basic bodily or physical needs—food deprivation, lack of clean clothing—and some were subjected to heinous and sadistic tortures. Those who have experienced physical or sexual abuse tend to struggle more intensely with trust issues, since their parents failed to cultivate and respect the child's bodily boundaries, and the child grew up feeling there was no safe, contained, space in their world to process or resolve emotional issues.

People who have had these childhood experiences tend to develop a whole range of problems. In general, they find it difficult to experience ordinary situations without feeling rapidly overwhelmed. It is challenging for them to define precisely what they feel. They may be profoundly out of touch with their bodily experiences and often are very poor caretakers of themselves. They may crudely neglect their own physical welfare through poor nutrition, inadequate medical care, and failing to take everyday safety precautions. Kelly B., for example, used to walk into street traffic reading a book and was unable to prepare a healthy meal for herself.

Although a significant majority of patients who self-injure report a history of physical and sexual abuse, not all self-injurers have this history. People can and do develop a pattern of self-injury in the absence of these conditions. Patients who self-injure may have suffered different kinds of parental failures or psychological trauma, which may have interfered with their ability to grow into whole human beings. Conversely, not all sexual- or physical-abuse victims become self-injurers.

In *Women Who Hurt Themselves*, Dusty Miller asserts that a wide variety of problematic behaviors—including self-injury, alcoholism, and excessive plastic surgeries—stem from the re-creation of traumatic events from childhood, or "Trauma Re-enactment Syndrome," as Miller dubs it. We agree with her that self-injury often represents a reenactment of child abuse: many wishes and fears get expressed through self-injury, and people who have suffered chronic physical or sexual trauma can use the behavior to try to master that traumatic experience. Self-injury permits control and predictability of the invasion of boundaries. The injurer converts a passive experience of victimization into something that she controls actively. She can "play out" the abuse scenarios over and over in different ways, determining the outcome for herself each time.

Louise Kaplan writes in *Female Perversions* that the self-injurer has learned that "action brings comfort," while "waiting long enough to think or speak only brings more tension and more disorganization." People with histories of sustained physical or sexual abuse learned early on to equate caregiving from adults with bodily harm. They make this connection very early and continue to repeat it in their adult lives.

Patients whose families intruded on their bodies—through physical abuse or smothering child-rearing tactics—often describe self-injury as a way of differentiating themselves from others. Most often the person from whom they seek to separate is their mother. The message is: "I can do something you can't—I'm stronger, tougher, and can tolerate more pain than you." The patient harms her body to retaliate against the family member, whom she imagines she is also hurting by acting out. To wit, one patient described an argument with her mother that ended in a savage act of cutting. During her therapy session she leapt from the chair and exclaimed to the therapist, "Can't you see? I had to cut her loose!"

Patients who come from neglectful families may use self-harm as a cry to be noticed. Since anything less than a dramatic gesture goes ignored, the patient feels that both she and her anguish are invisible, so her internal pain must rise to the skin's surface in order to be seen. This kind of patient may also be actively seeking to revolt people with her behavior, since negative attention may seem to her to be better than none at all.

Susan L.

When we met Susan, she desperately wanted to heal. She dreamed of getting married, having a child, finishing college, working, volunteering, playing an active role in her church. Most of all, she yearned for a life free of self-injury. "I don't know how to make it stop," she wrote in one desperate journal entry. "I want it more than anything."

Despite the terrible circumstances of her life, Susan had a lot going for her. She always had a lot of friends her age, both as a child and as an adult. She got good grades in high school and made the dean's list for one year of college. "I feel that I have to get perfect grades to prove my intelligence," she wrote in a journal. "My folks were always telling me how stupid and worthless I was."

Susan has also held down many responsible jobs in the health care field and considers her talent at caring for other people one of her biggest strengths. She volunteered as a hospital candy striper at age fourteen, and as an adult worked at several rewarding positions at nursery schools. She taught Sunday school on the weekends and loved spending time with her sisters' children.

But self-injury always got in the way, causing her to miss work and feel constantly overcome. Though Susan had the ability to be a very capable worker, she acknowledged, "when I'm sick, I'm undependable." Once Susan enrolled in a training program to become a nurse's aide, but got kicked out after two suicide attempts. Several times she felt she genuinely wanted to end her life, but her religious faith always pulled her through.

"The Mormon Church has always been my strength," she says. "If I had not had the support and love of my fellow church members, I would be dead. They have helped show me how to be outgoing, strong, and loving and caring—for everyone except Susan."

Moreover, Susan says her role as a "child of God" is the "only one I don't fake."

"I love my Heavenly Father and my brother Jesus Christ with all my heart," she says. "I know they love me no matter what. When I self-abuse, I know they love me. I get angry with the Heavenly Father sometimes and wonder why I suffer, but even when I'm angry with him, I know he loves me."

Susan's situation shows how clear the link between child abuse and self-injury can be. Even as a preschooler she had a sense that her impulse to self-injure was being prompted by the horrifying crimes inflicted on her—the neighbor's sexual abuse, her mother's physical and emotional abuse—and negative messages swirling into her head.

Susan's case also helps clarify the often misunderstood distinction between self-injury and suicide. Susan did engage in several suicide attempts, as many self-injurers have. But something deep and visceral always revived her will to live. Given the manifold and extreme ways Susan abused herself, she could easily have ended her life had she so chosen.

We accepted Susan at S.A.F.E. Alternatives because we felt she could pull through—and she did. She completed the program and went on to live independently in an apartment of her own. Susan says she is injury-free, employed, and happier than ever before. She tells us she is pursuing her many interests—reading, cross-stitch, teaching Sunday school—and writing in her journal whenever the urge to self-injure strikes.

"What happened to me as a child is horrible," Susan says. "I let it control my life for thirty-seven years. The next thirty-seven are mine."

Liz C.: Still Seeking an Escape

Routinely beaten by her mother and raped by her father, Liz C. is an interesting example of someone with vast talents who has used them to create ways to hurt herself. One has to wonder what she might have accomplished if her experiences had not been so crippling.

Liz, a thirty-nine-year-old mother of two, has her brilliant and charming side. An attractive and quick-witted woman with a long brown braid and a compact figure, she developed instant rapport with everyone at S.A.F.E., staffers and patients alike. Though she has little education, she is fascinated by science and reads voraciously. She knows the name of every rock and mineral and can talk for hours about geology. After reading several books on the topic, Liz learned to put together microscopes from scratch.

Then there is the dark side of Liz. She cannot take care of herself or her children. When she forgets to take her medications, she goes into an antisocial funk and hides in her closet or under a bed for hours or days. Sometimes she remembers everything about herself and her past, and other days she remembers nothing. Liz's outpatient therapist believed that she had a dissociative disorder, multiple "personalities" of which she was unaware, and he used hypnosis to try to "integrate" her personalities and make them acknowledge one another. This technique—which we strongly discourage for all self-injurers—made her regress and deteriorate severely.

Like many abuse survivors, Liz doesn't believe she "deserves" anything good. "I was taught that others always come first," she says. "I believe that my obligations and responsibilities as a parent have to come first, and many times there is not enough time or money left for me."

Such rigid thinking may well be a product of Liz's joyless childhood, which was spent in an austere household that viewed weekly attendance at revival meetings as mandatory. Liz describes her parents as "hypocritical religious fanatics" who used Christianity to justify all discipline and household rules, no matter how quirky or cruel. The children were not allowed to go to movies, dances, or anywhere that served alcohol. Nor were they allowed to discuss any personal problems or difficulties—bringing up "bad news" was explicitly forbidden.

These principles and moral values gave Liz one kind of idea about how impulses and excitable emotions should be expressed. However, life inside her family was anything but contained. For Liz the problem did not lie in the religious faith that her family adhered to, but in the incongruence between the beliefs they espoused and the blatantly cruel and malevolent ways they treated their children.

The religion and rules masked a family with problems. Liz's mother would "fly into blind rages" at her and her two older siblings, and her father issued a constant stream of sarcastic put-downs. The parents fought often. Liz's father used to molest her sexually when he put her to bed, and her mother whipped her with a belt. "For the longest time I thought that it was just normal discipline, and every parent did it," she observed. "It was not until my adult years that I realized it was really abuse."

Liz lived hard and fast in her youth. A less than stellar student, she got heavily into drugs and drinking and managed to eke out a diploma by transferring to an alternative high school. By age seventeen a dynamic had developed at home in which her father would try to shield her from her mother's beatings, but demanded sexual favors as payment. The problems culminated when her mother's psychosis reached a murderous level, and she tried to strangle Liz. Liz's father helped her escape by opening the back door for her; Liz ran away to join the circus, never to see her parents again.

When Liz left the military and resettled not far from her hometown, she had a brief romance that led to the birth of her daugher. While floating from job to job, she married a coworker two weeks after meeting him; the marriage lasted all of three months. Her next relationship turned into a nine-year marriage, during which her son was born. All the relationships ended with Liz being physically abused.

Her self-injury began in adolescence, around age thirteen. "I would get so mad, and I wasn't allowed to express it," Liz says. "The pressure inside me would build up, and in order to release it, I would cut my wrist and forearm."

The first time she remembers injuring was after an argument with her mother. "You didn't get angry at Mom, because if you did, you would get hurt," Liz says. "I don't know why the idea came across my head—I'm not sure if I was trying to kill myself—but I ended up self-injuring, and I got an immediate release." In hindsight, she says, the main reason she committed herself to recovery was "I don't get the same release anymore." Many other self-injurers describe the same phenomenon, that the sensation changes over time and the behavior fails to produce the desired "high."

Over the years Liz has "used many ways to self-harm—cutting, scratching, biting, burning with cigarettes, stabbing with a pencil, banging my head, punching my face, punching walls," she says. "Basically, I do whatever happens to be an available method at the time."

Liz did finish the S.A.F.E. program, but not without problems. One day, on impulse, she smuggled a plastic knife from the cafeteria in her sleeve. Though she did not self-injure with it, she did lock herself in the bathroom after turning it over to a staff member, an "isolating" behavior that we do not condone. She hid in her closet a lot, saying that small, enclosed spaces were the only places she felt safe. She also missed many compulsory meetings.

Liz's transgressions led to a separate contract, over and above the No-Harm Contract that we ask all patients to sign (this and other basic tools of the S.A.F.E. Alternatives program will be discussed at length in Part Two). "I commit to not hoarding sharp implements and to staying out of my room's closet," it read. "I will approach staff, utilize the quiet room, fill out Impulse Control Logs, talk with peers, do journaling or other safe alternatives when I think that I am unsafe. I commit to participating in the S.A.F.E. program by attending groups, doing writing assignments, taking prescribed medications, taking self-responsibility, and being an active participant in my treatment."

Liz says she got a lot out of S.A.F.E. She is now enrolled in a day treatment program for people with borderline personality disorders, but one day hopes to complete her training and become an art therapist.

"I learned a lot about handling my angry feelings during the S.A.F.E. program," Liz says. "I learned to acknowledge my anger, and I learned that it's important to verbalize the emotion rather than act on it."

A year out of the program, Liz is still making progress. "I went several months without self-injury," she says. "Right before I went into the program, I was self-injuring every five minutes. They couldn't leave me alone, and my life was in danger."

Progress came slowly. "I did a lot of soul searching," she says. "I had a hard time making a commitment to the program. For me to self-injure, it felt like a compulsion. The pressure would build up inside. It wasn't something I was really getting any pleasure out of—it had become my master. I still have lapses occasionally, but I do go longer in between."

Just as no two siblings necessarily turn out alike, so is it that no two child-abuse victims will grow up the same way, even if they are from the same home. Some turn to self-injury, and others find different ways to grapple with the pain and outrage. We try to instill hope in our patients who were abused as children: that they can learn to overcome the past and live joyfully in the present and future.

Chapter Five

THE CASE FOR BIOLOGICAL
FRAGILITY

A mong people who do not have overt abuse in their backgrounds, self-injury can be far more puzzling. Some families that seem normal as apple pie produce a child who is a severe self-injurer. Sometimes a self-injurer's experience of her family life differs drastically from the account given by her parents—the child may perceive extreme slights and abuse, and the parents deny them—and it's impossible for outsiders to judge where the truth lies. There are also people whom we believe have been coaxed into remembering "abusive" childhood situations that were exaggerated or did not occur. The so-called "recovered memory" movement is extremely controversial, yet some of our patients have been treated by therapists who subscribe to it.

Parents can behave toward their children in many ways that seem to lay the groundwork for self-injury. But not all of these behaviors are abusive, and indeed, not all parents of self-injurers engage in them. In some cases there may be an organic problem with the self-injurer, something about her body chemistry or genetic makeup that contributes toward her urge to harm herself.

We are not entirely persuaded by any genetic or biological explanations of the root causes of self-injury. However, we have observed that some people we work with appear to possess a higher predilection toward emotional "hypersensitivity" than others. Our patients routinely describe themselves as "too sensitive," "thin-skinned," and "too emotional." This fragility exhibits itself in many ways: the self-injurer finds her emotions too traumatic to bear, and she often has extreme aversions to certain physical sensations, particular noises, odors, sights, and sounds. One patient, Kelly B., used to startle with fright at the sound of a ballpoint pen dropping on a tabletop. Jared T., whose story appears later in this chapter, could not stand the way his college roommate breathed.

Researchers are at work around the country trying to pinpoint a gene, brain chemical, or other biological explanation for self-injury. While we encourage all research in the area of self-injury, we are concerned about a "Holy Grail" approach to finding "The Cause." Self-injury, in our estimation, may have multiple causes.

We believe the situation is more nuanced than whether self-injury is a disease or a manifestation of a genetic or biological vulnerability. There are many open questions about the causes of the syndrome, and answers are difficult to come by given the lack of conclusive findings and the political atmosphere that surrounds the behavior. Self-injury seems to have organic effects that produce distinctive biochemical changes similar to those seen in a physical addiction. But that is a separate issue from the question of if a genetic or internal predisposition to self-injury exists. There's ample research to show that if you do certain things to the brain, lab animals become more self-injurious.

The fact that a preponderance of self-injurers come from abusive or damaging backgrounds points to the conclusion that environmental factors are a major influence. But sometimes people confuse early childhood determinants with genetic explanations. A person's innate temperament can influence how she handles stress and why she might become a self-injurer when an equally maltreated sibling does not.

In some families of self-injurers everything seems fine on the surface, or at least not so bad that it would produce this level of pathology. The parents seem normal and caring, the family has undergone no particular traumas, yet the child suffers from serious psychological problems. Again, we have no way of knowing what really happened behind closed doors. However, when we see situations like this, we are receptive to the possibility that there are innate explanations—something we refer to as "biological fragility" in the child.

To this day, for instance, we have not been able to figure out why

Leila H. developed such severe problems, and we probably never will. Leila is a graduate of S.A.F.E. who returns often to visit friends but who has replaced self-injury with different physical and emotional complaints. Neither we nor Leila's parents can understand why someone who grew up with such promise under such seemingly auspicious circumstances could turn out to be a dysfunctional adult who shows few signs of long-term recovery.

Leila H.

Leila H., twenty-three, a petite redhead with large eyes and long, thick hair, comes across as someone who has everything going for her. The eldest daughter of a successful lawyer and his wife, a stay-at-home mother, Leila grew up in a luxurious home with a swimming pool, a Jacuzzi, and hordes of neighborhood playmates who dropped by all the time to see their popular friend. A music prodigy, Leila became something of a local celebrity in her youth: by age three she was a soloist in her church choir; by elementary school she was composing her own songs; by high school she had begun singing in professional operas.

Leila, who describes herself as "a perfectionist," was also academically gifted. A member of her high school's chess team, she competed in competitions around the country and won an award for being the top player in her age group on the East Coast. Her musical talents continued to blossom throughout high school, and several internationally prominent voice coaches took her under their wing. By graduation Leila was being hotly pursued by many prestigious colleges, all offering rich music scholarships.

Leila's parents were extraordinarily proud of her and used their considerable wealth to promote her talents every way they could. They sat in the front row of every recital, clapping loudly. When Leila was ten and her brother was born, her parents let her name the baby so there would be no jealousy. The day Leila turned sixteen, she got her first car.

Leila had a few problems in high school—she showed up drunk for class one day and nearly faced expulsion—but her personal battles started in earnest during college. Blaming her parents for her internal demons, she started feeling alternatively depressed and rageful and was dogged by severe back problems. She began cutting her arms with razor blades in private—then her legs, then her chest.

"My anger feels white-hot, frustrating, and vicious," Leila wrote in her diary. "I have horrible fantasies of me destroying whatever room I'm in, or literally attacking the person who made me angry. Anger terrifies me."

Leila became a severe self-injurer with myriad emotional and physical problems. Her parents paid for her treatment at dozens of hospitals and back clinics, to no avail. They also paid for her treatment at S.A.F.E. Alternatives. Leila graduated from our program last year and is no longer injuring, but her other problems persist. She continues to seek new treatments at back clinics, continues to have difficulty accepting other people's viewpoints, and continues to believe that her parents are the source of everything wrong in her life.

Leila's story is a classic "he said, she said" situation. While Leila claims she was severely emotionally neglected—though not physically abused—by her parents, they cannot fathom what she is talking about. Leila says she spent most of her childhood with baby-sitters and in day-care centers; Leila's mother says she spent full-time at home taking care of the children, and the only time she can remember that Leila was in day care was for the two weeks after her brother was born.

Leila recalls her parents as being "always too busy to pay attention to me." Though Leila had every possession a girl could want, she says, "I was totally starved for affection. By the time I reached high school, I was no longer willing even to hope for my parents to come back into my life. They had wounded me too deeply for too long."

Thus, Leila explains, she began wounding herself. "I just want to shock others into awareness of my pain," she wrote in her journal. "I want them to know how miserable I feel. Sometimes I self-injure when I am angry at someone and want the person to feel guilty or somehow responsible. I want my parents to admit that they weren't there for me when I was growing up and that they're sorry, but I know they never will."

Leila's parents say they do not know what could have prompted their daughter to feel this way. They knew she was always terribly jealous of her little brother, Scott, and they tried to be sensitive to that. They had always paid all her bills and sought the best in expert care for her. They continue to support her in her decisions to hop from one back clinic to the next.

Leila's riddle is not likely to be solved. She would not let the staff at S.A.F.E. contact her parents to talk about her—she did not want any of us to hear her parents' side of the story, and what little we know was gleaned from conversations her parents initiated. Leila steadfastly refused family counseling, saying it "wouldn't do any good" because the situation was "hopeless."

"My parents have hung a little 'sick' sign over my head," Leila sighs. "The stigma and the label infuriate me."

Usually, we can tell a lot about a family when the parents come to visit the children at S.A.F.E.. The parents typically act in predictable ways: a father who the patient describes as drunk and abusive will show up drunk and abusive at our program, or a mother who has been cold and distant will refuse to contact her child. Leila's parents always seemed warm and loving, and we could never square her description of them with the behavior we saw. Moreover, Leila gained a reputation at S.A.F.E. for manipulating the truth and distorting stories so that she came out on top. It was as if she was desperate to prove that her version of the world was true, and that there were nothing but uncaring, hostile "others" in her environment. Our speculation was that Leila may have arrived in the world with a temperamental fragility, one that was so extreme that she needed more than average parenting to develop an internal sense of being cared for and responded to. Her fragility may have been such that everything felt to her as if it were depriving, or "not enough."

Jared T.

Jared, twenty-three, constantly described himself as "hypersensitive." He was bothered to distraction by various noises, sights, sounds, smells, and tactile sensations. Other people's habits and personal quirks drove him wild, to the point that he could barely contain his anger. A hairdo or clothing ensemble that did not meet his standards could ruin his whole day, shattering his emotional equilibrium. Jared told us, "I feel like I could just go to pieces at any time."

The list of things that aggravated Jared could fill a fat volume: music that offended his taste; any sign of messiness or dirt; sloppy eaters; people with loud laughs.

"Sometimes the smallest thing will set me off," he told us. "I'm like a balloon always ready to burst, and I inflate very quickly."

Irrational and compulsive ideas dominated Jared's emotional landscape and colored everything in his life—work, relationships, living within his skin. As a teenager, Jared hated his dog-walking job because "it had that element of *everyday* commitment—no days off, even though it was all of forty-five minutes a day." He also hated his job at a music store, because "everyone else did everything wrong, and if people didn't do their jobs the way I liked, I felt I had to do them over again." As an adult, he hated his roommate, "because of the way he breathed, talked, blew his nose, slept, woke up, and walked."

Jared considered himself an extreme perfectionist, and only he met his own exacting standards. In school, anything less than a perfect grade prompted him to berate himself. Falling short in any category was intolerable. "I pressure myself into making everything a competition," he wrote in his journal. "I have to have the best grades or I am not good enough. If I get the best grades, I didn't deserve them. Why do I do this to myself?"

Other people sometimes told him he was smart, clever, witty, and funny. They praised his academic performance and his artistic ability. But these compliments drove Jared nuts—he hated praise almost as much as he hated his roommate's personal habits. He felt undeserving and tormented; while he privately felt he was "the best," he couldn't stand for others to see the pride he took in himself.

On the flip side, any sort of constructive criticism sent him into a tailspin. Jared described his mood swings as "dramatic and intense," and his ego as "extremely fragile." He told us, "I continually need to fight my self-loathing thoughts and my rejection of compliments. God has blessed me and wants me to feel good about myself."

Jared had other odd fragilities that hampered his ability to live independently and maintain relationships. For one thing, he had an extreme neurotic fear of new places and situations. He tried to avoid at all costs going into a grocery store or shopping mall where he had never been. "I don't know where everything is, I'm afraid to look, even more afraid to ask," he explained. "It's a fear of making a mistake, looking out of place, and feeling like a fool." He harbored a similar anxiety over following directions—"I'm afraid I will mess up and just won't get it"—which led to a refusal to drive anywhere or go anywhere that wasn't familiar.

Jared's mind was racked with conflicting feelings. On one hand, he felt a Christian love for his fellow man and claimed to love helping others. On the other, he confided in his S.A.F.E. journal that he hated nearly everyone. "I usually find something in EVERYBODY which I dislike, and I hate that about me," he wrote. "I hate things that aren't done my way. What an egocentric jerk I am! Stop the rage, STOP! STOP! STOP!" Jared's anger was so profound and so constant that it frightened him continuously, and one of his worst fears was that other people would see it manifested.

Jared was the youngest of six children in a deeply religious household characterized by a cold and controlling mother and a quiet, henpecked father. The combination turned out to be troublesome for all the siblings: one older brother attempted suicide; another became a drug addict in high school; and an older sister developed anorexia, restricting food as her mother castigated her behavior.

Jared's mother always called him her "perfect child" or "perfect angel" when he was young. He used to tattle on what the older siblings were up to. Mother wanted to know everything that was going on in the house. "She always tried to make decisions for everyone in the family and got very bitter if any of us thought differently than she did," Jared observed. "Her love seemed to be conditional—if I did something she didn't like, I was no longer her 'perfect child.' "

Part of his mother's problem was probably medical: when Jared was a toddler, his mother began having severe headaches that were understood to be related to a childhood car accident. Jared's siblings later told him that his mom's behavior changed radically after the headaches, that she became tyranical and insulting. She would let the children hug her, but she would never hug back. Words of affection were meted out sparingly by the father, but never by the mother.

"I wouldn't say I was emotionally abused, but perhaps emotionally neglected," Jared says. "Sometimes I just feel like I need to be hugged for hours at a time, and like I need to cry for hours at a time."

Jared started getting into mischief in junior high school. He cheated on an exam and trashed his room after his parents forbade his going to a party sponsored by a radio station. Worse still was the ridicule Jared endured daily from classmates, who regarded him as a nerd, a holy roller who talked too much about the Bible, and a "geek beneath contempt." Jared had no friends and avoided eye contact with everyone at school. All that mattered were grades, and he took out his aggressions on a punching bag in the basement. "I pitifully lack common sense, social sense, and coordination," Jared laments. "I'm such a klutz."

Things improved late in high school, when Jared began painting murals for a theater group and developed a flair for set design. He served as emcee at several high school plays and also joined a club for people who were interested in astronomy. He got an internship at a local radio station and made some friends there. Jared said he "craved the love and attention of others," particularly women, whom he would do anything to impress. Though Jared's religious faith prompted him to take a vow of chastity until marriage, he desperately wanted to date. He approached women hamhandedly. "I'm so starved for love, affection, and attention that I easily become attracted to any girl who befriends me. I'm so naive and ridiculous," he wrote.

After high school Jared enrolled in college for a semester. It was then that self-injury got the better of him. Not only did Jared develop anorexia, but he also began cutting, first with the blade of a fingernail clipper, then with a coat hanger, a razor, and anything else that seemed tempting. Cutting became a daily habit within two weeks.

"I knew I needed to draw that blood," he says. "My wounds progressed from my immediate wrist areas up my forearms and onto my shoulders. Although I've found the razor to be the most satisfying, I often obsess about the many different objects I could use. Everything becomes a sharp object, and I want to try just about every different thing. I've used everything from dental floss to combs to plastic ID cards.

"The scars—I like to see the scars, the cuts, the blood. It's obsessive—I want to see them. The impulses are most aggressive when the scars fade—for some reason I don't want to see them go away."

At S.A.F.E. Jared made this chart of the emotions surrounding his self-injury:

Before	During	After
Tension	Pleasure	Guilt
Worthlessness	Exhilaration	Shame
Vulnerability	Satisfaction	Crushed
Loneliness	Gratification	Pathetic
Confusion	Relief	Disturbed
Detachment	Control	No control

| Panic | Aggression | Sorrow |
| Torment | Hatred | Intrigue with scars |

Before S.A.F.E. Jared had been placed in psychiatric hospitals several times. Even so, he was able to enroll in a Christian college. There he found himself "disgusted by the lax morals in a school for Christians." Many classmates cursed, drank, smoked, and had premarital sex, which sent Jared into a frenzy of anger and disapproval. When he wasn't self-injuring or starving himself, he would try to convince fellow students of the errors of their ways, pointing out in detail how they had lapsed in their commitment to God.

Reflecting on this period of his life in his S.A.F.E. journal, Jared observed that his behavior seemed to mirror his mother, who "tried to control everything and believed only her standards were right." He wrote, "As I think of this, I just can't believe how much I've become my mom in this sense. I've become a victim like my dad and a control freak like my mom." His anger toward his parents was also tinged with guilt, since they supported him and had always managed his finances and paid for medical treatment.

Part of the control freak in Jared stemmed from his urge to convert and evangelize, and part came from a desire to "save the world" and everybody in it. "I love giving of myself to others—I find it very fulfilling—though I see now that I often neglect myself," he wrote. Unfortunately, as Jared came to realize, anyone who wants to save the world and is frightened of walking into a new grocery store is heading for inevitable frustration.

Jared's insecurities were on easy display at S.A.F.E. He waltzed into a group and started cracking jokes, apparently trying to be the life of the party. Jared fancied himself a real cut-up, and he tried to cut a swath by turning group therapy into a variety show.

Some of his fellow group members—all of them women—were immediately turned off, both by his apparent arrogance and by his humor, which they considered flat. Jared took the rejection of his jokes to heart. Other group members found Jared amusing and debonair, and he developed a coterie of quasi-admirers who flocked to him during the course of treatment. This, of course, was exactly what Jared wanted. Finally, he was able to play out his fantasy of being the rooster in the henhouse. "I can be both incredibly shy and outrageously outgoing, but here at S.A.F.E. I get to be the charming side of me," he told us.

Jared's swagger did get in the way, and we had to urge him to tone it down. This dejected him considerably, but probably served some therapeutic value. "I feel quite rejected if the attention is focused elsewhere," he confessed. "I need to be able to be assertive and speak my voice in group dynamics, but without putting it on myself to gain attention and adoration through my humor."

When Jared came to S.A.F.E., he seemed to draw extreme comfort from the writing assignments and from the staff counselors who worked with him. He clearly understood many of the problems that were holding him back—his irrational anger, his skewed self-image, and the fire-and-brimstone demands he placed on himself and others—and tried to work through them. Jared did abstain from self-injury—both at S.A.F.E. and afterward—and he credited God with his recovery.

After Jared left S.A.F.E., he went to live with a cousin in Syracuse, a new city for him. The changes and transition left him full of dread. "Can I stay safe? Yes! Will I stay safe . . . yes. There is weaker conviction here," he wrote in his journal. "But the tools are in place, and new ones are being learned and built upon daily. I will also follow up with after-care in Syracuse. I am excited and hopeful."

Jared's glee at his incipient recovery was tinged with regret. "I had hoped to be in the middle of my second semester at school right now," he observed. "But the Lord's will be done; his timeline is never wrong."

Jared contacted us a few months after graduating from S.A.F.E. He said he had completely abstained from self-injury and had made firm plans to return to school. Though he continued to be fixated on his religious beliefs, he reported no feelings of depression or urges to self-harm.

Self-injurers like Leila and Jared, who seem not to have been overtly abused as children, are becoming more common as self-injury spreads its tentacles into the population. Every year we notice how increasingly diverse our patient population has become in terms of social class, age, and family history. One steady trend is the growing number of teenage self-injurers, whom we will discuss in the next chapter.

Chapter Six

GROWING PAINS: THE
ADOLESCENT SELF-INJURER

B y day Ashley P., a junior in high school, diligently attends all her classes, jokes with friends in the lunchroom, does her homework, and cleans her room. She logs a few hours at her part-time job as a sales clerk at an accessories store at a mall in her upper middle-class suburban hometown, chats on the telephone with her friends, and helps her mom prepare dinner for the family. On the weekends she volunteers at a women's homeless shelter and runs clothing drives and other charitable activities at school.

By night Ashley retires to her bedroom, ostensibly to finish up stray assignments. She earns perfect grades and is universally praised by her teachers and the managers at the store where she works, so the story is easy to believe. Ashley has never gotten into serious trouble, never experimented with drugs or alcohol, never so much as talked back to a grown-up. But every night she locks herself in her private bathroom, quietly unwraps a secret stash of razor blades that she keeps hidden at the bottom of a Band-Aid box, and begins etching sharp parallel lines into the pallid flesh of her left forearm. The blood comes quickly, blurring the straight marks Ashley has cut with such precision.

Ashley does not cry while she cuts, nor does she tense or cringe from the gashes. Instead, she thinks about cutting deeper, wounding other parts of her body, taking a lighted match and holding it under her hand until the smell of burning skin wafts upward.

"Before I self-injure, I am usually in so much pain emotionally," Ashley explains. "I feel helpless, hopeless, upset, and anxious. I really do not consider anyone around me. During the act itself I feel completely numb, or I feel so much physical pain that I overpower my emotional pain. After the episode I feel relieved, as if I have released some tension. My blood shows me I am still a human being."

Ashley is tall and slender, her long, honey-wheat hair usually tied in back with a ribbon. She favors long, floral skirts and peasant-style blouses, but feels equally comfortable in jeans and sneakers—with sweatshirts, of course, to hide the scars marching up her arms. Her many friends consider her the perfect confidante: she is always sympathetic, willing to listen, and never says an unkind word about anyone.

How could such a seemingly perfect teenager—someone who seems so well adjusted and competent on the surface—end up in the S.A.F.E. Alternatives program for weeks of intensive treatment? The question seems to be on many people's minds today, as so many "normal" teenagers (and adults) resort to self-injury to handle their problems.

There is no way to explain why one person will decide to cope with life's pressures through self-injury and another might handle stress through healthy means. While some self-injurers share certain common characteristics and family profiles, there is no one "reason" why someone like Ashley resorts to self-injury while another teenager with similar problems and responsibilities does not.

It is striking that most self-injurers begin harming themselves in adolescence, specifically around the time they reach puberty. Equally remarkable is that many people go through years of psychotherapy without examining their adolescent experiences in depth.

For teens like Ashley, the term *delicate self-cutting* that is often applied to self-injury is a fairly descriptive one, for it describes nonlethal rifts of the skin. It almost connotes the type of artful care a gourmet chef might take with a rare cheese or prime meat. Louise Kaplan calls the term an "innocent-sounding diagnostic label"—deceptively innocent, she points out, yet appropriate inasmuch as it distinguishes the activities of Ashley and her ilk from the "coarse" self-injurious behavior of others.

What would compel a model student to act out in this way? It's easy enough to see the comparisons between adolescent self-injurers and teen anorexics, who tend to be perfection-minded little girls whose refusal to eat can be another manifestation of the "being best at everything" complex. (A full discussion of the overlap between eating disorders and self-injury follows in chapter 8.) But often there is more to it than that. One study by two researchers, Barent W. Walsh and Paul M. Rosen, took a group of fifty-two adolescents who self-injured and tried to identify common conditions or events in their childhoods. The researchers discovered that adolescent self-injurers were more likely to have experienced certain stressors and traumas; that they were more likely to have suffered early loss of a parent, childhood illness, or surgery; and that on average they were much more likely to have endured physical or sexual abuse. The research also found strong histories of family violence in adolescent self-injurers. These teens were often exposed to impulsive, addictive, or self-destructive behavior.

Walsh and Rosen suggested that certain experiences during the adolescent years were "triggers" for the start of self-injurious behavior. These included a recent loss, conflict with peers, and difficulty coping with the changes of puberty. Obviously, not all adolescents who struggle with these issues begin to engage in self-injurious behavior. But many people who do become self-injurers arrive at adolescence in a vulnerable state and find the ordinary tasks of this period exquisitely painful and traumatic.

Ashley's case supports the Walsh and Rosen research findings to a T. Her father, a chronic alcoholic, used to fly into rages at the drop of a hat. While he never physically harmed Ashley or anyone else in her family, he did a lot of screaming and insulting. "When he would get drunk, or had a hangover or withdrawal, he'd yell if I left one speck of dust on the floor," Ashley says. "Whenever I would say things in family therapy meetings, my dad would take them out of the meeting and use them against me at home."

When sober, Ashley's father would apologize profusely, making "promises he wouldn't keep," and bringing her presents after each outburst. "He manipulated me into thinking it was all normal," Ashley says bitterly. Ashley reports that her mother, who often seemed distracted and would spend much of the day humming tunes to herself or watching soap operas, seldom interjected herself in the family dramas. When her husband was drinking, she tried to stay out of his way.

In many ways Ashley's complaints seem like typical adolescent ones. Her grievance list could read like that of any other American teenager.

"My parents try to belittle my problems and anxieties by blowing them off or ignoring them," Ashley wrote in her diary. "Both my mom and my dad attempt to explain my feelings away or make excuses for things I get mad about. Also, they just listen out of one ear."

In another entry, Ashley wrote: "I really get angry when people don't seem to understand me. At home and at school, others think I can do everything, and I think they forget that I need care and love just as much as others who aren't so independent. I get angry when I think no one cares for me and start feeling like they view me more as an adult than as the needy child I feel like inside."

Indeed, as we learned at S.A.F.E., quiet little Ashley, who never missed a week of church, had developed some sophisticated and violent fantasies about the ways she wanted to repay her father for his loutish behavior. "I would like to shoot him or stab him in the head, or strangle him and hold him there until just before he died," she wrote in an essay at S.A.F.E. "Then I'd suffocate him with plastic wrap, and make up lies that he had physically abused me and I had killed him in self-defense."

But in reality Ashley craved a caring relationship with her father. Instead of violently murdering him, "I think I'd rather forgive him," she wrote. "I'd like to work to a point where I don't feel I want to do any of this to him anymore."

Ashley's parents didn't get angry with her when they learned of her problem, but they didn't sit her down to talk about it either. Ashley told us she had never had the opportunity to vent her feelings about her family or the ways their behavior affected her. "They make fun of me so much, and they never give me any chance to tell my side," she says. "My self-esteem is so low that I think I am worthless and ugly, and don't deserve anything better than self-injury."

Despite their own problems Ashley's parents desperately wanted her to stop self-injuring. They found out about her behavior after she confided in a school counselor, who recommended hospitalization. The parents said they would gladly pay for any treatment program that would help their daughter get better.

Ashley spent a month at S.A.F.E. and has been living without self-injury for the better part of a year. Her father's problems are unresolved—he used to show up drunk and unruly to visit Ashley at

S.A.F.E. and has refused to seek treatment for his alcohol abuse—but Ashley now has a support team in place to help her handle the rough patches. She has returned to school and has resumed her relationships with her friends. She continues to study hard, work part-time, and volunteer. Life is still an everyday struggle, but Ashley appears to be winning.

"I need to practice opening up instead of closing in and self-injuring," Ashley says. "I need to work on reminding myself that pain is not here forever, and that I need to challenge my thoughts before acting out in dangerous ways. I need to apply a new definition to myself—I am not a self-injurer anymore."

SEPARATION, AUTONOMY, AND SELFHOOD

The main task for the child who has launched into adolescence is to develop a stable sense of identity—to know "who she is," her place in the family and in the world at large. She begins to separate from her childhood dependence on her parents and slowly to acquire adult rights and responsibilities. It is a time full of paradoxes and contradictions. The adolescent wants more freedoms and privileges: she wants to drive the family car, choose her own friends, stay out late, and perhaps experiment with cigarettes and alcohol. The healthy adolescent's pre-occupation with privacy (keeping secrets, closing the door to her room) and her rebellious and quarrelsome demeanor are ways to find her own space.

Teens like to wear different clothes from their parents, sport the latest hairstyles, listen to the latest music. They often seem to have a language all their own. The adolescent finds faults and flaws with everyone and everything, critical of mom's outfits and dad's bad jokes, and all this behavior is part of the normal process of separating from mom and dad and "finding themselves."

At the same time, all adolescents have a secret wish to remain protected and cared for, not to be rushed into the grown-up world. Most adolescents take comfort in knowing their parents still pay the bills, buy their food, provide housing, and care for them when they're sick.

They don't want to be bothered with all the obligations and responsibilities of adulthood.

Parents often struggle with this negotiation, respecting independence, doling out privileges, yet feeling at times that they are in the presence of a tall, sullen, needy two-year-old. Some parents marvel that their teenager who begs for the car keys sometimes can't seem to manage the littlest thing without parental intervention. Even in the healthiest of families, this awkward waltz between an adolescent's moments of exasperating immaturity and her adult strivings pose major challenges.

On the path to adulthood, the adolescent must also learn responsibility for her actions and their consequences. She must be able to respond to tough situations and to soothe herself in times of distress without the constant presence of an adult caregiver.

The adolescent who self-injures confronts these issues of separation and identity formation with great alarm. Many arrive at this time period having been deprived of the ordinary gratifications of attentive parenting. During adolescence the "underparented" child often comes across as pseudo-mature, wise beyond her years because of the inappropriate duties foisted on her. Deprived of parental attention and energy, she learned early to fend for herself, not to expect care or concern from adults. Such adolescents frequently remark to us that they have indeed "never had a childhood." They develop the persona of the "strong one" in the family, believing that they are not allowed to express any need or vulnerability.

Underneath the surface, however, are all the unmet longings for nurturing and parenting, along with all the sorrow and rage. This adolescent may harbor tremendous resentment for the loss of her childhood and may perceive separation and autonomy as a profound threat to emotional safety and equilibrium. She cannot celebrate adult roles and responsibilities as achievements because they remind her of her inconsolable losses. Instead, she fights mightily to keep her memories and feelings at bay, often in self-destructive ways. Self-injury helps her cope, but at the same time it disrupts her life course, forcing others into caretaking roles and impeding independence. The underparented adolescent has already experienced, in the emotional or physical absence of care, *too much* separation and autonomy. This occurs before she is mature enough to assimilate it as a natural part of her growing personality.

But what of the adolescent who suffers from the opposite extreme—
the overparented child who has struggled with too little separation or
too few boundaries between herself and the adults who care for her?
Some adolescent self-injurers have told us of parents who would not
let them separate. Their parents may be rigidly perfectionistic and controlling, living vicariously through their children and dictating every
move. Boundaries—the imaginary line around each individual's
thoughts and feelings, between "me" and "not me"—are blurry and
indistinct. Any attempt on the part of these children to move into the
larger world outside the family is met with hostility and rage, or ab-
surdly extreme limit setting. These adolescents report having little or
no opportunity to be alone, or to choose their friends or activities. The
parent responds to disagreement, or any independent thinking, as if it
were a punishable betrayal.

We've seen hundreds of examples of teenage rebellion by self-
injurers whose behavior seemed to be a direct response to the extremes
in their parenting. Here are just a few:

- Heather P., whose mother was a fundamentalist Christian, decided to identify instead with her Satan-worshiping friends.
  Heather became a fan of morbid rock singer Marilyn Manson,
  dressed in black clothes with black lipstick, and embarked on a
  vivid routine of self-injury; predictably, her mother was terrified
  by her behavior and wanted an exorcism done.
- Lisa K., whose sister's developmental illness drew all their
  mother's attention, never felt either parent had looked out for her,
  so she had to fill in with self-injury. Despite her vast anxiety about
  separating from the family, Lisa moved far away at an early age,
  because living too close to her relatives made her feel obliged to
  go home and take care of things.
- Victoria R.—whose impeccably dressed country-club mother
  shoehorned her into the prissiest dresses in town—replaced cu-
  cumber tea sandwiches with drinking, drugs, and self-injury. Victoria's reliance on oversized sweatshirts and baseball caps horrified
  her mother, who remembered the days when she used to set out
  her daughter's elementary school clothes on her bed and dictate
  the order in which she was to put them on.

Children of smothering parents may find in adolescence that their growing urges for autonomy seem dangerous and destructive to the people they love. They lurch hesitatingly toward adulthood, seeking secret outlets for their urges to separate. They must establish clandestine boundaries around their thoughts, feelings, and experiences, and sometimes the guilt they feel leads them to carry out secret agendas involving self-punishment. As a strategy self-injury fits the bill well: the surface of the skin becomes their very own territory to mark off as they wish, to enact this violent struggle for selfhood.

The adolescent who has suffered from childhood physical or sexual abuse represents a special case of boundary violation in the family, leading to additional problems in the task of separation. The abuse victim perceives adults as either dangerous or neglectful and themselves as constantly vulnerable to harm. Without a core sense of safety, the advance of physical, sexual, and emotional maturation is met with horror and alarm. Feelings of self-loathing, guilt, and shame intensify. The adolescent may begin to self-injure in an attempt to master her fears of bodily invasion and to tame feral anxieties over her developing mind and body.

GENDER, SEXUALITY, AND BODY IMAGE

All adolescents grapple with the rapid maturation of their bodies, their burgeoning sexuality, and their capacity for adult procreation. Some writers have suggested that this task is particularly complex for females because of their partially hidden genitalia, the intense internal physical sensations associated with menstruation, and their more dramatic and abrupt changes in body contours during puberty.

Interestingly, Walsh and Rosen found in their research study that the single most important predictor of future self-injurious behavior in adolescents was what they termed "body alienation." This described the experience, in their group of adolescents, of feeling hatred, revulsion, and disgust for the body, often accompanied by a wish for, or sense of, being "cut off" from bodily and sexual experiences.

Most self-injurers in the S.A.F.E. program, overwhelmingly female, confirm this view. They report nightmarish experiences of puberty and their first period. The ordinary biochemical and hormonal changes associated with adolescent maturation, including surges of sexual arousal or premenstrual tension, are experienced as terrifying and unbearable. "I felt like I was dying, or like my insides were falling out," one teenager told us. Girls and women often tell us that they "hate their periods" and are revolted by their breasts and genitalia.

Sexual maturation is a deeply frightening experience for an adolescent self-injurer. If she has arrived at adolescence without having felt held together, protected, and safe in childhood, these changes represent an invasion by alien forces. Forced into an awareness of her inner body and genitals, feeling vulnerable to harm, she experiences all kinds of inner arousal and sensation as intrusive, uncontrollable, and destructive. Often, this is the same way she has come to view all her experiences of emotional arousal. Unless she finds a way to tame and focus these terrifying urges and feelings, she feels that catastrophe will result, that she will "explode," "fall apart," or "go crazy." For the adolescent girl who has been sexually abused, sexual maturation and arousal can bring on further feelings of intense guilt and shame, self-hatred, and an inescapable dread of further victimization.

We can easily see how an adolescent tries to take care of her body alienation and fears of bodily invasion through the ritual of self-injury, in which she converts her passively suffered torments into an active, controlled strategy that puts her squarely at the helm of her body experience.

THE ADOLESCENT AS CHILD, THE ADULT AS BABY

To some extent, all self-injurers seem stuck in a regressed developmental state. Though they may go to college, hold down jobs, even have families of their own, many of them behave in ways that are far more typical of children, or even babies. Like two-year-olds, they are narcissistic and can think of no one's needs other than their own. They demand that all needs and desires be fulfilled instantly—or else. When the toddler is, in fact, a full-grown teenager or adult, that "or else" no

longer takes the form of a temper tantrum; among our patients it manifests as self-injury.

Many patients acknowledge this aspect of their personality. Many
of them tell us they have been described as "childlike," and often they
agree with the label. Jared T., the twenty-three-year-old devout Christian, observes, "It seems like I'm fighting an alter ego who really hates
me and, like a child, selfishly refuses to give up."

We point this out not to blame sufferers for their behavior, as frus-
tratingly infantile as it can be. We understand where the desire to be
mothered and nurtured comes from, usually from the patient's experience as a two-year-old whose needs were not properly met.

For adolescents, poised between childhood and adulthood, the desire to be properly "mothered" can conflict with the desire for independence, prompting the "self-mothering" behavior of self-injury. This
phenomenon can continue well into adulthood, as teenagers who fail
to progress developmentally become fixated on the problems they are
addressing through self-injury.

"I certainly don't play an adult woman role," acknowledges Chrissie
M., who is thirty-four. "I usually feel like a child and probably act like
one too. I don't think I've been a very good daughter, because I've
caused my parents a lot of distress. My siblings don't trust me anymore,
nor do my parents. I am the 'sick' person or scapegoat in my family. I
do things to make people take care of me—usually self-injury."

Chrissie also expresses a fantasy common among self-injurers. "I
wish I could go back to being a small child—to start over with my
parents, only with them having good parenting and communication
skills."

There is good news about adolescent self-injurers. Because adolescence is such a critical stage—and the stage when self-injury is most
likely to make its debut—we view it as the optimal time for recovery
from the syndrome. When you catch the behavior early, before it becomes an entrenched pattern, the task of extinguishing it becomes less
arduous.

This is not to say that older people cannot recover too. Many ages
and categories of people have responded extremely well to our program,
and adolescents stand out as just one of them. Among the common
threads uniting those who recover are hope, perseverance, and courage.

"What I'm Afraid of in Going Home," by Ashley P.

"I fear going into relapse and having done all this hard work for nothing," writes Ashley P. in a S.A.F.E. essay. "If I did relapse, I think I'd feel so bad and ashamed. My dad doesn't currently have a job, and if I had to go somewhere again, I'd make my family go broke. I would not like for my sister to see me upset, because she's only twelve.

"I am also afraid that my friends will be overly nice, because they will be afraid to get me upset. I fear seeing neighbors and acquaintances. I am still unsure what I will say when someone asks me where I have been. I have made up so many excuses— maybe I'll just tell the truth.

"I don't want to go to school because I am afraid people will stare or point and I will lose friends, or people will try too hard to be kind out of pity for me.

"The tools I have acquired here—assertiveness, challenging my thoughts, different alternatives, and the wisdom to accept things I cannot change—can be applied to my fear of relapsing. I can also use these to deal with my anger that my father seems to make worse. When I am in school, I can use my alternatives and challenge my thoughts. I can remember my struggle to open up, and remind myself how far I've gotten. I still need to learn how to not let people get to me. I need to learn how to lessen my anxiety in a way that works for me. I still need to talk to people in my family more about how they have affected me and depressed me. Most of all, I need to accept that it's okay to be happy and sad, and to find a moderate level to stay put between my highs and lows."

Chapter Seven

BODY IMAGE AND SELF-INJURY

Self-injurers come in all shapes and sizes. We have seen slender cheerleaders whose good looks were the envy of their high school class, and we have seen obese patients who have battled their weight all their lives. Men and women, fat and thin, conventionally beautiful and not—appearance never correlates to the severity of their self-injury, their emotional problems, or their capacity to recover.

What they all share in common is a tortured relationship between their minds and their bodies, particularly their sexual organs. They also have a tangle of difficult thoughts about gender, usually because of their early experiences with child abuse or of conflict with a parent. Their private anguish is exacerbated by the scary and confusing lessons they learn about sexuality and gender roles.

As females grow up in our culture, they are bombarded with intense and conflicting messages about their bodies. Girls and women are the prime marketing targets for the fashion and cosmetics industries, health clubs, diet pill purveyors, and cosmetic surgeons. Even as their bodies are becoming softer and more rounded with sexual maturation, girls are implored by cultural ideals to be "slim," "hard," and "in control."

Everything they see and read implies that their appearance and body shape are what define them as feminine, sexy, worthy, and lovable.

Worthy and lovable females are attractive (translation: slim, hard, not too curvy or voluptuous), sexually restrained, and fastidious in grooming and cleanliness. Even the commercial treatment of menstruation, in which *sanitary* napkins are advertised for personal *hygiene*, imply that menstrual flow—and, by extension, female genitals—are soiled or dirty. Girls grow up believing that they are inherently unclean for having a period. Indeed, many women believe they can never measure up to the physical superiority of men.

"I hate that as women age, their bodies change so much," says Ceci J., mapping out her thoughts on the differences between men and women. "The drooping, sagging, wrinkling, dried-up mess. Men seem to get more attractive with age, and, in my eyes, women don't."

Like many of our patients, Ceci believes that "men think more with their heads, and women feel with their hearts," and that women are too often reduced to nothingness with comments like "She's just an emotional woman." Ceci doesn't believe men are any smarter, but she notes that their physical size gives them an advantage, as when they make "unwanted advances and force themselves on women."

Many self-injurers decide on purpose to make themselves unattractive, usually because of their mistaken belief that rape and incest are brought on by irresistible physical beauty or provocative clothing. This type of distorted thinking is a product of the myth perpetuated by society and mass media, that men are a bundle of sexual impulses who "can't help themselves" when they come across attractive woman flesh. It's a blame-the-victim attitude that many of our patients hold uncomfortably dear. We try our hardest to persuade them otherwise: if the myth were true, we tell them, then nuns, the elderly, and the handicapped would not be targets of rape, which they frequently are. Power is the motive, not sex, and rapists seldom care about the appearance of their victim.

The sad paradox is that since rape is not a sexual crime, women who deliberately make themselves unattractive—through obesity, self-injury, and other means—end up placing themselves on the fringe of society, where they find themselves *more* vulnerable and *more* likely to be chosen for future attack.

Women who have experienced a sexual attack or even the threat of one can become so frightened that they go to extraordinary lengths to avoid further incidents. They may gain a tremendous amount of weight, wear baggy or masculine attire, shave their head or pluck out hair, or mutilate their bodies. Some women even insert sharp objects into their vagina, losing sight of the fact that this "precaution" hurts them as much as it would any potential attacker. One patient of ours told us that she thought all the time about cutting off her breasts, because she imagined that would make her safer from sexual predators.

These measures make the self-injurer feel that she is in control of the damage. Injurers often state that they would rather hurt themselves than have someone else do it; the goal being independent mastery of the pain. Most of our patients feel intense pain and suffering from illnesses and medical problems they have not brought on themselves but are able to tolerate extreme forms of self-orchestrated injury.

BODILY HATRED

"I'm not comfortable in my fat body," says Chrissie M., who is thirty-four and obese. "When I'm at my normal weight, I wear a 36C bra, but that's still too big for me. I can't stand having to deal with a period every month. Sometimes I get suicidal right before my period starts. It was hard for me to connect the two, but I do get real emotional and want to eat a lot of bad foods. I don't appreciate guys staring at my boobs, or me thinking that the only reason they want to be with me is to have sex."

It is quite common for self-injurers of both genders to detest their body parts. More often than not, the parts they detest most vehemently are sexual organs. A study of self-injuring women by one of the authors and Dr. Armando Favazza found that:

- 34 percent strongly hated their breasts
- 58 percent strongly hated their periods
- 56 percent strongly hated pelvic exams
- 19 percent said they would be better off without a vagina
- 10 percent sometimes injured in an attempt to stop their periods from occurring

Dr. Favazza has found similar sentiments among self-injuring men, who typically express loathing toward their penises and testicles. Just as many male self-injurers express castration fantasies (or even on rare occasions try it themselves), so do many females voice analagous desires. Jacqueline G., a severe self-injurer who is obsessed with setting herself on fire, says she has spent most of her adult life asking doctors if they will excise her labia. Unless she finds one who will do it, she claims, she will do it herself.

Donna W., a former patient, described the anguish so many self-injurers feel every day. "I've always loathed my body," she wrote. "When I was younger, it was because I had horrible scars from the surgeries I had as a child. As I grew older and my body began to age, I saw myself as horrible and fat. I thought I was lazy because I wouldn't exercise to keep my body in shape. When I would look at myself in a mirror, I would hate what I saw and spend hours redoing makeup or changing clothes to make myself look prettier or thinner."

Many self-injurers maintain equally conflicted relationships with their hair. Some compulsively pluck it out strand by strand (a disorder called trichitillomania), and others keep theirs close-cropped or in a crew cut. Jane O. used to shave her head regularly in order to look as fearsome as possible.

Hair has traditionally been an important symbol of femininity. In *Female Perversions* Louise Kaplan writes: "Hair, because it is closest to the soul or head, is regarded as the symbol of all that is noble, sacred, and clean. At the same time, because pubic hairs are so close to the anus, hair is sometimes associated with all that is soiled, defiled, and dirty."

Self-mutilators serve many purposes when they denude themselves of hair. The pulling of hair, like other forms of self-injury, can serve as a distraction from anxiety. It can also represent the loss of power, including the loss of sexual power.

The struggle for sexual freedom and autonomy are the cornerstones of many of our patients' problems. Rosa G., fifty-two, says her battle with excess weight is related to her fear of men, whose physical strength she finds intimidating. Her strong fears of being beaten or raped keep her from slimming down to a weight that would make her more physically comfortable. "I do not like feeling like a sexual object for men's gratification," Rosa says. "I don't believe women are any less talented, smart, or competent than men, but men are more easily accepted in society, in jobs, and in naturally having more authority and power. Using the patriarchal system and the 'boy's club,' they try to keep the power."

On the other hand, Rosa has "not been happy with being a woman most—maybe all—of my life," she says. "I have never been comfortable with my body. I didn't like being short and stocky. I have not particularly felt it okay to be a woman, to be feminine, to be sexy." She had bad feelings about her breasts, which she considered too small, and about her period and menopause, which made her feel "powerless" and seemed like "another way men put women down."

Rosa's feelings toward her gender are complicated by her feelings about being a lesbian. "How can I be a woman and not be defined by men?" she asks. "I have not been able to balance my masculine and feminine qualities. I don't need them to be equal, I just need to accept them."

Liz C., thirty-nine, is another patient who feels tortured by her body and society's expectations of it. She hates having a period and having breasts. "Most men consider a woman 'great' if she has a good body," Liz says. "The standards people set for the way a woman should speak, walk, talk, and look are sometimes impossible to achieve."

Liz does not consider men more competent, and she gets indignant when the housekeeping duties a woman does are "taken for granted." Liz feels strongly that "If a woman has determination and ability, there is nothing she can't do, anatomical differences aside," but this assertive streak clashes with her view of herself.

"I do not usually look at myself as a woman—I barely think of myself as a person," Liz says. "I do not like my body. It is ugly, untoned, flabby, and out of shape. I'm overweight by about fifteen to twenty pounds. I would like to be more petite. I don't like the size or shape of my legs. I do like my hair and eyes. Most of the time I feel as if I hate myself."

Victoria R.: Inner Conflict

"My body means nothing to me," Victoria states flatly. "There isn't anything that could be done to it that could cause me any more pain than I have already endured. In fact, since abuse has occurred on so many different levels, I have come to the conclusion that I deserve to be punished. Thus, I self-harm."

To some people, hearing such devastating sentiments from a self-injurer may not seem surprising. But taking into account other aspects of Victoria's personality, they might seem more curious. After all, she is a graduate student who attends rallies on women's issues. Her best friend, Natalie, volunteers each weekend at a rape crisis center. Victoria considers Natalie a role model, saying she admires her "compassion" and the fact that Natalie is constantly supportive and attentive to each rape victim she counsels, despite the relentless sameness of their sad stories and circumstances.

Though Victoria may think like a feminist when it comes to other people—she is proud of Natalie's strength, her good looks, her ability to do so much volunteer work while holding down a full-time job— she does not apply the same rules to herself. Feminism is something she supports intellectually: she is outraged that women earn less than men at the same jobs; she is discouraged that women are so often the targets of violent crimes; she feels women are underrepresented in government. It angers her that society seems to embrace a blame-the-victim mentality, and that women's contributions and achievements tend to be undervalued. She does not think men are inherently superior in any way.

Yet Victoria cannot connect this knowledge and these beliefs to her feelings about herself. "I despise being trapped inside this body," she says. "I hate everything that is characterized as a female physical attribute."

Victoria says she works hard to separate "mentally being a woman" from "having a woman's body."

"I make a close connection between the fact that I have a vagina and breasts and the fact that I have been abused," she says. "I blame my body for attracting men. I think that if I were more androgynous, then the abuse never would have happened."

But the logical and rational side of Victoria knows this is not true. "The truth is," she says, "I was pretty androgynous in second grade, and it still didn't keep me safe." That was the year a family gardener began fondling her, and her cousin sneaked into her room and raped her.

Victoria says her body image is "slowly improving," but she still does not feel comfortable about her looks. Her mind is at war with her body. She is self-aware enough to know that she is a popular girl who makes friends easily, yet she cannot translate that knowledge into self-esteem. "Much of my self-harming behavior—mutilating, promiscuity, drinking,

drugs, bingeing, vomiting, starving myself—has been my way of punishing my body," she concludes.

By contrast, Victoria says she is grateful that she has "a woman's
mind." She says, "I believe in general that women are more nurturing
and emotionally complex. I'm proud to be a feminist. My social activ-
ism in this area has helped me find a voice. I feel empowered when I
work collectively with women in a way I don't with men.

"If only I could have the mind of a woman and NO body . . ."

FEMINISM

Why is it that women are drastically overrepresented among the population of self-injurers? One reason, we believe, relates to the traditional role of women as quiet, obedient caretakers. Our female patients
often talk about the anger they feel at inequalities between the sexes—
workplace pay scales, household chores, and the like—and the feeling
of "oppression" that it gives them. (This theme of oppression may well
be why we see so many male prisoners begin to self-injure. This theory
is explored more fully in chapter 9).

Many of the women we treat describe themselves as feminists, but
it's often unclear what that means. For the most part, the term seems
to translate for them into a fear of men, rather than a true appreciation
of their own gender.

We often point out that one of their biggest complaints centers on
the violence men perpetrate against women. Then we point out that
they, as self-injurers, are doing the same thing through their cutting
and other behaviors. We try to help them look at feminist ideology in
terms of an appreciation for "femaleness," not a bashing of "maleness."

When self-injurers tell us they are feminists—as many do—we start
to notice a curious paradox. On one hand, people who self-injure almost always do so out of a sense of self-loathing, hatred of their own
person and body, and what they represent. On the other hand, being
a feminist implies a celebration of womanhood—quite the opposite of
loathing your female body and your emotions. How can one philo-
sophically appreciate female qualities while simultaneously hating

those qualities in one's self? How can you love your gender when you want to destroy it?

Leila H., twenty-two, who considers herself a feminist and attributes many superior qualities to women, tried using these attitudes to combat her urges to self-injure. "I feel that women, myself included, tend to be more spiritual and interconnected than men," she says. "We are closer to nature and we are the ultimate creators of life, since our children form inside our bodies."

Leila describes herself as the "physical stereotype" of femininity, because "I am petite, have long, thick hair, and large eyes. I am proud of my tiny bones and controlled weight." But in other ways Leila feels she does not fit the mold of the tiny, passive female. "Psychologically, I am too aggressive to fit into the stereotypical woman's role," she says. "I speak my mind, and I refuse to let anyone intimidate me. I accept both my strength and my femininity."

Leila "wouldn't trade being a woman for anything" and says that "men are usually inferior to women." It disturbs her that women sometimes have lower annual incomes than men who perform similar jobs, and that behaviors that are considered aggressive in men are considered "bitchy" in women. "We are seen as flaky and hysterical when we get upset and show our emotions, yet men who display their anger or fear are seen as bold and strong," Leila complains.

Other patients do not call themselves feminists. Many self-injurers come from extremely traditional backgrounds in which a biblical-style hierarchy between the sexes was keenly enforced. Susan L., thirty-seven, for instance, says she's "not big on E.R.A. junk" but believes, in keeping with her Mormon faith, that "men and women make a good balance."

Though Susan is "glad I'm a woman, because women can have babies," she too dislikes her body. In her writing she calls herself a "FAT woman" but praises her mind—her intellectual qualities and capacity to nurture others.

Donna W., a forty-six-year-old paralegal and mother of two, summed up the attitudes of many of our patients in her essay on gender attitudes. "I've always enjoyed the 'caretaking' attributes I associate with being a woman," she wrote. "I like taking care of a man in exchange for his love and support. I view this as an equitable exchange—I've always felt that being a woman meant being softer and gentler than a man. I enjoy feeling pretty when I get dressed up, and I believe being a woman means I am supposed to look attractive. I believe women have the ability to remain calm in a crisis and to think clearly to come to a solution. Woman are the primary caretakers of children, even when it has to be in conjunction with working outside the home. Women are also the primary housekeepers and meal preparers.

"I am discouraged that I am judged first by my appearance and second by my abilities. I am also discouraged by the trivialization of what a woman's role in running a home entails. I don't believe that all men possess greater competence, ability, or adequacy just by being male. I do believe that the world and society as a whole hold fast to this idea, however. An overweight man is much more readily accepted than an overweight woman, and a man without any formal education can still get a job making more money than a woman with the same limitations."

MEN, SELF-INJURY, AND BODY IMAGE

While male self-injurers suffer from the same boundary issues as their female counterparts, they are far less likely to be preoccupied by visions of bodily perfection or ideals of masculinity that they feel they cannot achieve.

Indeed, our culture's preoccupation with body image may help us understand something about the gender gap in self-injury. Our lopsided patient population cannot be entirely explained by the fact that women seek mental health treatment more often than men.

An interesting finding was reported in an interview study of adolescents conducted in the early 1970s. Adolescent boys described their bodies in terms of function and effectiveness, while adolescent girls described their bodies in terms of size, shape, and appearance. From a very early age, girls' self-esteem seems to be much more tied to their body image than boys. This dichotomy is made clear from the moment parents dress their infant girls in pink clothes with flowers on them and their boys in blue overalls with choo-choos, and when they tell their toddler girls how "cute" they are, and their boys how "big and strong" they are.

To be sure, our male patients have severe problems managing their relationships with their bodies: they struggle with feelings about their sexuality, genitalia, skin, etc. But they do not look with fear at society's standards for how a man should look or behave; indeed, perhaps because such standards are far more fluid than they are for women, male self-injurers tend to feel far less pressured than female patients to try to conform, and far less guilty and troubled when they do not.

Men who spend time in the gym working out, trying to polish and perfect their muscles, may be the counterparts of women who feel the need to be small and thin. The drive to be big and strong can be a relatively healthy and nonconsuming interest for the average male, or it can expand to obsessional overconcern with body image, which usually masks intense underlying anxieties.

Though our male patients are less dissatisfied with their bodies, their symptoms are no milder than the females. Indeed, as we have noted earlier, men tend to injure themselves more catastrophically, and their psychological problems tend to be especially grave. While these men are often repulsed by their body parts or body functions, their conflicts tend not to spring from comparisons between their own bodies and those of physical ideals. This is interesting, because it is so unlike the women, who are both angry with their own bodies and with how they stack up against women they admire.

Jared T., for instance, when asked what he thought about being a man, said it was something he "hadn't given a whole lot of thought to." Since he's a deeply religious person and wanted to give a complete answer, he decided to rely on biblical interpretations of the relations between men and women and talked about men as having a "role designated by God" to hold authority over women.

Even so, Jared went on to describe views that wouldn't be shouted down by your average women's libber. He said he disliked the cultural stereotypes foisted on men and women, and the "unrealistic images" of both genders portrayed on television. He said that too many men "abuse their positions and power to manipulate women and other men," and that women "really get the raw deal just because they are women." Though he had a difficult relationship with his mother, Jared, who has never seriously dated, said he viewed "many women with greater competence and adequacy than men, especially in their drive and determination."

Indeed, as it turned out, one of Jared's healthier attitudes was of his own male self-image. Though he is heterosexual, he said he was not afraid of the "feminine" side of his feelings, which were "oversensitive," and hated swaggering, cussing, and stereotypical "male bonding" types of behavior. He hates "manly manners" and doesn't like being called "one of the guys." It makes him angry that society perceives men as being perpetually horny and "out to get some," and that he is lumped into that category.

Jared, an outgoing and popular man who formed instant rapport with many women on the S.A.F.E. unit, told us he was a virgin. Despite his lustful feelings—which felt sinful to him—he was saving himself for marriage. Jared's explanation for his sexual abstinence and his inability to form intimate relationships with women—which he craved—always circled back to religious teachings. While we certainly accepted his beliefs and applauded him for sticking to his principles, we asked Jared to look at whether there might be other reasons why he had not attained the type of romantic life he was looking for.

The explanations he came up with were psychological and did not relate to any feelings of inadequacy about his own physique. "So how do I match up to the brawn of the Fabios of the world and the wit of the Larry Kings?" Jared asked. "I couldn't care less. I'm not in pursuit of a chiseled body or a superior intelligence. As far as my body, sure, muscle, perfectly toned, would be nice. A charming smile and killer eyes would be great (my hair is already superior!). But what is said is true—beauty is fleeting. Real beauty is the beauty of a quiet, gentle, loving spirit, and true beauty is being 'man enough' to admit that I have limitations."

Jared said he used to work out at the gym and was "gleeful" over the progress he had made. "I saw some seedling muscles bursting forth," he said. "But it wasn't too long before I realized how obsessed I was becoming with my physical appearance. It was the opposite of the healthy humility I desire—it was self-consuming, pride, vanity. Truth be known, I know that my frame is less than average, and I am content with that."

SEXUALITY

Almost all male and female self-injurers experience tremendous identity and gender confusion. Many are unsure of their sexual orientation, and few derive much pleasure from sexual intimacy. Most of our patients report that they far prefer hugging, snuggling, and kissing to genital sexual contact.

Liz C., for instance, reports never having had a positive sexual experience. "I always felt that sex was dirty or bad, even when I was married," she says. Though her second husband tried to be gentle and to please her, she cringed at his touch. Intercourse was painful. "I found sex to be disgusting, and I wanted it over as quickly as possible," she says.

Yet Liz and many other self-injurers report that they have gone through periods of extreme sexual promiscuity. They place various interpretations on these "phases": sleeping with many different men provides a "quick fix" for feeling loved, but it also shows the self-injurer's utter disregard for her body and its value and integrity. Ceci J. said her insecurities and thirst for attention have made her seek out new boyfriends all the time. "I'm constantly needing male approval," she said.

"I used to wish I was a man, because I felt they didn't have such intense emotions as women," Ceci said. "But one day I was talking to a girlfriend, sharing my thoughts and dreams, and I told her that I was glad to be a woman, to be able to feel things like love, concern, compassion." Sadly, Ceci tends not to find those qualities in the men she seeks out as partners.

Many self-injurers report strong longings to be a member of the opposite sex. This does not mean that they are latent transsexuals; instead it reflects their visceral loathing of their bodies and dissatisfaction with their selves. The fantasy of the female patient is: "If I were male, I wouldn't have been abused." Among males the thought is that if they had been born female, they would be able to be better mothers than their own were.

Often patients confront this whirl of difficult feelings about sexuality and conclude that they don't like either gender. Usually they have been "wronged" by one or the other or both and cannot tolerate much love for their own sex.

Chrissie M. describes how this tension plays out in her thoughts. "I think women are weaker than men and more sensitive, and I think men are more competent and generally stronger than women," she says. "The reason I choose to have a male therapist is because I feel more comfortable with males—I feel they are more competent. I generally don't trust women for some reason."

Then again, she adds, "I wouldn't want to be a man either. Some-times I think I want to be asexual."

Self-injurers tend to identify themselves as sexually ambiguous, or neutral. Often their childhood experiences have stunted their ability to explore their sexuality in a healthy way. The ambiguity exists on both sides: among male patients, many express homosexual feelings but are also homophobic. Some of them say they hate women because they fear the feminine sides of themselves. Most of them want to work with female therapists, whom they believe understand them better.

Some of our patients who identify themselves as straight have been in lesbian relationships. We believe that for some self-injurers, ho-mosexuality may reflect a struggle for self-protection rather than a clearly developed identity. Many female injurers simply view women as less physically threatening, and thus find it easier to express their sexual feelings with them.

Susan L. is an example of someone whose history of abuse ravaged her attitudes toward sexuality and the body. "I don't like to talk about private body parts," she says. "I don't like—or want—people to talk about them or touch them either. I feel safe with hugs and like them very much, but that's about it."

Though she was tortured as a child by a man (a neighbor who sex-ually abused her) and her mother (who physically and emotionally tor-mented her), Susan came to S.A.F.E. trusting men only. Because her father did not physically abuse her, Susan placed him on a pedestal. "I for sure think more highly of men than women—I feel they are more understanding and kind," she wrote in an assignment about gen-der attitudes. "I feel more comfortable talking to men—I always have. That's changing now, though. I'm starting to believe that women—including myself—are kind and understanding too."

While not all self-injurers will learn to love their bodies, we have found that a vast majority can at least learn to treat themselves with respect. Abstaining from injury is often the first step in a process in which the patient makes peace with herself, inside and out.

Chapter Eight

THE EATING DISORDER
CONNECTION

Although S.A.F.E. Alternatives does not admit patients whose only problem is an eating disorder, we rarely see self-injurers who don't have issues with food. When someone comes to S.A.F.E. with both problems, we strive to tackle them simultaneously. Patients have told us they entered hospital programs to deal with self-injury only to find their anorexia or bulimia spiraling out of control. Many seesaw between these problems for years, because the common issues underlying both syndromes are never fully addressed.

Among the self-injurers we see, eating problems range from mild preoccupations with food intake, weight, and body image to severely disordered and dangerous patterns, like anorexia nervosa, bulimia, or compulsive overeating. Though these disorders are typically seen as female problems and do occur statistically more often in girls and women, some of our male patients, like Jared T., also have concurrent eating issues. Jared said his struggle with food restriction predated his bout with self-injury and believed that both problems were related to his desires to be perfect.

Many people ask, "Aren't anorexia and bulimia forms of self-injury?" Strictly speaking, yes, if you keep to our definition of self-injury as *the deliberate alteration of body tissue, without regard to health or safety, for the purpose of regulating emotional stability*. The disordered-eating pattern can be a part of a person's overall crude neglect of her physical welfare, which is a subtle aspect of self-injury. Sometimes these practices can have long-lasting or even fatal consequences.

Eating disorders in our culture are more accepted than self-injury. Eating disorders tend to bring about sympathy, whereas self-injury engenders shock and horror. Given that we all have to eat, and that food consumption tends to be a social activity, eating disorders can come across as a relatively mild perversion of something we all can relate to. In our body-focused culture, everyone is preoccupied with food and weight to some degree. Restaurant menus refer to chocolate desserts as "sinful," and people like to describe the "guilt" they purport to feel after consuming ice cream or potato chips. That someone might take these messages the wrong way seems understandable.

Food and feeding rituals are riddled with symbolism: loving, nurturing, giving, soothing, need gratification, sensuous pleasure. We recognize this every time we watch a mother feed an infant or see a businessman widen his eyes in delight at a big, juicy steak. For someone whose life may have featured disruptions in nurturing, food and eating may become powerful players in the arsenal of self-injury. If she hates herself too much to nurture herself, if she sees her needs as dangerous or destructive, and if she has tremendous conflicts with body pleasures and sexuality, her body may become a theater wherein she stages all her dramas and emotional dilemmas. Food, calorie counting, purging rituals, razor blades, and shards of glass are props that set the scene.

Our patients' self-injury and eating problems seem to have the same psychological experiences at their roots. Because of long-term problems and childhood traumas, sufferers have difficulty achieving a stable sense of identity, safety, and of feeling "intact." They tend to communicate through mute gestures, or the motoric acts of self-starvation, purging, or self-harm. The bulimic gives powerful voice to her terror as she frantically tries to "rid herself" of poisonous rage and sadness through vomiting or laxative abuse.

In eating disorders, as in self-injury, we see many hidden conflicts about self-image, gender identity, and sexuality. Both anorexics and compulsive overeaters tell us they are trying to make their bodies as asexual as possible, unattractive through their extreme thinness or fleshiness, blurring or bloating the sexually obvious characteristics of breasts and curves. They believe this disguise will protect them from the dangers of intimacy. Among people who have been sexually assaulted or abused, this can be a prominent concern, as they struggle with feelings of vulnerability and imagine their bodies to be open to harm and penetration.

Self-injury and eating disorders may have very similar aims. Both behaviors counteract a sense of being out of control of oneself and one's mind. Just as the injurer experiences a "rush" of calm after cutting herself, so does the anorexic speak of food deprivation as a soothing "high." She derives pleasure and comfort from her hunger and her shrinking body, and the control she has over them.

Psychologist Lisa Cross has suggested that self-mutilation and eating disorders represent women's attempts to "reclaim ownership" of their bodies, which have come to feel alien in some way. For survivors of sexual abuse, for example, the message is: "Hands off! This is my body, these are my boundaries, and I'll be in charge now." The self-injurer experiences her body as a detached, inanimate object, an "it" rather than a "me." Her inability to feed this body in a life-sustaining, nurturing way encapsulates this attitude.

Furthermore, self-injury and eating disorders can both serve to satisfy the need to express rage toward real and perceived villains in a person's life. The anorexic holds a cruel grip on others by refusing to eat, causing alarm and desperation in the people who helplessly stand by as she starves.

The overeater erects an angry barrier between herself and others, saying, "Don't come too close to me." Eating and self-injury have become wordless substitutes for the spiteful feelings she has toward people who have wronged her, slighted her, taunted her, ignored her. At the same time she is exacting revenge, she is also trying desperately to coax others to pay attention to her needs, which she does not want to have to verbalize.

The following case studies are of two S.A.F.E. patients: Pam W., a teenage anorexic, and Chrissie M., who is thirty-four and obese. Both patients found addressing their problems with self-injury was a necessary precursor to tackling eating and weight issues.

Pam W.: Anorexia

Pam W., a nineteen-year-old college student and the oldest of four daughters, is responsible, mature, attractive, and popular. Anyone who met her at the S.A.F.E. program would think she had everything going for her: she plays several musical instruments; is heavily involved in school orchestra, choir, and church groups; spends every summer working at a senior citizens' home; and earns money for college as a manager at an athletic shoe store.

Pam can't figure out why her sisters—who were abused by her father, just as she was—do not have problems with food or self-injury. She herself has been bulimic, and sometimes anorexic, on and off since age eleven, and started cutting herself a few years later.

Pam says her injuring routines are planned well in advance. They happen at night "to punish myself and get rid of my feelings," whereas her vomiting is done on the spur of the moment, whenever she needs a quick release. Most of her Impulse Control Logs (the diaries we ask patients to keep about their urges to self-injure) are food-related.

"My eating disorder follows a similar pattern to my self-injury," Pam says. "I restrict so I can block out my feelings and have control over them, and the purging is a way for me to relieve tension and make myself feel better."

Pam has only recently come to realize that her deleterious behaviors are linked to the atrocities she suffered as a child, which included her father's repeated sexual abuse.

"I remember once when I was eleven and my father had come to visit and my mom was staying with a friend—it was after they had separated," she says. "The abuse was terrible, because he was all alone with the four of us, and the worst thing wasn't what he did to me, but knowing what he was doing to my little sisters.

"One night he was in their room, and I knew what was going on because he had raped me earlier, and also I could hear my little sister crying. It made me feel so sick and so guilty that I just sat in the bathroom and threw up. I wasn't doing it on purpose, but I learned that it made me feel better. That's how my bulimia got started. I think that when I purge, I'm still trying to make all the bad memories and feelings go away."

Pam describes her relationship with her mother as distant. "Even when my mom and I weren't fighting, I didn't feel connected to her."

When Pam was twelve, her mother fell off a ladder and became chronically disabled, leaving Pam largely in charge of the household. Her mother recovered and divorced the abusive husband (who was severed from the girls' lives by child welfare authorities), but the scratches on Pam's memory did not fade.

In her freshman year in high school, she began drinking and experimenting with drugs, and her eating problems spiraled out of control. Pam recalls that year. "My eating was terrible, and even though I hadn't lost a lot of weight, my bulimia got to the point where I was purging four or five times a day," she said. "Anything that I allowed myself to eat, I immediately threw up. That was the time that I started injuring myself too. I was friends with a girl who burned her hands with cigarettes, and that was what gave me the idea.

"I started scratching my arm with my fingernails, and I discovered that it was a great source of temporary stress relief. I ended up with all these wounds on my arm, and even though they weren't deep, they bled a lot."

Self-injury was a revelation for Pam. "It was a substitute for the eating disorder," she said. "Since I had to eat, I had found something else to do to my body that felt good. Every day I did it. It made me think less about my eating disorder. Then my parents [mother and stepfather] found out during family therapy."

Pam's parents did not know what to do. Self-injury was a foreign concept to them. They decided to place Pam in a hospital for people with eating disorders, but the experience was a bad one. The staff was so alarmed at the injuries on Pam's arm that she made little headway with either problem.

"Sometimes I used to pick my scabs off and make myself bleed just to upset the staff," Pam recalls. "My self-injury got worse after I was discharged to the eating-disorder partial [hospitalization] program—I burned my leg in two places with an iron and cut my arm with a razor so deep that I almost had to have it stitched. I could never let my wounds heal: I would pour water on the burn to make it sting, and it had all these blisters on it, and I would pick them off."

After Pam was discharged from that program, she made progress with a private psychotherapist. "She was the first person who didn't think my self-injury was weird," Pam says. "She made me sign a contract saying I wouldn't kill or hurt myself, and I quit injuring for the most part after that. For a year my problems weren't so bad, and my whole family started going to therapy together." Pam, her therapist, and her family made slow, steady efforts to identify and face the angry and conflicted feelings they had been avoiding for years.

Pam began attending a parochial high school (she had dropped out of public school because of her various problems) and graduated with honors. Her final high school years were punctuated not by purging and injury, but by band practice, gymnastics, and an active social life. Relations improved between Pam and her parents, and she began viewing her stepfather as "a real dad," one who helped with homework and was available for advice or companionship.

Pam's problems returned to haunt her in college, where life became overwhelming. With the rigorous course load of a math major and a stressful job at the shoe store (where customers, she says, were obnoxious and complained constantly), Pam fell back into bad habits. Her dietitian referred her to S.A.F.E., where she drew comfort from meeting so many people who had similar woes.

"I remember being in eating-disorder treatment, and some of the other patients and I were talking," she says. "We got off track, and I got some ideas from them about ways to refuse food. S.A.F.E. is much better because that can't happen—you're not allowed to talk about the ways you self-injure."

Pam is confident about her future after S.A.F.E. "I want to go back to school, get married, raise a family, and have a career," she says. "I believe I can put self-injury and eating disorders away, lock them in a box in my past."

Pam's story is a good example of someone who used bulimia and self-injury to "eject" terrible, unwanted feelings—including guilt, rage, and sadness—that resulted from her experience of abuse at the hands of her father. On the other hand, some patients—like Chrissie M., below—overload on food to try to fill a limitless void brought about by early deprivations. When food cannot fill the empty place, they turn to self-injury.

Chrissie M.: Obesity

"I'm very overweight and I HATE myself," writes thirty-four-year-old Chrissie M. in her journal. "I'm proud of graduating from college with honors, and I did do a triathlon before I gained all this weight, but I've been going downhill ever since, and now I'm a big, fat, fucking slob."

Chrissie finds little to like about herself—except perhaps her eyes and hair, and her sense of humor and opinion of herself as a "good listener." Most of the time she spends berating herself for being obese and trying to punish herself for it. Chrissie vows she won't have a sex life until she loses weight. She won't pursue any of her hobbies, like ceramics, hiking, or knitting. She claims that her aunt refused to invite her to her cousin's birthday party because of her weight. She blames her weight for most of her problems—at the same time she acknowledges that she overeats because she has psychological difficulties.

"I am socially retarded," she says, enumerating her faults. "I am very impulsive. I'm very shy. I'd like to become an outgoing person and learn how to handle stress and change better."

Chrissie's weight was normal as a child; then in high school she became bulimic and anorexic. At one point, she says, she lost so much weight so fast that she developed gallstones and had to have her gallbladder removed. Then she gained the weight back, plus more.

Chrissie was very athletic in her youth. She liked swimming and track and field, and was a member of several school athletic teams. She worked out in the morning and after school. But these activities ebbed late in high school, when Chrissie became depressed, started drinking heavily—usually to the point of vomiting or passing out—and started using drugs almost daily: pot, cocaine, methamphetamines. "I liked school, but I didn't have too many friends because I was painfully shy," Chrissie says. She missed her school prom because she was confined to a psychiatric hospital.

Despite her problems Chrissie went to college and graduated with a degree in special education. What followed was a long string of jobs, some part-time and some full-time, that Chrissie had to leave because of self-injury, binge drinking, or suicide attempts. "If I don't like the job, I try to kill myself or self-injure real badly," she says matter-of-factly. "My most recent job was as a teacher's aide in third grade, and I liked it, because I wasn't in charge. But it was full-time, which was too much, and after I visited my parents at Christmas, I totally self-mutilated and overdosed and ended up in the hospital and have been on disability ever since."

Chrissie ranked among the most dysfunctional of our patients at S.A.F.E. Before she came to us, she spent all her time "listening to

CDs with some kind of sports on mute on television," she told us. "I get pretty restless and it can be very boring. I was trying to start walking again and eat right to lose weight, but I'm too fat and have no motivation." Her depression led her to sleep all the time, both at home and at S.A.F.E., where she slept through many mandatory appointments and reported feeling constantly sleep-deprived. When awake, she says, she felt "spaced out and detached" a lot of the time, and sensed that she lacked the coping skills to handle that feeling.

Chrissie grew up in Tampa, the second of four children. Her father, a heart surgeon, was known as "Doctor Welby" by his patients and staff because of his patience and heroic work hours. Her mother, a journalist, was hyper-competent, plus "very beautiful and skinny."

"My family was very distant from one another—frozen emotions," Chrissie says. "I didn't see my dad much because he was always working, and I didn't feel real close to my mom. But I did get upset when she would leave, which seemed like a lot of times. I wasn't abandoned as a child, but my mom sure left a lot."

Chrissie describes her mother as her total opposite: a gregarious woman with an active social life who dances the night away at clubs on the weekends, yet has the discipline to get up early and put in a long workday (Chrissie's parents divorced when she was nineteen). Chrissie says her mother has always seemed exasperated with her, even in high school when Chrissie told her that a track coach had sexually molested her. Her mother, she says, refused to believe the story and told her she was responsible for bringing on any negative attention.

"Mom gets very angry when I self-injure," Chrissie told us at S.A.F.E. "The last time she called and cussed me out. She has no tolerance and doesn't understand at all. I used to call her a lot, because sometimes she would make me feel better, but then she told me to quit calling her so much."

Chrissie also has mixed feelings about her father. Though he supports her financially, he has threatened to stop unless she ceases self-injuring. She describes telephone conversations with him as awkward, with long silences that make Chrissie feel guilty.

"Dad only wants to hear about good things, not bad things," she asserts. "He gets mad at me if I tell him things aren't going too well. The first time I tried to kill myself, I was a freshman in college, and he called me in the hospital. All he did was yell at me and never asked what was wrong or why I had done it."

Chrissie's relationships with her siblings are similarly troubled. As children Chrissie's older siblings ignored her, and a younger sister used to break her toys. She felt frustrated by them at an early age. "When I was young and would get into trouble, I would tear up my own favorite toys," she says. "I've always wondered if it was sort of like self-mutilating." In adulthood, Chrissie reports, her siblings are all normal and well adjusted, with families of their own; all of them throw up their hands at her problems.

Among other childhood traumas Chrissie reported an early unsuccessful surgery, a few sexual molestations by people outside the family, a difficult move to a new city, and the departure of a treasured junior high school chum. "My best friend lived next door to me until seventh grade, when she moved," Chrissie writes bitterly in her diary. "That's the story of my life. Whenever I get close to someone, they leave me or betray me."

As an adult, Chrissie's closest friend has been Steve, whom she met during one of her twenty-five hospitalizations. Before Chrissie came to S.A.F.E., she and Steve spent a lot of time together—watching movies on television, making popcorn, attending football games and AA meetings—but did not become lovers. Chrissie regarded Steve as a brother, one who kept keys to her apartment and would feed her cat when she was hospitalized for self-injury.

One day Steve decided his recovery was being impeded by the fact that Chrissie was self-injuring and still drinking. He threatened to cut off the friendship unless she stopped. That's when she came to S.A.F.E.

Chrissie had a relatively severe history of self-injury, even by our standards. She relished attention from doctors, the "excitement" of ambulance rides, the "thrill of it all." Her first experience was at the time of her parents' divorce, when she rubbed skin off her arm with a pencil eraser. She abstained from self-injury during college, when booze was her chief demon. Then the injuring began in earnest.

"I usually cut with a knife or razor blades, which became my item of choice," she says. "Those cuts would bleed a lot but rarely need stitches. Then about five years ago I began cutting myself multiple times with a knife, requiring over a hundred stitches a lot of the time. I have cut my arms and legs up, and my breasts and abdomen and stomach are covered with scars.

"I would usually be okay as long as the stitches were in, but once they were out I would want to cut again. I also burned myself a lot. I'm not sure what prompts the urge to self-injure—it could be anxiety, or anger, or loneliness, or feeling like I don't exist."

The first thing we helped Chrissie recognize at S.A.F.E. was that she had to stop beating herself up mentally. She took note of this in a writing assignment. "I don't nurture myself because I don't feel I'm worth it, and I hate myself. I don't deserve anything good and enjoyable. But that is changing. I'm learning to love myself and realize that I am worthwhile."

She also began learning that she could tolerate the sensation of anger. "When I'm real angry, I want to punch the wall or self-injure to get back at the person I'm mad at," she says. "I've learned that I don't have to self-injure when I'm angry. I've learned I can write down my feelings, or talk to someone about it instead. Now when I get angry, I'm learning to take a 'time-out' so I can figure out what to do instead of self-injure."

Chrissie had trouble completing the program—she burned herself with a cigarette lighter at one point and constantly slept through meetings—but she ultimately did make it through. She went home with a vow to attend AA meetings every day, to meet new people, and to "have to answer to them if I screw up." She set a goal of isolating herself much less, picking up with her friend Steve, and forging better relationships with family members.

Three months out of S.A.F.E., Chrissie has remained sober and has lapsed into self-injury only once. She sees herself making incremental progress, in keeping with the AA motto of "one day at a time." Chrissie told us proudly, "Now I can actually have a conversation with someone where I know what to say without becoming detached."

Chrissie is a good example of someone whose self-injury and eating disorder expressed her profound anxieties about intimate connections with others, and her fears about becoming a sexually mature adult. Chrissie felt unwanted and unloved as a child and had trouble identifying with a mother who made her feel so different and inferior. She thought that none of her painfully awkward, anxious feelings had been tolerated or dealt with. Self-injury and overeating became Chrissie's frantic ways to express her strangled feelings and protect herself from further vulnerability.

Eating disorders and self-injury tend to be nested in the same set of psychological traumas. With proper treatment patients can resolve both problems at the same time. In our experience, there is no reason to treat an eating disorder as a distinct problem from self-injury: once someone learns to respect her body and well-being, her healthy attitude manifests itself in many ways.

Chapter Nine

BEHIND THE "MACHO" MYTH: THE MALE SELF-INJURER

S.A.F.E. Alternatives has treated only about twenty-five men and boys in our thirteen-year history, versus hundreds of women and girls. There are several reasons, some more enlightening than others, why we believe men are underrepresented among the general population of self-injurers:

- Males are more likely to turn their anger outward, into aggression toward others. For instance, a man who comes from an abusive background might turn into someone who enjoys a good bar fight or who has frequent brushes with the law. Thus, men may be more likely to end up in jail than a psychiatric hospital. Women and girls more often turn the same feelings inward, into depression and self-blame.
- Men tend to deny that they have any emotional or psychiatric problems. Women are more likely to seek treatment for such problems, and they make up a larger percentage of patients who are psychiatrically hospitalized.
- Men are more likely than women to turn to alcohol and drugs to soothe what is ailing them. In psychology lingo, these are their favored "addictive solutions" to stress, providing the same thrill and adrenaline rush as self-injury.

Though men at S.A.F.E. are a rarity, those who do come to us thrive at our program and find that their problems are not so far off from those of female patients. Indeed, if you looked at the intake questionnaires that all patients fill out when they arrive at S.A.F.E. and covered up the names, you would never be able to tell the men from the women.

While men tend to handle their emotional distress differently from women, the underlying problems for both sexes tend to be more similar than dissimilar. Just because men mask their vulnerability doesn't mean it isn't there; just because they're taught that masculinity is synonymous with independence and autonomy doesn't mean they don't long for personal connections and relationships.

Like our women patients, male self-injurers usually harbor profound ambivalence toward their parents. They feel strong anger toward them, yet simultaneously fear that any direct expression of that anger could bring about the permanent loss of the relationship. Some male patients work overtime to cover up and deny whatever hostile feelings they have toward their less than perfect parents.

Consider the case of Eric G., a self-injurer with a long-standing history of alcohol and drug abuse. In one S.A.F.E. writing assignment, he painted a saintly portrait of his mother. She is "the most important woman in my life, and she possesses an almost impeccable sense of morality," he wrote. "The most significant thing about my mom is her unwavering sense of loyalty and integrity."

This was an interesting appraisal, given the facts of Eric's life. After his parents split, his mother got romantically involved with a second cousin who had just jumped bail for selling drug paraphernalia. Because of the boyfriend's legal problems, Eric's mother and the boyfriend went underground, traveling the country with young Eric. Though they did not marry, they produced a son before the boyfriend had a nervous breakdown. Then Eric's mother took on a new lover, whom Eric says "beat me on a regular basis over trivial things." Eric's mother eventually returned to the other boyfriend and married him.

Instead of venting his infinitely angry feelings over these overwhelming situations, Eric submerged them in alcohol, narcotics, and self-injury, which together helped him deaden the loss, abandonment, and vulnerability. At S.A.F.E. his therapeutic work focused on allowing these feelings—as well as the overt depression that needed to accompany them—to surface.

PRISONS

Some male self-injurers wind up in prison because their poor impulse control spills over into other situations. A male self-injurer who is "conditioned" to believe that asking for help with a problem is a sign of weakness might subconsciously believe it is more socially acceptable to go to prison than to a mental hospital, where people might brand him a sissy.

But more often than not, it is men who have never mutilated themselves who begin experimenting with the behavior once incarcerated. The behavior is prevalent and contagious. We are contacted by prison officials around the country who want to know how they can stanch the epidemic among inmates. Armando Favazza, in his book *Bodies Under Seige*, describes prisons as "notorious hotbeds of self-mutilation."

A few reasons suggest themselves. In prison men can't discharge tension in the same way they can in the outside world. Convicts, who are likely to have had antisocial tendencies to begin with, probably found thrills, distraction, and emotional stimulation in other ways before they ended up behind bars. Once imprisoned, their movement is restricted, their freedom of choice removed, and their external stimulation curtailed. Prison, in some ways, seems to stand out as the physical embodiment of the feelings commonly expressed by our female patients, who say they feel "trapped" and unsafe to express their anger.

Second, self-injury may serve as a survival tool within prison culture. It can get the inmate moved from the general population to a hospital ward or to a cell that is farther away from dangerous inmates. Some men embark on aggressive bodybuilding programs in prison to ward off attacks from predatory colleagues; self-injury may serve as a similar defense mechanism, proving to others that the sufferer is too crazy or fearsome to attack.

Prisoners also crave control over their lives, which may also lead them to self-injure. Just as many women tie the behavior to their desires for physical and emotional control, so do prisoners need to feel that there is some aspect of their existence that nobody else can dictate. It has been well documented that prisoners of war also mutilate themselves to exert some type of control over the foreign power holding them captive.

The men in our program often have histories of drug and alcohol abuse. But unlike self-injurers in prison, they do not usually have histories of violence toward others. Perhaps the men who end up in psychiatric treatment rather than jail have made a choice to direct their anger toward themselves rather than other people.

The specific circumstances of prison life seem to make treatment particularly challenging. Self-injury can seem like a boon to prisoners: they can get themselves moved from the general prison population to a safer and more nurturing environment. Thus, it is hard for them to see an incentive to become "healthy" and nondestructive. Given the limited stimulation and resources within prison walls, they may have a hard time finding alternative strategies for self-soothing.

Perhaps the largest hurdle to overcome is the implication that in order to recover from self-injury, the sufferer—in this case, the inmate—must begin to tolerate and experience unwanted feelings. For many prisoners there is a competing motive: the desire to dissociate from feelings, to grow numb to the deprivational experience of incarceration. Self-injury may seem preferable to feeling the full impact of the hostile environment from which he cannot escape.

We suggest that prison staff start by addressing the issue of the secondary gain of self-injurious behavior. Perhaps the injurer should be given medical attention for his wounds, then returned to the general population or wherever he was before—some facilities may offer further treatment, such as counseling or group support. This help may be framed as entirely voluntary, and as an opportunity for growth and change.

Self-injury resembles criminal behavior in one important respect: both are forms of "illusory control" over the world. Both strategies backfire and cause a loss of control over one's life and circumstances. The distinction between illusory and true control over one's destiny is one that the prisoner may be willing to entertain and absorb. Other incentives, like privileges, could be used as a reward for safe, noninjurious behavior. A modified Twelve Step model could indeed be helpful under such circumstances, because of its egalitarian view that all sufferers are equals, there are no "authorities," and mutual education, role modeling, sponsorship, and peer mentoring are the frameworks of the helping relationships.

Many aspects of the S.A.F.E. program can be imported into the work. These people are incarcerated because of their problems with impulse control and their refusal to accept responsibility for their behavior and its consequences. These topics are the central focus of the S.A.F.E. Alternatives approach.

Luke C.: Portrait of a Male Self-Injurer

Luke C., a tall forty-two-year-old with a barrel chest and a mop of curly red hair, arrived at S.A.F.E. looking like a portrait of burly masculinity: plaid shirt, faded jeans, work boots.

Unlike Jared T.—the self-described "sensitive male" who enjoyed pouring out his feelings on paper and in front of others—Luke was the silent type. His writing assignments were short and terse, but well thought out. He tended to keep quiet in group meetings, though he was clearly mulling over what was being said and what his reactions would be.

Despite his macho appearance, it's safe to say that Luke's experience of his own body led him to self-injury. Subjected as a child to repeated homosexual rape, Luke did not feel comfortable in his own skin. As his several marriages dissolved and his emotional equilibrium worsened, Luke began to find that his normal bodily functions had turned into agonizing reminders of the trauma he had suffered. Sometimes he would fast for weeks, growing dangerously thin and undernourished, because having a bowel movement reminded him of the rapes. Other times he would try to purge himself with laxatives of the evil he felt lurking within him and would lie in bed for days with blinding stomach pains.

Luke's emotional difficulties had a variety of causes. His fundamentalist religious beliefs contributed to the blame and value judgments he placed on his actions and the crimes perpetrated against him. The complex set of stigmas Luke had set up in his mind about self-injury and various other behaviors made him reluctant to tell us what was going on with him, but gradually he softened.

"I grew up in a dysfunctional family," says Luke, who came to us after a self-inflicted gunshot wound led to three major foot surgeries. "I was never victimized by my family in a physical way, but there were never many 'I love yous.'"

Luke has been married four times and has three children, two from his first marriage and one from his second. He has held a series of jobs—truck driver, mechanic, golf instructor, residential manager at an apartment complex—but self-injury has plagued him for more than fifteen years. He has cut and burned his arms and legs hundreds of times, abused laxatives, mutilated his genitals, poured hydrochloric acid on his hands. "There is no simple reason why I hurt myself," Luke says. "It's like a drug. Sometimes I don't realize I'm even doing it."

The youngest of eight children, Luke grew up in a solid middle-class family where there was always ample food and decent clothing, a nice, clean house, and annual lakeside camping trips. Luke got along well with his siblings, three boys and four girls, and was particularly close to his sister Mary, who played catch with him in the yard and used to help him with his homework. But his home was lacking in parental love, supervision, and authority. Luke's mother was a chronic invalid, and his father, who ran a successful office-supply company, traveled frequently, golfed every weekend, and withheld affection. Luke's dad always said that putting food on the table was more important than kisses and hugs.

Early on, Luke learned the importance of being seen but not heard, doing what he was told, and not making waves. He describes himself as "a perfectionist," someone who is "very polite" and "cares about issues like hunger and homelessness." His favorite passage from the Bible is: "Do unto others as you would have them do unto you."

Like his father, Luke is "not very emotional" but takes pride in the fact that his children love him. "I'm warm and personable on the outside, but feel like a rock on the inside," Luke confided in his diary. "I don't have an angry side. I seem to hold it in."

Luke has much in his past to be angry about. At age twelve he met a security guard in his community named Keith, who did business with his father. One day Keith and another man sodomized Luke and told him that if he ever reported the crime to anyone, they would have his father's home and warehouses condemned. Soon Keith came back for more, not only for himself but for other pedophiles whom Keith charged money to have sex with Luke. The elder man turned the young teenager into a male prostitute, forcing him to deal drugs and to submit to frequent anal rapes. "If the customer was not satisfied, I would be punished by burning," Luke wrote.

Luke's torture continued until he was sixteen years old, when Keith died suddenly of a heart attack. For Luke, a deeply religious person whose beliefs were as violated as his body, the death of Keith was as traumatic as the abuse itself. Not only had this man taken away his childhood, sullied his virginity, and stolen his innocence, but he had also disappeared in a way that prevented Luke from gaining vengeance or seeking punishment. "I hate myself for allowing this to happen—I should have told someone," he says.

Luke spent many years in denial about the abuse. The year after Keith died, he met Linda, his first wife, whom he describes as the love of his life. The couple married young, and the early part of their relationship was extremely happy. They took long nature walks, went hiking and camping together, and shared a mutual interest in outdoor sports.

Linda's father, Jason, was a Baptist minister who performed their wedding ceremony. Luke idolized him and felt that Jason's love and religious teachings could rescue him from his sordid and unhappy past. Luke and Linda moved in with her parents after they were married, and Luke began working for his father-in-law's church, handling the money that came in from charitable donations Jason solicited.

Luke also worked as a truck driver and was on the road a lot. He describes himself as a loyal and loving husband, but says he probably did not appreciate his first wife enough. He and Linda had two children, and most of the household chores fell to Linda. Some of their best times together involved going to church as a family, or holding Bible discussion groups with other couples.

After nine years of marriage, Luke decided to confide his childhood trauma in his wife, hoping that her love and support would help him come to grips with what had happened. The results were disastrous. Linda accused Luke of being gay and immediately sought a divorce. She told her father what Luke had related, and her father—Luke's role model and hero—condemned him and cut him off from both Linda and the church.

Luke was distraught. He got in a car accident, which affected his hearing and left him unable to work. As he slipped in and out of two shorter-term and less meaningful marriages, Luke began to relive the abuse more vividly and to suffer extreme emotional trauma.

Luke arrived at S.A.F.E. Alternatives in bad physical shape and emotionally riven by the abuse issues he had never been able to explore. On one hand, he believed Keith, his tormentor, gave him "a sense of being wanted," and Luke was angry at him for "dying without saying good-bye." Keith's death "left an open wound needing surgery to close."

On the other hand, Luke felt unspeakably shamed. The homosexuality jarred with his beliefs about what was proper, and he knew—in many ways he could not verbalize—that what Keith and the other men had done to him was perverted and something he could never get away from. "I'll always feel his mustache from where he kissed me," Luke wrote bitterly.

At the time Luke attended S.A.F.E., he was the only man in the group, but he made great progress and said he felt comfortable among his fellow patients. Like many of the women in his group, the hardest thing for Luke was learning to open up, to talk about his memories and feelings. The learning process was a painful ordeal, but it helped him process many of the unbearable emotions that had been flooding him during his bouts of self-injury.

Luke worked hard, and he got much better. One day, for instance, as one of his writing assignments, he was asked to describe on paper what compensation or recognition he could reasonably obtain for the wrongs that had been done to him. Luke sat over his notebook in private, reflecting with pen in hand. Finally, summoning great courage, he wrote down: "The thought of knowing I will be the last boy abused."

Then Luke had to stop. He concluded his diary entry: "As this took several very grueling hours to write, it hurts too much to go on."

It took a lot of courage for a macho guy like Luke not only to admit his problem but to agree to be hospitalized. Many men suffer silently, fearing not only the stigma of self-injury, but also society's views toward men who have psychological problems. Far from being "weak," men like Luke are the healthier ones, who know that asking for help is the bravest and most important thing a person can do.

Chapter Ten

CHARACTERISTICS OF SELF-INJURERS AND THEIR FAMILIES

There is no way to build a profile of the "typical" self-injurer, or to say that all self-injurers have had one kind of experience or another. One of the remarkable and perplexing issues that comes up in the field of psychology is that no two people are alike in their makeup, or in their responses to different problems or events. For example, two people may suffer from childhood abuse at the hands of their parents, and one may develop into a self-injurer and the other may not. The reason for this is that many complex factors go into a person's capacity to adapt and cope with trauma and problematic circumstances. Individuals may have different inborn strengths, and different people or events may have helped them compensate for bad experiences.

For example, some of our patients have had benevolent experiences with adult figures other than their parents—grandparents, teachers, coaches, and others who helped compensate for deficits within the home. Also, a great many of our patients are of above average or superior intelligence. [Though self-injury has been noticed with high prevalence among certain groups of people with mental retardation and other conditions that involve low IQ, our treatment program is not set up for people with this kind of developmental difficulty or delay.]

The life histories of our self-injurers contain a multitude of varied tales, including painful losses, illnesses, neglectful or abusive parenting, and a range of other bad experiences. Some have had depressed or withdrawn parents, some have had overly intrusive ones, and every nuance in between. Others have suffered from traumas, tragic circumstances, and catastrophes outside their immediate families. Though the circumstances vary drastically from one case to the next, there are some commonalities that may help readers understand the mind-set of many self-injurers.

CHARACTERISTICS OF SELF-INJURERS

Naturally, few self-injurers will exhibit *all* of these qualities. Some may identify with only one or two of them, or some with none of them. We merely point out these themes as ones that recur among the sufferers we meet. A few have been addressed before and can be summarized briefly; some bear further discussion here. The characteristics are as follow:

- *Difficulties in various areas of impulse control, as manifested in problems with eating behaviors or substance abuse.*
- *A history of childhood illness, or severe illness or disability in a family member.*
- *Low capacity to form and sustain stable relationships.* Self-injurers often complain of poor social skills, including hypersensitivity to other people's faults and an inability to tune in to the needs and concerns of others. They are irritated beyond belief by "lazy" and "annoying" habits of others, and often believe this behavior is targeted toward them, or done deliberately to annoy them.
- *Fear of change.* This can be a fear of everyday changes in their environment, or of any kind of new experience: people, places, events. It can also involve an intense fear of changing their behavior in relationship to others, and a fear of the changes they may need to make in order to get well.
- *An inability or unwillingness to take adequate care of themselves.* Many patients ignore their own needs for a nutritional diet, sufficient exercise and sleep, and good hygiene. Most say they fail to nurture

themselves out of laziness and apathy, or because they consider themselves undeserving. In a supplementary category are patients who fail to take care of their basic safety needs. Kelly B., for example, would take money out of bank automated teller machines in dangerous neighborhoods at night.

- *Self-injurers tend to have low self-esteem, coupled with a powerful need for love and acceptance from others.* They go to extremes to exact demonstrations of love and caring from others, including taking on too much responsibility for what happens in relationships (excessive self-blame), or adopting a "caretaking" role even when it is unhealthy or dangerous for them to do so. For instance, one patient at S.A.F.E. who was a recovering drug addict agreed, when asked by her mother, to take in her drug-addicted brother, despite the fact that this would put her and her family in jeopardy.

Some self-injurers manage to find more adaptive ways to meet their needs for affection, in their career choices (many choose medical fields or social services) or love of pets. Most of our patients have at least one pet, often more than one. Cats seem to be a favorite, perhaps because they are easier to keep than dogs. Pets give self-injurers the unqualified affection they are seeking, often unsuccessfully, from other people. We encourage patients to keep pets because of the responsibilities that pets entail. Gretchen I. says of her four cats, "If I didn't have them, I would have nobody to get better for. They need me."

Many patients deliberately enter the "helping professions"— nurse, physical therapist, massage therapist—to try to transform or transcend the anger and disappointment in their lives. They may be hoping that as "caretakers," someone will take care of them in return. Others are curious about the workings of the human body; they want to watch medical operations and to learn about anatomy.

- *Childhood histories replete with trauma or significant parenting deficits, which led to difficulties internalizing positive nurturing.* Many self-injurers adapt to trauma by developing fantasies about being rescued from their grief. Our patients often explicitly acknowledge their desire for someone to swoop in and remove their pain. Some are seeking to attract the attention and care of someone who will nurture and protect them in ways their own parents did not.

Often a friend, lover, or family member will attempt to play the hero for a while. But nobody can sustain the role of "mother" to a fellow adult, so the strategy ultimately fails. When that happens, the self-injurer is confirmed in her belief that she is destined to be abandoned by others. Victoria R., for instance, described a friendship with someone who fell into the category of rescuer: "Natalie has taken actions—such as clearing out my apartment of sharp objects—to try to get me to stop. It hurts her to watch me hurt myself. She has offered everything in her power to try to keep me safe. I doubt few things would make her happier than to know that I was no longer self-harming." Natalie's actions, however, did not compel Victoria to alter her behavior.

Significantly, when Victoria was injuring, she also found great value in relationships with people who were not rescuers. Her friend Karen "has never been freaked out by my self-injury. She does not give me attention for it. She will listen to me when I need to talk about what has caused me to self-injure, but she isn't interested in what I actually do. She has been very supportive when I try to keep myself from self-injuring, like giving me some distractions or offering her apartment as a safe haven."

Victoria describes her brother-in-law similarly. "Andrew supports me while not focusing on my self-injury. He never acts shocked— in fact, he never comments on my injuries. He pushes me to continue with therapy and get the help that's available to me."

■ *Rigid, all-or-nothing thinking.* A self-injurer's signature catastrophic thoughts might include: "Nobody understands me," "I never get my needs met," "Nothing will ever change." Such a thinking style, combined with a chronically low self-image, tends to make sufferers more likely to reach for self-harm in a state of frustration, alarm, or impending rage.

For some, rigid thinking can manifest itself in perfectionism. This quality can be highly adaptive in some areas of the self-injurer's life; for instance, it can help her excel at school or on the job. Yet it tends to wreak havoc on her emotional stability when something unpredictable or stressful happens in her well-ordered universe. One of our goals during treatment is to help patients become more flexible in their everyday lives.

While perfectionism and workaholism are two common traits among self-injurers, the behavior takes hold of all types of people. Some of our patients, like Chrissie M., feel too incapacitated to hold a job, have a social life, or maintain a romantic relationship. Most of the time they feel too paralyzed by urges and fears even to leave the house.

Other self-injurers alternate between periods of cocooning, in which they hole up at home and refuse to socialize, and periods of functioning normally or participating in too many activities. In fact, they may function very well on the job and in many other aspects of life. They go to school, complete degrees, hold responsible positions. "Most people assume you're going to get low-functioning people as a rule, that you're not going to get post-doctorates," says one recovered self-injurer, Nora A., who earned her Ph.D. in psychology and knew of two other people in her program at a large university who were also self-injurers. "It's a behavior that can interfere so badly that you have to drop out of school. I just took off for a year at a time when I was too sick."

Nora, who now runs a psychology practice and supervises a staff of twenty, decided to quit self-injuring after her two small children walked in on her in the act. "That made me realize the true consequences of what I was doing," she says.

SELF-INJURERS AS PARENTS

One question we often ask self-injurers is: "If you had children, what would you think if you learned that they were self-injuring?" The answer is always the same: "I would be very upset and would try to get them to stop."

The question becomes knottier for self-injurers who actually *are* parents—who respond the same way, but who seem unable to reconcile what would be good for their children with what is good for them. Though they recoil in horror at the thought that their children might self-injure (and some do, in emulation of their mother or father), they maintain the position that self-injury is okay for themselves. The attitude is, "My mental health is secondary to others."

Parents who self-injure typically report troubled relationships with their children. Sufferers are often emotionally unable to care for their dependents, let alone themselves. We sometimes hear of parents who must relinquish custody to the child's other parent, even if that parent is abusive.

Donna W. voluntarily turned over parenting responsibilities for her two children. One of them is old enough to live on her own, but the other still lives with his father, from whom Donna is estranged. Both the children, Donna believes, have tried self-injury.

Donna was twenty-two when she gave birth to her daugher, Camille, who is now a college student. "I think she and I sort of grew up together," says Donna, who divorced Camille's father when the child was nine. "Despite the problems I was having when I was raising her, she has grown up to be a wonderful young woman of whom I'm very proud."

Once, when Camille was in high school, Donna found her sitting in the garage, crying and banging the back of her head against the garage door. She was bleeding from the blows. "I comforted her by taking her and cradling her in my arms," Donna says. "I don't think the incident was repeated, but I don't know for sure. She seems to be doing well in school, but states that she is under a great deal of stress."

Donna says Camille shows no reaction to her own self-injury or alcoholism. She has never raised either subject. "Other than the night before I left for S.A.F.E. Alternatives, when I offered her literature on self-injury to read, we have never discussed the behavior," Donna says. "To my knowledge, she did not read the literature."

By contrast, Donna and her fifteen-year-old son, Dustin, have talked about self-injury. "I have attempted to explain to him how the behavior is destructive, because I fear that he will try it," Donna says. "He did show me once where he had rubbed the skin off his forearm with a pencil eraser. He told me that he 'just did it' but didn't know why. I suspect he was trying to connect with me in some way—trying to emulate me as children are wont to do with their parents."

Donna is worried Dustin will continue to self-injure, but feels "powerless to stop him." Her worries are compounded by her complex feelings toward Dustin, whom she sees infrequently. "I'm so tense when I'm with him," Donna confides. "I do love him, but find myself avoiding him sometimes because of the guilt I feel about him being molested by his older stepbrother when he was seven and eight. I work hard at disguising my tension when I am with him, but I suspect he picks up on it."

To Donna, Dustin "represents how I failed at keeping my marriage together, how I failed at keeping him safe, and how I failed at raising him."

Liz C., thirty-nine, is the mother of two children, whom she raised largely on her own. Self-injury, she says, is "okay for me, but not for my kids." Liz admits she has a "double standard," and is fearful about the messages that her problems have been sending to Eric, seventeen, and Tanya, nineteen.

"When they were little, I used to tell my kids they were cat scratches, or I was clumsy and I fell," Liz says. "There were a hundred and one different stories I could come up with. When my daughter got old enough to figure out what was going on, she was angry at me for lying. She knows that I am trying to do better, but I think she's scared."

Most distressing to Liz was the discovery that Tanya had dabbled in cutting. "She claimed she wasn't doing it, but I knew better," she says. "That scared me, because it's like, 'What have I taught my kids?'"

Moreover, self-injury has become a weapon in the family arsenal, something that mother and children use against one another in times of tension. "They know I do it," Liz says. "When I get into a verbal argument, I feel stuck. Rather than exploding toward others, I explode toward myself.

"It got to the point where my daughter and I would argue, and she would say to me, 'Now you're going to go off and self-injure.' That brings it home to me that it affects other people."

Relations between Liz and her children are strained, to say the least. Liz was unable to care for them at various points in her life, and they were in and out of foster care. Tanya graduated from high school and has her first job; she lives on her own, and her father is nowhere to be found. Eric lived with Liz for a while until he was expelled from high school for truancy and drinking. He ran away from home a few times, and finally Liz relinquished custody to his father, who was Liz's second husband.

Liz complains about her children. Eric, she says, doesn't take anything seriously and always comes up with a "smartass answer" when she asks him about his future. Tanya, she says, tries to provoke her wrath and "doesn't give me any respect."

Despite these problems with the maternal bond, Liz is adamant in her wish that neither child ever fall into the trap of chronic self-injury.

"I consider my children to be 'other people,' and 'other people' don't do this," she says. "I'm the only one who deserves it. Sometimes I would say that everybody else matters, but I don't matter."

THE FAMILY: BREEDING GROUND FOR SELF-INJURY

We have already described several family scenarios that seem to be the most likely to produce a self-injurer. For review purposes, here is a quick list of common situations among families of self-injurers:

- The presence of traumatic losses, illnesses, or instability in the family life (such as frequent moves)
- The presence of neglect or abuse—physical, sexual, emotional
- Family life characterized by a rigid, dogmatic code of values or religious beliefs, which are applied in a hypocritical or inconsistent manner
- Breakdown in the structure of family roles, in ways that make children take on adult responsibilities prematurely and inappropriately

But a few additional characteristics of the family structure seem to play a role in self-injury. Often, these factors are very subtle and difficult to detect, and sometimes they can relate to the "biological fragility" phenomenon we discussed earlier. Below are some examples of how certain family conditions—none of them rare—came to produce a child who self-injures.

WHEN DOES ONLY ONE CHILD IN THE FAMILY SELF-INJURE?

In some families there are multiple siblings who self-injure—usually one or more siblings picks up the habit from the one who starts it first—but more often than not, one sibling in the family is the "full-blown" self-injurer.

Some of our patients tell us of siblings who have engaged once or twice in a behavior that qualified as injurious, but the habit did not escalate from there. Others describe siblings with different impulse-control problems, such as drug and alcohol abuse or eating disorders. Still others say their brothers and sisters are perfectly normal, and no one in the family can fathom the one exception.

It may seem odd that children who grew up in the same family, often under basically similar conditions, might turn out so vastly different from one another. Why should one sibling develop a harmful habit derived from severe psychological problems, while another sibling—perhaps close in age and of the same sex—does not? The reasons are numerous and complex, and often cannot be pinpointed. Perhaps a good analogy would be to ask why one child in the family ends up a violin prodigy or a tennis star, while the others may be talented in the field but not exceptional.

Sometimes in troubled families certain children are singled out for the abuse. In a dramatic and highly publicized child-abuse case in New York City, a single mother with seven children deliberately starved one of them to death. While the other children were given meager but adequate provisions—food, clothing, and school—one girl was kept caged in a crib, hidden away and denied nourishment or care. The five-year-old girl died at sixteen pounds.

While most cases are not nearly so extreme, many self-injurers describe being tagged for degradation or abuse, either in overt or subtle ways. Sometimes they *felt* like they were the ones who always got picked on, and sometimes they actually were the ones whom the abusive parent actively sought out the most. Again, it's important to point out that sometimes the parents of self-injurers report that they were as evenhanded as possible among their children, and yet the child who self-injures perceives that she was left out, slighted, or unfavored in some way.

Other times there seems to be no concrete explanation for why one person becomes a self-injurer and a sibling remains healthy. Some people live through unbearably awful childhood abuse and grow up emotionally stable, and some people grow up in seemingly normal homes and emerge with terrible psychological difficulties.

At times experts use sibling differences to try to argue that self-injury has biological origins: if one sibling has it and another doesn't, mightn't that point to a genetic mutation or difference of some sort?

We don't buy that argument. Some self-injurers may be born with a kind of predilection toward hypersensitivity, but we believe the manner in which the caregivers respond to this sensitivity ultimately determines how a child begins to cope with life's demands.

Each family has its own idiosyncrasies that may or may not prompt someone exposed to them to turn to self-injury. Below are three examples of people who grew up under very different circumstances and who all became the only self-injurer in the family.

Ceci J.: Singled Out

Ceci J., the youngest of eight children, is a self-injurer. Cory, her twin sister and "best friend," is not. Neither is her brother Charlie, the next oldest, who is extremely close to both twins and has been throughout their lives. Neither are any of the five eldest siblings, two boys and three girls.

Ceci is thirty-eight years old, single, thin, and attractive. She wears preppy clothes, parts her shoulder-length blond hair in the middle and feathers it to the side. Ceci holds a law degree, as well as a high-paying job as a lawyer for a pharmaceutical company. An avid runner and exercise fan, her proudest day was when she completed her first marathon.

Ceci started injuring in her early twenties, but not until age thirty-five was she first hospitalized, at S.A.F.E. Alternatives. She spends a lot of time ruminating on her family situation and why she became a self-injurer, the only one. She knows of one time that her twin sister smashed a glass during an argument with their mother and cut herself with a shard, but that was an isolated event; most of the time Cory is "one of the strongest people I know.

"I don't understand why I'm the one in my family who has feelings like this," Ceci says, sitting in a lounge at S.A.F.E. and discussing the situation with her brother Charlie during visiting hours. "I can remember even being a little girl and hitting myself, taking a hairbrush and looking in the mirror and saying, 'You're so ugly, I hate you.'"

Ceci and Charlie spent some time together during Ceci's stay at S.A.F.E. trying to figure out how Ceci's problems originated. (Both Cory and Charlie were instrumental in getting Ceci to S.A.F.E., and both have played an active role in her treatment. For more on the sibling relationship and how it contributed toward Ceci's recovery, see the next chapter.)

"I was the one who was picked on a lot, teased," Ceci recalled. "I was the one who did everything everybody told me to do."

Charlie agreed. "I think that Ceci was treated differently. Cory was always the perfect one, the one everyone admired. Our mom says we were all raised the same, but I don't think that's exactly true."

The differences were manifest at birth. Their mother had not been expecting twins—the second baby was tucked behind the first—and had vowed that, boy or girl, she was going to name her fifth child Cory. After Cory—a girl—was born normally, the mother learned with dismay as she lay on the delivery bed that a second child was about to be born, only this one was a breach birth. Ceci came out feet first, with one lung collapsed and her head highly molded from the birth canal.

"Mom remembers the doctor saying, 'Well, you have one perfect baby, and the second baby has a long head.'" Charlie said. "People commented on how perfect Cory was and didn't say anything much about Ceci. I believe babies understand that."

Ceci agreed. "I always felt I was the unwanted one, unexpected, outcast. I was a surprise afterthought."

Ceci and her siblings were not sexually abused, but life in their household was not easy. Their father was chief executive of a small electronics firm, an alcoholic who enforced strict and bizarre rules of conduct. Children were meant to be seen and not heard, and were not supposed to have feelings.

"He was very reserved," Charlie said. "Everything was dictated by him. He was like the father of the Von Trapp family with the whistle, and everybody lines up. I remember his checking our nails before dinner—you had to go upstairs and wash them if they didn't pass inspection, and if they still weren't clean the second time, you'd get a pretty hefty swat."

Dinnertime was an extraordinary event. The eight children sat at one table in the kitchen, and—for reasons that were never explained—none of them was ever allowed to speak during a meal. Laughter and other forms of interaction were also forbidden. The two parents sat at a separate table in the dining room, with the door open so the father could keep watch on the offspring and make sure no conversations took place. The parents did little talking themselves.

"If there were any outbursts at the children's table, there was trou-ble," Charlie said. "Our father's spankings weren't your average spank-ings. There was a room at the top of the house where we three boys used to compare the welts and red handprints on our bottoms."

Ceci's parents divorced when she was twelve—her mother initiated the rift in part because she disapproved of her husband's child-rearing tactics—and the family fell into poverty as the mother moved to a new city and attempted to support everyone on her own. Ceci and Cory wore hand-me-downs and ate free hot meals at school. When their mother remarried, the family moved yet again. Shortly after, the chil-dren's father died.

There wasn't enough money for the family to fly to the father's funeral—classmates tried to raise funds for the siblings but were un-successful—so the children had to grieve at a makeshift mass. Ceci was fourteen. "I remember we were supposed to say some type of prayer, and I was asked if I had said it, and I said no," she recalled. " 'Well then,' the priest told me, 'Your father probably won't go to heaven.' I felt so guilty."

Ceci was a straight-arrow during high school. She was shy and studious, got good grades, and stuck close to her small band of friends. Twin sister Cory, meanwhile, hung with a fast crowd and ended up pregnant. At age sixteen she was sent to a faraway home for teenage mothers. Ceci was devastated by the departure of her sister.

Not until Ceci reached adulthood did her self-injury start. Ceci had suffered a string of bad romances and several abortions and felt un-loved and unappreciated. Though she was not overweight, she felt bad about her body and her sexuality. Her first experience was with an artist's knife; she cut long slits along the sides of both legs, in a circular pattern. She immediately made up a cover story.

"I had stories for every day of the month," Ceci recalled. "One time I said I had put up cyclone fences, and that's how I cut my arms."

Gradually and insidiously, self-injury became "an obsession" that "felt like an addiction," Ceci said. "I used a knife, and once the blood came, I felt better," she explained. "I had put knives all around my house, in my truck, on my nightstand. They were like a security blanket for me."

Ceci said "self-loathing and rejection" were her two strongest feel-ings prior to self-injury. Far from relishing the attention the activity brought, she shunned medical care, failing to attend to her wounds even when, she admits, they could have used stitches.

Like many patients at S.A.F.E., Ceci began panicking when the soothing effects of self-injury started to wane. "It was scaring me because it wasn't doing what it used to do, and I was thinking about suicide and how I could slit my wrists," she said. "I felt like I wanted to die. I've talked to a lot of people here at the program, and they started out just like me."

At S.A.F.E., Ceci enjoyed the camaraderie of being with fellow self-injurers. Her comments point out a common phenomenon in psychiatric wards, ours and everyone else's. Some patients jockey to be the "baddest," or sickest, and some take solace when they perceive others as sicker than they are.

"I think I have looked at people at S.A.F.E. and said, 'I'm not that bad,'" Ceci said. "Depression is what I suffer with more than anything. I'm not psychotic."

Ceci's brother visited her nearly every day that she was at S.A.F.E., but other relatives were less supportive. Ceci and Charlie said their mother had reacted with disgust.

"My mother is so disturbed about it, but for the wrong reasons," Charlie said. "She keeps asking, 'How could Ceci be so different? Where did I go wrong?'"

Ceci chimed in. "All she feels is self-blame. I'm sure she wants me to stop doing it so it's not an embarrassment to her."

As part of Ceci's ongoing recovery, she is learning to handle the emotional pain that accompanies her mother's rejection. "I'm grieving over having less than ideal parents, but I'm learning that you're the one who needs to take care of yourself," she said.

The rigid ways of thinking that pervaded Ceci's family are quite typical among the self-injurers we see. Often, these inflexible attitudes manifest themselves in different forms. In Ceci's case, they were cloaked in a mantle of military discipline; in the case of Jared T. they were part of a religious code of conduct.

Jared T.: Extreme Religiosity

Jared, twenty-three, was a voluminous writer and deeply religious man who hoped to become a minister within his small Protestant sect.

"Many people have told me that I 'carry' myself as a pastor," Jared said proudly. "The Lord has blessed me with a heart full of love and compassion and caring for others, and thus he has shown me my calling."

Jared's writing assignments at S.A.F.E. have a confessional quality to them, and they universally end with a paean to Christ. "Praise the Lord!" is Jared's signature tag line.

Jared's self-injury, self-esteem, and worldview were delicately intertwined in his religious beliefs. Unlike the extreme religious zealots that Dr. Menninger, Dr. Favazza, and other clinicians have described in written analyses of self-injury—the people who plucked an eye or self-castrated because of a biblical interpretation or private instruction from God—Jared did not connect his religious fervor to his self-injury. It was not the Devil who forced him to do it, or any other spiritual or biblical factor. Indeed, Jared repeatedly reminded himself that, in his view, God forgave his behavior.

Still, getting angry did help Jared feel he could identify with Jesus. "Sometimes it feels like my heart is burning within me," he wrote. "This would be the times when other people attack Jesus, or when fellow Christians act blatantly hypocritical and mock me."

Jared's extreme piety made him the butt of many jokes while growing up—he describes himself as "a geek" to begin with, but his sensibilities did not let him understand that constant preaching and proselytizing was not the way to forge connections. He enjoyed his self-styled role of "spiritual counselor" to the people around him, and said he was "always open and eager to talk about Jesus." He acknowledged that this sometimes could be a strain. "To some people this makes me a pompous and smug person, as if I think I'm some guru beckoning followers," he admitted. But in Jared's mind, his method of social interaction was justified. "In reality, all I'm doing is trying to share the greatest news in the world, that Christ Jesus died for the sins of the world," he told us. "I want others to take comfort in the simple message of Christ crucified, for you, me, the world."

Jared encountered problems with classmates at his Christian college, some of whom apparently did not take various Scriptural prohibitions as seriously as he did. Hearing other students utter curse words—or talk about religion in a way that Jared interpreted as mocking—made him seethe with rage, and usually resort to self-injury. "Profanity *really* upsets me when it's within the context of Christians," he explained. "I mean, especially the school I was attending. Everyone there was studying for the ministry, yet the profanity flowed and many people liked to drink underage, and many others got drunk! Don't get me wrong. I understand that we are all sinful, and really Satan has the most to gain by attracting a group of potential ministers.

"Sometimes I would confront people, and usually I would get mocked. But such blatant public sins in a school of people claiming the desire to serve in the public ministry makes me angry—I guess that's called righteous indignation."

Jared did not put his self-injury or eating disorder in the same category as the sins he observed among his classmates. Indeed, he likened his struggle with self-injury to the trials faced by Jesus himself. Jared spoke repeatedly of his need to challenge his irrational thoughts, including his belief that he was "too sensitive, too critical, too strict, too stubborn, too everything." He wrote, "All I see is weakness except for the love of Christ that God had given me. All I know how to do is drive myself crazy."

Jared credited Christ with keeping him alive and said that without his faith he would have been hopeless and suicidal. At the end of his treatment Jared credited God with his recovery (we privately took a little credit).

Upon his release from S.A.F.E., Jared set forth three mottos for himself:

1. Jesus is bigger than my impulses.
2. Jesus is the Lord of my life.
3. With Jesus, I can control my impulses.

Yvonne K.: The Child as Substitute Grown-up

Yvonne K., who is twenty-eight, grew up in a family full of denial. Her father, a licensed electrician, liked to tell everyone what a happy family he had. He bragged about his wife, a stay-at-home mother, and her outstanding cooking skills. He bragged about his son, Michael, so strong and athletic. And he bragged about his daughter, Yvonne, the baby of the family, whom he called "my little China doll."

Inside the family home, the myth fell apart. Yvonne's parents screamed at each other constantly, and Yvonne would hide in the closet when they fought. Yvonne has no memory of either parent listening to her concerns. "The rules of the household were: don't talk, don't feel, and don't think," she says.

Michael was the favored child. When Yvonne was an infant, her mother would leave her in another room for lengthy stretches, failing to notice her cries or screams, while she attended to Michael. Yvonne and her brother got along as children and played together, but Yvonne was always aware of her envy. "My mom always felt that I could take care of myself," Yvonne observes. "Emotionally, she wasn't there for me growing up."

When Yvonne was in the sixth grade, her mother had a stroke and spent the next several years incapacitated. Yvonne suddenly became responsible for all household duties—cleaning the house, washing the dishes, laundering and ironing the clothes, and making dinner every night. "I wasn't a happy child with all these chores to do on a daily basis," she says. "I felt like I was living in a boarding house where no one will talk to you or sit with you."

Worse still was when her father's best friend would sexually abuse Yvonne. This started when she was five years old and persisted until her early teen years. "My dad's friend got me pregnant, and then he did an abortion on me," she says. "I may not be able to have children because of that."

When Yvonne was fourteen, her parents got divorced, something they had promised her they would never do. The split hurt Yvonne deeply, in part because it shattered all the fictions her family had built up about how happy and stable they were. "My father says he's a man who has no problems, who never played any part in his divorce," Yvonne says. "He tries to put on a big show that he's a goody-goody, but really he's a sad man who fears rejection. For example, if he asked me to get some soda for him and I said no, he would say, 'You hate me,' and try to get me to admit it."

Moreover, Yvonne's father—whom she loved and trusted throughout her childhood—told her the divorce was her fault, that it was happening because Yvonne did not love or respect him enough. Clearly, Yvonne's father forced her to play the role of his wife in every way.

Yvonne's self-injury began right after the divorce. "I felt responsible for holding the family together, and I couldn't," she says. She began cutting herself, and it quickly escalated to burning. The injuries hurt, but the hurt felt good, like a reminder of a private secret. In high school, "nobody knew I was carrying razors with me everywhere,"

Yvonne says. "I would hide them in my locker, under my pillow, and in my jackets. I didn't feel safe without a razor—it was a part of me that no one knew."

Yvonne's mother did ask about the cuts she saw on her daughter's arm, but Yvonne lied. "I told her a cat had scratched me—and the story worked!" she recalls.

Since no one seemed particularly concerned about Yvonne or her symptoms, her self-injury worsened. It was also accompanied by other problems: fasting and purging that led to a forty-pound weight loss during freshman year, and alcohol and drug abuse that began the year after. Yvonne used pot, speed, and downers.

Her substance abuse seemed to fuel her desire to self-injure. By the end of high school, "burning my hands was the high for the day." She soon had her first hospitalization, and doctors mistook her deep cuts for a suicide attempt. They were wrong.

"When I talked about my childhood abuse with my therapist, I got stressed out, and I would cut," she explains. "My urges got so intense. I needed to see as much blood as I could."

Yvonne first came to S.A.F.E. Alternatives when she was twenty-four. She completed the program successfully, and after graduating from S.A.F.E., she spent three years injury-free. Always fond of ceramics, Yvonne got a job in a pottery studio, where she gained satisfaction from working with clay: throwing pots and molding them, firing them in a kiln, cleaning them up, and painting them. She moved in with a roommate, Jocelyn. She was able to enjoy gardening, even though she did remember her father sexually abusing her in the family greenhouse when she was young.

Yvonne's relapse began during a one-month visit with her mother, who had moved to a city far from Yvonne's home and had remarried a man who was an alcoholic and a crack user. Yvonne's mother was working—as a night-shift manager at a telephone answering service— but her stepfather was not. "As the days went on during my trip, he would drink a six-pack, and then beg someone for some money so he could get high," Yvonne recalls. "My mom would be at work when he would drink and get high, and I would be alone with him all night."

One evening the stepfather left the house to get drunk and high, then brought his drug dealer back home for payment. "Walter paid his drug dealer off with clothes, and to have sex with me," Yvonne says. "He was going to pick up my mother from work, and he left the drug dealer alone with me. The drug dealer raped me while Walter was gone."

Yvonne didn't know what to do. "I was so scared and felt so dirty." When her mother came home three hours later, the man was still in the house. Her mother sensed that something was wrong and called the police and threw the man out. "The police made a report, and that was all they could do—the dealer was long gone," Yvonne says. "Nothing was done about it. I didn't go to the hospital because I had already taken a shower. I had to spend two more weeks with my mom after the rape happened, and when I got home, I didn't tell anybody, because I was too ashamed."

What Yvonne did do was pick up her old habit of self-injury—with a vengeance. Amid many emergency room visits and several hospitalizations, Yvonne was grappling with her feelings toward the trauma, as well as a difficult relationship with her roommate, Jocelyn, who refused to keep the apartment clean.

According to Yvonne, Jocelyn was a pack rat who filled their two-bedroom apartment with myriad accumulations of a lifetime: clothes, shoes, old magazines, kitchen gadgets, books, memorabilia. Also on hand were more than a dozen pets.

It was a familiar pattern for Yvonne, who was used to living in a chaotic environment. The second time she arrived at S.A.F.E., she was so confused about whether or not her feelings actually mattered that she said she had trouble sorting out her emotions.

"I feel I still need to work on trying to recognize when I'm angry," Yvonne said at the time. "Sometimes I don't realize that I'm angry until I've self-injured."

Yvonne completed S.A.F.E. again and has remained injury-free since then. She moved out of the dreadful apartment she shared with Jocelyn and holds hope that she will be able to avoid the contact with her family that has proven so damaging in the past. Most important, she has learned lessons about herself that will help her quell future urges to self-injure.

"I've learned that anger can be controlled, and that I don't have to act out," Yvonne says. "I've learned that I need to talk to the person I'm angry at and resolve it. It's difficult for me to approach the person when I'm angry, but it's getting easier every time I do it."

Clearly, self-injurers come from all walks of life. Rich or poor, educated or not, their pain feels equally intense and unbearable. There is no dream job, fabulous romantic partner, or amount of personal wealth that can alleviate the misery of someone who has fallen into a pattern of self-injury.

No matter what their circumstances, people who self-injure can pull themselves out of despair through a treatment regimen that includes psychotherapy. Time and time again, we have seen "basket cases" turn their lives around by using their determination and accepting appropriate help. While no two self-injurers will have the identical background, we believe they share in common the ability to get better.

Chapter Eleven

WHAT FAMILY MEMBERS
AND SIGNIFICANT OTHERS
SHOULD KNOW

S ometimes the self-injurer herself is the first to recognize her serious problem and seek out help, but more often it is someone
close to her who detects something amiss. Self-injurers tend to
start cloaking themselves in privacy and withdrawing from activities
and situations they once enjoyed. Parents of self-injurers sometimes
say the first signs of something wrong were when their normally viva-
cious child grew silent at the dinner table or began spending hours in
her bedroom instead of hanging out with her friends.

Figuring out that there is a problem is only half the battle. As relatives of alcoholics and other people with impulse control issues will
attest, there is often nothing more difficult than confronting the sufferer and coaxing her to admit her problem. She is likely to be defensive in the extreme, and perhaps in a state of denial. Friends and
relatives of self-injurers often agonize about how to broach the topic
in the first place, and then how to handle it once their loved one is in
treatment and recovery. This chapter will attempt to provide some
answers.

Sadly, it's often the case that not everyone in a self-injurer's world
steps up to help her. Some relatives want to deny the problem, or
think it's too crazy to accept or understand. Others are too worried
about how the self-injurer's problem reflects on *them*. Most self-

injurers can usually figure out quickly which of their friends and family members will be there for them and which will ignore or belittle their recovery.

Ceci J.: A Brother and Sister Intervene

A corporate lawyer and attractive single woman who dates often, thirty-eight-year-old Ceci J. fell into a pattern of self-injury in her twenties and thirties. The behavior resulted in part from depression and low self-esteem. Though Ceci was able to hide the behavior from colleagues and casual friends, her twin sister, Cory, and brother Charlie sensed something was wrong.

"The more her arms became marked up, I kept asking her about it and she kept telling me stories that I didn't believe," said Charlie.

After gentle but persistent prodding Ceci mustered the courage to tell her siblings about her problem. She found a magazine article about self-injury and sat them down on the lawn in front of her house. They immediately recognized what was going on with Ceci, and the three of them wept.

Then Charlie and Cory strategized privately about how to help her. "We agreed that Ceci really needed therapy, that she wasn't responding to the circumstances of her life the way she should," Charlie recalled. "I said, 'We have to treat Ceci a little differently right now, give her a little more attention. We have to watch over her, and we can't push any of her buttons.' "

Charlie took the problem to their mother and stepfather, but they did not respond sympathetically. The mother was embarrased by the situation and refused to acknowledge it. Charlie recognized with sadness that he and Cory would have to handle the situation themselves, and Ceci would have to recover without parental support.

As Ceci's condition worsened, Cory moved into her home. "Cory was there with her even when Ceci told her to leave," Charlie said. "Cory just said, 'This was what I have to do.' She was very stoic about it. It lasted about a month."

At that point Ceci's therapist decided she needed to be hospitalized. By coincidence Charlie saw a television program about S.A.F.E. Alternatives, and he brought her to us. It was her first time in a psychiatric hospital.

"I was a wreck when I came in," Ceci recalled. "I was sweating, I was clinging to him, I was crying. I would not be here physically on this earth if it weren't for my brother."

The event was equally traumatic for Charlie, who had been staying up nights worrying that Ceci would kill herself. "When I walked out the door to leave her, I just really fell apart," he said. "I was thinking, 'What is going to happen to her? Did I do the right thing?' I felt like I just left her behind at a time when she was literally falling apart. What was I supposed to do then? Go home and watch television?"

Charlie visited Ceci frequently and attended weekly support meetings for family members, where he was able to air his worries and get answers to some of the questions on his mind. Unlike many family members of S.A.F.E. patients, Charlie was extremely understanding of his sister's problem and the root causes of the behavior.

"Life's not easy for any of us, and I think that for some people it's even harder," he philosophized. "Ceci's self-injury gave me an idea of the depth of her pain."

Sitting in a parlor at S.A.F.E. and clasping Ceci's hand, Charlie expressed a conviction that his sister's life would soon be different.

"I have an image of Ceci walking out of here with a tool belt," Charlie said. "Maybe not all the tools are there yet, and maybe some of those tools are strange and she doesn't know how to use them yet, but—minute by minute, just like her time in the program—she will learn."

FAMILY TURMOIL

Families of self-injuring patients often find themselves steeped in a complex drama. On one hand, their self-injuring relative may not want to see them, and may blame them—or isolated family members—for causing the problems and the emotions that led to it. On the other hand, the ability to trust family members and close friends is an integral part of overcoming self-injury.

When they first find out about the self-injury, most relatives feel at a loss, questioning their past behavior toward the patient and worrying that, from now on, every word or action will prompt an incident. Family members usually describe their initial feelings as shocked, scared, confused, and frustrated. Many fear the relative will commit suicide. "It's hard to understand," wrote the seventy-one-year-old father of one of our patients. "I don't bring it up unless she wishes to discuss it, and so far she has not done so. But I am mostly concerned about what was causing her to do this."

One woman described the anguish of trying to help her sister while finding the time and energy she needs for her own husband and children. "I've tried to tell my sister she needs to find a way to stop," the sister wrote. "I've also told her I'm proud of her for seeking help, and I'll always be here for her, although I have had to set certain emotional boundaries to preserve my own mental health."

This sister knows why her sibling self-injures, but like most people, her sympathy is tempered by disbelief and amazement. When asked what she would like to tell her sister about the behavior, she said: "Why can't you realize everyone has ups and downs, and just deal with life?" She added, "I would never say this, though, because I realize it's more complicated than that. It's frustrating to watch her struggle with it time and time again."

As shattering as the syndrome can be, working through the illness can also bring families together. One mother said her seventeen-year-old's struggle with the problem had improved their relationship and made the mother more sensitive to the way she treated people. Before Rachel's problem came to light, "I felt that we always had a very close relationship and could talk about everything," wrote the mother. "Boy, was I wrong!"

The mother blamed herself at first, then started thinking about what had gone wrong in the relationship. "First and foremost, I learned that Rachel can speak for herself—quite well, as a matter of fact," the mother wrote. "This is something I did for Rachel since the beginning of time. I lived her life for her, thinking I was helping her when in fact this made her feel worthless and small. I remember Rachel saying that no one listened to her or took her seriously—no wonder, when I did all the talking for her!"

Now that Rachel is in recovery, things are better at home. "We talk more about what is on our minds, and we word things differently," the mother said. "We think before we speak. Rachel's dad asks her how she is doing instead of asking me."

Feelings of guilt are very common among the significant others of the self-injurer. Family and friends can expend vast amounts of energy searching for what they did wrong, or didn't do enough of. While a certain amount of this can be useful and constructive, too much guilt and self-recrimination can divert energy from the need to be helpful in the here and now.

THE SELF-INJURER'S PERSPECTIVE

Donna W. says she always had a great relationship with her father, and there was no history of abuse. But when it came to bringing up her problem, Donna felt tongue-tied.

"I have discussed the behavior openly with my father only once, which was when he came to visit me when I was an inpatient at a mental health hospital," she said. "I described to him my feelings of being overwhelmed and out of control, which I found too difficult to handle. I told him that other times I had feelings of loneliness and emptiness which were just as intolerable."

Donna said her father had some helpful advice. "His response was that I should just tell myself that many people care about me and remember that I am a very strong person. He reminded me that I have overcome many things and told me I could overcome this too."

On the other hand, there were ways in which the reaction fell short of what Donna needed. "I believe my father is sincere in his love for me, but I also believe that my self-injurious behavior is beyond the realm of his understanding," she said.

While Donna's father was able to offer a modicum of emotional support, many other significant others do not. And surprisingly, the ability to offer sympathy and to be helpful does not necessarily correlate to the closeness of the relationship. Self-injurers say they have loved ones who seem to care about them in every respect, but have proven unable to deal with this facet of the relationship.

Liz C.'s sister, Roxanne, is in denial. "She knows I've been hospitalized many times, but she calls them 'mini vacations,'" Liz said. "She says that I should cut out all the nonsense and just be normal. If she happens to notice my self-injury, she either doesn't say anything, or else she makes some kind of comment and I come up with some excuse for the injuries. Either that or I turn it all into some kind of joke."

Liz's lament is echoed by many self-injurers. At S.A.F.E. we believe it is vital for the significant others in a self-injurer's life to bring her world into the realm of their own understanding, so they can feel more helpful and less guilty. To this end, we have included answers to some of the most frequently asked questions raised by family and friends.

Q. What are the warning signs that someone is doing harm to herself?

A. Often there are telltale signs—scars on the arms or legs, a pattern of curious abrasions—but equally often the signs are scarce or more subtle.

Many self-injurers become masters of their furtive ritual, and their secrecy may be the most obvious red flag. The person begins to seem physically or emotionally absent; she may seem distracted, preoccupied, or distant. She may disappear frequently, retreating to her private space to injure.

Among more overt warnings, someone who has begun to injure repeatedly may start to offer flimsy or repetitive excuses for her wounds. She may claim she was scratched by a cat, suffered an athletic injury, or had a clumsy accident. The carelessness of the accident may seem uncharacteristic for her, and when pressed for details, she is likely to grow guarded, anxious, and vague. She may even seem annoyed at the "intrusiveness" of the questions.

A self-injurer's family may notice that she is wearing long sleeves and long pants in warm weather. More obvious still is the discovery of a cache of implements: odd objects like bent paper clips, pieces of glass, and razor blades stored in unusual locations.

Whether or not overt signs are present, the onlooker may notice behavior changes that usually accompany self-injury: social withdrawal, sensitivity to rejection, difficulty handling anger. Injurers may make disparaging comments about themselves, or show feelings of extreme shame, worthlessness, or self-loathing. They may grow overwhelmed by everyday responsibilities and withdraw from work, school, or family obligations. Naturally, these behaviors may signal problems other than self-injury.

Another set of signs to look for are behaviors that often accompany self-injury. These include eating disorders, alcohol or drug abuse, kleptomania, and other problems of compulsion.

Q. What should I say or do—or avoid saying or doing—in such a circumstance? Should I confront her? How?

A. We strongly recommend paying swift attention to the situation. Ignoring it will not make it go away.

If you suspect someone is injuring herself, don't be afraid to say, "I've been terribly concerned about you. I see all these scars on your arms, and I suspect you may be hurting yourself. If that's the case, I want you to know that you can talk to me about it. I just want to help." You might want to add: "If you can't talk to me, please talk to somebody else."

The parent of an adolescent may want to assure her that she won't be punished. Teenagers invariably feel as if they are doing something wrong, or being bad.

For the family member or witness, the hardest thing may be to grapple with your own initial reactions: shock, horror, anger, fear, disgust, guilt. Your first reaction may be to say, "Stop doing that—are you crazy?" Remember that the self-injurer is operating under an entirely different frame of reference. She may not be experiencing the physical pain that you would expect and may not realize how much danger she is in because of her behavior.

Q. She won't open up about the problem. How can I get her to talk to me?

A. Once again, try to see things from the self-injurer's perspective. You are asking her to talk about an emotionally charged subject, a behavior she wouldn't have developed in the first place if she had been able to talk about her feelings. She may view as inconceivable that a dialogue about self-injury could take place. Your recognition of this is the first step in adopting a stance of helpful empathy. Abrupt questions—like "Why are you doing this?"—may make her clam up. She may not know why she is self-injuring and is likely to act defensive.

In the beginning, it is most productive to focus on getting the person to acknowledge her problem and her need for support and professional help. She will need a measure of privacy as therapy progresses, but she also needs to include her significant others in some way. The injuring behavior germinated in her experiences with intimate relationships, and those relationships are inextricably tied to the problems she is trying to resolve.

Keep in mind that it takes people time and therapy work to begin to put their feelings into words. Don't expect too much in the beginning, and don't take her reluctance to talk personally.

Q. When she finally did talk to me, I didn't know what to say. Help!

A. Don't expect that you have to fix the problem—that would be far too great a burden. It's fine to acknowledge that you don't have the answers. While your instinct may be to want to offer advice or suggestions, sometimes the most help you can offer is to be available as a listener. You don't have to say or do anything special.

You might tell the person that you know her behavior and the feelings behind it are difficult, painful, and scary—sometimes this is all she needs to feel a little better. Let her direct you toward what she needs or wants from you, and let her know that you will do what you can to help her find resources and to support healthy behavior, growth, and change.

Q. Should I try to get my loved one to stop the behavior? Are there any strategies that work?

A. You cannot control someone else's behavior, no matter how much you may want to. The most you can do is have an influence of some kind.

The more you get into a power struggle with a self-injurer, the more resentful and resistant she will become. Your actions may backfire, with her injuring more frequently or intensely to express her heightened outrage. (This, we believe, is exactly what happens in most hospitals and institutions where patients are given ultimatums, supervised round-the-clock, and deprived of "sharps.")

As a way of exerting some influence, you can make the self-injurer aware of the possible consequences of her behavior, such as the end of the relationship with you. Such a threat may serve as a productive— even therapeutic—warning, but before you act on it, you do need to give the person a chance to consider her options and find alternatives to self-harm.

Q. What do I do if she refuses to acknowledge a problem or to get help for it?

A. It depends on whether the person is an adult or a minor. If she is an adolescent, then it is her parents' responsibility to care for her medical and psychological welfare. The parents may have to deal with trying to get help for a reluctant teenager and contending with her anger, defiance, sense of betrayal, and perception that she is being controlled by an arbitrary authority.

If the adolescent refuses to see that she needs help, try a low-pressure selling job. Suggest that if the behavior is not really a problem, then this will be confirmed by a consultation with someone who isn't emotionally invested in proving anything. Tell her that a third party—someone with expertise—is in the best position to give input.

It may help if you give her some choices about where to go for help and whom to see. In one case a treatment-resistant adolescent who eventually made her way to S.A.F.E. Alternatives calmed down and felt more in control after she was given three treatment options. She discussed the different facilities with her family and therapy team, just as an adult would, and experienced herself as having some say in the matter, even though it was certain that she needed professional assistance somewhere.

As parents, rest assured that you are not betraying your child by seeking help for her. The concept of betrayal is a distorted one in this context. What you *are* doing is modeling a healthy parental attitude, showing that you can accept problems and deal with them constructively—even if it means that the right answer is to hospitalize your child.

For adults, things are a bit different. Unless the person is legally deemed incompetent—or is actively suicidal or homicidal—only she is responsible for her safety and well-being. As her friend or relative, you have a right to decide on what terms you will continue the relationship. Many people decide that in order to remain involved, they must insist that the injurer get help.

Our single most important recommendation: do whatever you can to make the injurer aware that she is not the only person affected by her behavior. The biggest illusion she must surrender is that self-injury hurts her alone. We have found that once the self-injurer begins to grasp the magnitude of the impact on everyone she knows and cares about, her resistance erodes, and her motivation to change is galvanized.

Q. Whom should I tell—or not tell—about the problem? Does her school or place of employment need to know?

A. For an adolescent, getting help may mean absences from school. The injuring problem may already have caused failing grades or conduct difficulties. Thus, it may be hard to avoid telling school authorities.

On the plus side, it can be in the student's best interest to adopt a collaborative attitude toward teachers and school officials, and the school system may have ample support resources to offer. Some degree of openness about the problem can help dispel the adolescent's belief that self-injury is a shameful act that must be kept hidden.

Adults must make their own choices about whether to approach employers and colleagues. If special accommodations or leaves of absence are needed, the workplace need not know the details of the problem, only that it is medical in nature.

As her friend or family member, you should respect her privacy on this issue and not attempt to take over the decision making. You should help her weigh the consequences of sharing the information with people in her workplace: is it likely to bring about censure and mistrust, or more support? Encourage her to take some time in deciding and not to be impulsive in disclosing her problem with self-injury.

Q. The rest of the family is beginning to suspect something is wrong. What should I tell them?

A. Talk to the injurer about what she wants the family to know. There is a delicate balance between her need for privacy and others' interest in knowing, which must be considered in light of whether or not the family members can be helpful and supportive. If one of the self-injurer's underlying issues is poor boundary delineations between herself and family members, disclosing the problem may cause more difficulties.

Consider both sets of needs out loud with the injurer. What would be the reasons for sharing, and what would you be trying to accomplish? What kind of language do you and the self-injurer want to use with the people you take into your confidence? Consider the likely reactions of the people you intend to tell. Coming to an agreement about what will be said and how it will be said can contribute to the sufferer's sense of privacy and control.

If you do talk to family members, remember that they may need some education. Often it is helpful to start by saying, "My daughter is dealing with some serious emotional problems, and one of the ways

she is coping is by harming herself." Have some references and literature available for family members so they can quickly learn she is not
a crazy person, that she is not necessarily in lethal danger, and that
she is unlikely to harm anyone else.

Q. What should a parent who self-injures tell young children about the problem?

A. Even very small children will know something is wrong, but their
understanding of the nature and extent of the problem will be limited
by their age and developmental level. Talk with your therapist or counselor, and ask the child if he is aware that mommy has a problem—
feel out what he knows. You have to work to find words that fit his
cognitive abilities, simple language that focuses on the fact that there
is a problem that mommy is trying very hard to get well from. Remember that your children are children and are not there to absorb your
pain or hear extensive details about the problems you suffer from.

You might say to young children, "I love you, so I'm working very
hard on my problems. My problems have nothing to do with you, although I know they sometimes affect you. If this happens, please come
to me and tell me your feelings, and we'll talk about it."

Most of the time young children can take in simply stated facts
about emotional problems and the need for treatment. Primarily, they
are looking for reassurance that it isn't their fault and that nothing
horrible is going to happen to their parent.

Q. My sister doesn't want her kids to be around my daughter who has been injuring. What should I do about this?

A. Don't get defensive—open up the dialogue about her concerns.
She may be worried that the self-injurer will do something to hurt the
others, that the girl will self-injure in front of her children, or that the
condition is contagious.

While all these fears are unlikely to come true, some self-injurers
are discovered in the act by family members and have trouble controlling and directing angry feelings. In sum, these are legitimate
concerns that you must deal with in an open-minded and nonjudgmental way, especially if you and the injurer want the relatives to deal
with you in the same way.

Give the self-injurer some responsibility for addressing these concerns with the relatives. Be realistic and aware that the behavior scares people. It's true that there is a kind of "secondary harm" that occurs when a young person witnesses the injuring act or becomes aware of it in a graphic way. The self-injurer needs to believe she can behave appropriately in front of others.

Q. How do I support the healing process of someone who injures without falling into the "rescue" trap—or inadvertently prolonging the behavior? How do I stay healthy while supporting her at the same time?

A. Give over control to the helping professionals. If you find yourself being held hostage by the self-injurer, let her know and set limits.

The best support you can offer is to encourage her to use language, not action. Don't let guilt or an overblown sense of obligation drive your relationship. Be aware of what you are responsible for and allow the self-injurer to be responsible for her part. For instance, the self-injurer might say to you, "If you didn't gang up on me, I wouldn't have injured." Not true: an outsider who is trying to help doesn't need to accept blame for this distorted view of things.

Do avoid rescue behaviors and strategies. You cannot keep the injurer safe by being around her all the time, even if she seems to want you to parent her. Remember that self-injury as a chronic pattern is usually not lethal. While it must be regarded seriously, the injurer is not necessarily in imminent danger of death, and she is responsible for dealing with issues of self-protection. Familiarize yourself with her crisis plan, making sure you know the extent of your role and when others take over. You may want to consult periodically with the professionals involved in her treatment plan—not surreptitiously, but in open collaboration with the patient.

Additionally, it is important for you to take care of yourself. Don't neglect your own needs—for privacy, leisure time, or the fulfillment of personal responsibilities. Be ready to set limits that respect those needs. Being too available for the self-injurer without taking care of your own needs and health will not benefit either of you.

Don't be afraid to get your own therapy, counseling, or support. It doesn't mean that you are crazy or disturbed. Sometimes, the advice of an objective outsider can help you keep your emotional balance while coping with the self-injurer's difficult struggle.

Q. As a parent of a self-injurer, should I blame myself? How do I deal with my child's anger and disappointment?

A. In this book we ask the injurer to take responsibility for her behavior. For a family to grow, you must acknowledge responsibility for your part in the development of her problems.

The purpose of this is not to punish yourself for being a lousy parent—or sibling or spouse—but to learn and grow alongside the person who wants to heal. Blaming the person who has the problem is often easier than looking at the family dynamics that may have contributed. If you examine these dynamics and try to grapple with them, you will help the self-injurer a lot more than if you try to minimize or dismiss them.

Q. How do I cope with the frustration, fear, and anger I feel about the injurer's behavior?

A. Accept these as natural, normal reactions. Think them through, find a way to communicate them without being judgmental or punishing. Put the feelings to good use by viewing them as signals of issues you need to deal with in your relationship with the self-injurer.

Some frustration and concern can be alleviated by adjusting your expectations of her. You can allay your anger by remembering that she is in a great deal of internal pain and has never been able to voice it. Your fear may be something you have to live with temporarily, but you should view it as a sign of your commitment and love for the person. Hopefully, you can use the concern in a constructive way, helping the injurer realize the impact of her behavior and trying to instill in her a similar concern.

Just as we tell self-injurers that it's okay to have uncomfortable feelings without acting on them, so do we give the same advice to you. Remember that the healthy expression of emotion is the goal for everyone involved with the injurer, not just the injurer herself.

Q. My loved one is in the process of healing and has just gotten home from the hospital. What can I expect from her? When is she cured? Do I have to watch what I say or do?

A. Try to dispense with any expectation of a quick cure. It took a long time for the self-injurer's pattern to develop, and it will take some time to heal. Many people are in individual psychotherapy and/or group support for several years, and some are in treatment on and off for the better part of their adult lives.

The real work starts when a sufferer comes home from the hospital and begins to put into practice what she has learned. As with any new skill, improvement takes time. You can expect a bit of regression when she loses the twenty-four-hour support of an institution, and being on your best behavior will probably not be of much help. It's likely to make her feel more fragile, too delicate to deal with feelings—in short, like a victim. Being careful around the healing person creates a false environment and lets her continue to avoid difficult moments and situations. It also reinforces the idea that external conditions or behaviors can determine her safety.

Since the recovering injurer may be dealing with feelings directly for the first time, she may be more expressive than ever before, perhaps crying more often or being more direct with her anger. This may or may not cause you discomfort, but you should view it as a sign of progress, not a setback. Indeed, it is the goal of treatment.

Different people take varying lengths of time to become injury-free and stay that way. There is no set formula. However, it is vital for you, the supporting "other," to recognize that the absence of the behavior is not the cure, but the *first step* toward the cure. Coping with emotions in a nonviolent way lets the person free up enough energy to face her underlying issues directly, to make them available for genuine examination and treatment.

Safety is also her first step toward experiencing life's pleasures and rewards. A taste of these may help her realize how much she has been missing.

Chapter Twelve

THE MEDICAL SIDE OF
SELF-INJURY: DIAGNOSES
AND PRESCRIPTIONS

I f self-injury fit comfortably into a single diagnosis or category, it would be convenient indeed. Sufferers and their family members would view the situation as more manageable and less chaotic. Medical professionals would feel more confident about their ability to offer help. Everyone who is desperate to understand the origin and nature of the problem would feel that guidance was available.

Most patients arrive at S.A.F.E. bearing a panoply of diagnostic labels, drawn from a range of psychiatric disorders. Most have tried various medications, some of which may have helped and some of which have not. Victoria R., for instance, had been tentatively diagnosed as having bipolar disorder, which is the modern term for what used to be called manic depression. She took, and continues to take, mood-stabilizing medications for that condition. Liz M., whose previous therapist thought she had dissociative-identity disorder, took a variety of drugs for that. Donna W. arrived with major depression and an entirely different set of prescriptions. Other patients have been diagnosed with schizophrenia, obsessive-compulsive disorder, post-traumatic stress disorder, and borderline personality disorder.

Any of these diagnoses may be correct, depending on the individual self-injurer. It may be helpful to think of self-injury as being "nested" within a number of different psychological or psychiatric syndromes.

The fact that someone may have tried several different medications probably reflects her search for the best description of the accompanying difficulties, or core problems in which the self-injurious behavior is contained.

In general, we are not keen on diagnostic labels. Too often they are misused in pejorative or prejudicial ways. However, the diagnostic process can be helpful in describing the sufferer's range of problems and in organizing an overall recovery plan. Diagnostic language is also needed to get insurance companies to pay for treatment, a topic we will discuss more fully in chapter 14.

MEDICATIONS

Sadly, there is no real chemical cure for self-injury. Medications are primarily useful in treating the accompanying symptoms, which can be so disruptive that they prevent therapeutic progress.

We stand firmly behind the position that psychotherapy is the best treatment for self-injurious behavior, and that medication should be viewed as an adjunct treatment that addresses the dominant features of a person's symptom picture. In other words, if the patient's dominant feature is depression, an antidepressant may be indicated. If a patient complains predominantly of mood swings, she may benefit from a stabilizing agent like Depakote. If she complains of agitation and frequent confusion, the psychiatrist might prescribe a low dose of antipsychotic medication. With properly-tailored medications, patients find it easier to manage self-injury urges and tolerate therapy work.

COMMON DIAGNOSES

Self-injury has not been classified as a distinct diagnosis, nor do we believe it ought to be. However, several conditions that often accompany self-injury do indeed qualify as distinct syndromes. We hope that by describing some of these conditions and the medications typically prescribed for them, self-injurers and their families will have a better understanding of the rationales that may lie behind treatments.

The bible of the psychiatric world is called the *Diagnostic and Statistical Manual of Mental Disorders*. Known as DSM IV, it is published by the American Psychiatric Association, and the most recent edition came out in 1994.

The DSM divides diagnostic categories into two broad groups: clinical disorders are known as Axis I conditions, and personality disorders are known as Axis II conditions. To qualify as a disorder, a behavior pattern must, according to the DSM IV, be "rigid" and "inflexible," and lead to "distress and major impairment in several areas of the person's life: social, familial, and occupational." The diagnoses most frequently assigned to self-injurers fall under the rubric of personality disorders, though self-injurers may recognize some symptoms from both groups.

AXIS I: CLINICAL DISORDERS

These diagnoses pertain to mood, anxiety, and thought. They include depression, panic disorder, obsessive-compulsive disorder, post-traumatic stress disorder, and dissociative disorder. The latter two are sometimes assigned to self-injurers who have had a history of severe traumatic abuse.

MOOD DISORDERS

When we think of mood disorders, depression generally comes to mind: a persistent, unrelenting, and severe sadness that can cause insomnia, overwhelming fatigue, inability to concentrate, memory impairment, and feelings of hopelessness and helplessness.

Clinically known as *major depression*, the disorder can manifest itself in moderate or severe ways. Sufferers may not be able to function normally and may have suicidal ideas. Depression may also be masked, or disguised, by other symptoms, such as physical complaints or impulsive or aggressive behavior.

Many self-injurers suffer from frequent bouts of very severe depression. Yet—paradoxically—they may also lose touch with the despair at the root of the depression, as self-injury develops into a strategy for blotting feelings out of their conscious awareness.

While major depression is described as a *unipolar* disorder because sufferers' problems revolve around a single mood, *bipolar disorder* is a syndrome in which periods of depression alternate with a kind of un-controllable elation, or mania. Patients swing between these two poles.

In manic periods, bipolar people are intensely euphoric, giddy, and hyperactive. They cannot sleep and may engage in wild schemes or impulsive and reckless behaviors, like spending or gambling away their life's savings. Suddenly, without warning, they "crash" into a danger-ously severe despair, the depressive phase. A bipolar self-injurer will often harm herself during the manic phase—or just as she is crash-ing—to try to regulate her state of mind.

Because of their overall difficulty in modulating their emotional state, self-injurers are often misdiagnosed—or prematurely diagnosed—with bipolar disorder. In clinical terms, most self-injurers are highly *labile*, meaning they are unstable and intensely moody.

Interestingly, we have discovered that patients who suffer from in-tense mood swings may benefit from mood-stabilizing medications whether or not they really suffer from bipolar disorder. To date, these medications have included Lithium, Depakote, Neurontin, and Tegretol.

Self-injurers who suffer from unipolar depression sometimes re-spond well to antidepressant medications and to a newer class of drugs that operate on a certain brain chemical, serotonin. However, the relief these patients feel is usually not as dramatic as that experienced by true depressives, whose symptoms are not clouded by impulsivity and somatic issues. Even so, we think antidepressants are worth a try. Self-injurers seem to have an easier time tackling therapy when they are not continuously battered by despair, apathy, and insomnia.

ANXIETY DISORDERS

Self-injurers often suffer from anxiety disorders, which produce ex-treme tension and agitation, and episodes of disorganizing panic (panic attacks). These symptoms may represent a true anxiety disorder or may be part of a larger set of problems, like borderline personality disorder.

Some doctors prescribe anti-anxiety agents for these symptoms. These drugs are sometimes called anxiolytics, or *minor tranquilizers*. However, we believe great caution needs to be taken with regard to this type of medication. For one thing, self-injurers have strong desires to numb out their feelings and thus are at risk for overuse and dependence on tranquilizers. Many become addicted, and some overdose accidentally or on purpose.

In addition, research and clinical evidence have shown that some of these medications produce paradoxical effects. One study of the drug Xanax found that it produced an *increase* in self-destructive and impulsive behaviors. Just as alcohol makes imbibers less inhibited, some researchers have suggested that at least one anxiolytic—Xanax— makes the self-injurer's control over their urges erode more quickly.

THOUGHT DISORDERS

Some self-injurers describe periods of being out of touch with reality. Their thinking grows jumbled; their thoughts seem loose, incoherent, or disconnected. Sometimes they hallucinate or hear disembodied voices that "command" them to harm themselves.

Thought disorders can also assume other guises. Some self-injurers have bouts of delusion or paranoia in which they believe others are watching them or are out to harm them. They may believe their bodies contain toxic substances, that evil demons are pursuing them, or that they have a rotting limb that must be removed.

As with most problems, thought disorders can be severe or mild, transient or chronic. Schizophrenia, which can involve both hallucinations and delusional thoughts, is an example of a severe and chronic disorder. A relative minority of schizophrenics are self-injurers, but some self-injurers—especially those who suffer from borderline personality disorder—may have brief, transient periods of thought disorder, also referred to as psychotic thinking.

You may be surprised to know that even relatively healthy people can show signs of a thought disorder when faced with severe trauma or stress. When these symptoms are prolonged, they disrupt a person's life severely, fueling her agitation, fear, anxiety, and sleeplessness, and dulling her receptivity to treatment.

Medications used for schizophrenic conditions may be helpful even if the patient is not technically schizophrenic. It seems that lower doses of these medications tend to ease the person's anxiety and counteract the "loosening" of thought processes and content. Many sufferers and their families are unduly frightened by antipsychotic medications because they associate them with the type of sedated, institutionalized zombies featured in the film *One Flew Over the Cuckoo's Nest*. The

reality is that the technology of psychotropic drugs has advanced significantly since the 1960s, when Thorazine and similar medications
burst on the scene. Current forms have fewer side effects and can be
taken in more modest dosages. Self-injurers can use these drugs for
relatively short periods of time, weaning from them as therapy progresses.

A less common diagnosis among self-injurers is obsessive-compulsive
disorder, in which the sufferer experiences anxiety and distress because
of recurring, unwanted thoughts, impulses, or mental images. The concerns are intrusive and unrealistic, and extend far beyond normal,
everyday preoccupations. Many times the obsessive thoughts are accompanied by a repetitive behavior designed, in the sufferer's mind, to
calm or erase the unwanted thought. Some of the better-known examples are people who suffer from intense fears of contamination by
germs, which lead them to excessive hand washing and bizarre cleansing rituals.

For some people the urge to self-injure takes on the quality of an
obsessive-compulsive problem. Sometimes the medications prescribed
to people formally diagnosed with the disorder can help lessen the
intensity of the urge to self-injure. Psychiatrists have found that certain
antidepressants can help lower the intensity of obsessive ruminations.

POST-TRAUMATIC STRESS DISORDER

This diagnosis was born in the years following the Vietnam War, when
veterans developed severe and disabling symptoms after the trauma of
jungle warfare. Sufferers experienced nightmares, flashbacks, disturbing and intrusive memories, depression, pessimism, and an inability to
cope with daily life.

More recently the list of traumatic events that could potentially produce PTSD has been expanded to include robbery, kidnapping, torture,
incarceration, and violent personal attacks or abuse. Because of this,
some self-injurers who were severely abused and who suffer from these
symptoms have been given this diagnosis.

Medication therapies for these sufferers are tailored to address the
dominant symptoms: antidepressants for the despondency and pessimism, anxiolytics for the "startle" reactions and tension, and sleeping
medications for insomnia.

In *Women Who Hurt Themselves*, Dusty Miller writes that applying the PTSD diagnosis to self-injurers with trauma histories is a step forward. It acknowledges the source of some of the trouble self-injurers have with emotions and memories. But Miller cautions—and rightly, we think—that the scope of this diagnosis is limited for the self-injurer. It does not distinguish between trauma survivors who injure themselves and those who do not, and it may not adequately capture the severe impact of neglect, invasive caretaking, or emotional battering.

DISSOCIATIVE DISORDERS

Many self-injurers are diagnosed as suffering from one of various types of dissociative disorders. These illnesses make people feel numb, separated from the experience of their bodies and thought processes. The formal name for this is *depersonalization disorder*, and it represents one end of the spectrum of dissociative disorders.

At the other extreme lies dissociative identity disorder, formerly known as multiple personality disorder. These sufferers purport to have developed two or more separate or distinct identities, or personalities, who recurrently take control of their behavior. Self-injurers diagnosed with this problem report having extensive histories of abuse, losing track of large chunks of time, and forgetting actually engaging in self-injurious acts.

In our experience, dissociative identity disorder is as rare as it is controversial. Some self-injurers are diagnosed with it prematurely, based on limited evidence, or before their therapy team has fully explored other explanations for the "forgetting." Some have been hypnotized—an extremely controversial technique for coaxing memories—or encouraged to "give names" to the so-called separate states of mind. In such cases, what may appear to be separate personalities may in fact be products of the helpers' suggestions.

In our long-term experience with self-injurers, incidences of true dissociative identity disorder are exceedingly rare. We do, however, often see symptoms of depersonalization in our patients. This is a frightening state of affairs for them, especially since the phenomenon tends to block their experience of pain.

Some scientists have suggested that the experience of trauma releases naturally occurring opiates in the brain known as endorphins. These chemicals, which block pain, are triggered under traumatic circumstances, as in the case of a car accident victim who does not feel the massive injuries she has sustained.

Among self-injurers who dissociate, Naltrexone, which serves to block the release of endorphins, can be prescribed so that the person feels the pain when she injures. The drawback to this is that many patients simply stop taking the medication when they decide to resume their self-destructive behavior.

AXIS II: PERSONALITY DISORDERS

Several disorders fall into the Axis II classification, each characterized by a cluster of behaviors and personality styles.

BORDERLINE PERSONALITY DISORDER

The disorder most frequently linked to patients who self-harm is borderline personality disorder, or BPD. One of the salient indicators of borderline personality disorder is a history of suicidal gestures or self-mutilating behaviors. However, for that diagnosis to be fully accurate, at least four other symptoms must accompany self-injury, such as:

- A pattern of unstable and intense interpersonal relationships
- Impulsiveness
- Abrupt mood swings
- Inappropriate, intense anger
- Identity disturbance (uncertainty about self-image, sexual orientation, long-term goals, friends, values, etc.)
- Chronic feelings of emptiness or boredom
- Frantic efforts to avoid abandonment

Many of the self-injurers we see fit these descriptions, especially those who were abused or neglected in their formative years.

The borderline diagnosis has gotten negative press in recent years, partly because it is given far more often to women than men, and partly because the diagnosis carries with it a connotation of a difficult-to-treat patient. Many have long histories of impulse control problems such as gambling, substance abuse, kleptomania, and eating disorders.

We take a more moderate view of the diagnosis. Perhaps more than any other description, the borderline diagnosis captures the quality and tenor of some self-injurers' relationships: they are full of mistrust, fear, vulnerability, and unpredictability. Rather than implying a pejorative view of the person, we think the borderline diagnosis highlights the suffering of the individual and the obstacles that impede her from forging safe and trusting bonds with people.

OTHER PERSONALITY DISORDERS

Many self-injurers have features of the following personality disorders:

- *The dependent personality.* Patients who fall into this category could be described as helpless, unable to take care of themselves and demanding that others fill in. These patients defer decisions to people around them and come across as "clingy" or "people pleasers"; they are afraid that displays of anger will lead to abandonment. These people differ from sufferers of borderline personality disorder in that their reaction to abandonment is usually increased appeasement rather than rage or escalating demands.
- *The passive-aggressive.* This person doesn't express anger directly because of her fear and disdain of authority. Instead, the anger comes out in snide remarks and other covertly sabotaging behaviors. She tends to be pessimistic: since she believes she won't get what she wants when she asks for it, the only way to have her needs met are through passive, indirect methods.
- *The paranoid.* This syndrome is characterized by hypervigilance and the expectation that the motives of other people are always malevolent. The patient may be secretive and guarded and feel slighted easily. She has a tendency to blame all her problems on others and to see herself as a perpetual victim, constantly mistreated.
- *The narcissist.* These self-aggrandizing people like to compete for the spotlight. They desperately need for other people to view them as unique and as having the most extreme (best, worst) qualities. They can exhibit rage over relatively minor issues. They are usually less self-destructive and impulsive than typical sufferers of borderline personality disorder.
- *The histrionic personality.* These patients are excessively emotional about everything that goes on around them; their behavior qualifies as attention seeking. They are highly concerned with their physical

appearance, need immediate gratification for their wishes and desires, and think very globally, often failing to fill in the details. Unlike borderlines, they don't experience deep feelings of emptiness or loneliness, or angry disruptions of relationships.

There are no specific medication regimens for these various disorders, and psychotherapy is the primary treatment for patients with personality issues. However, someone with an Axis II problem can often have difficulties with mood, anxiety, and thought (Axis I), and the appropriate adjunct medication may be of some relief.

A PERSON, NOT A LABEL

At S.A.F.E. Alternatives we do not view the diagnosis of *personality disorder* as a way to pigeonhole people. Rather, we see it as a way to describe the patient's style of relating to other people. The purpose of any diagnostic description should be to help therapists intervene more effectively, not to label people in a condescending way. We emphasize as often as we can that the person who self-injurers is much more than an "illness" or a "diagnosis"; he or she is a person whose problem does not define his or her identity.

Chapter Thirteen

WHAT THERAPISTS SHOULD KNOW

From a therapist's perspective, encountering a patient who self-injures can be frightening indeed. Many therapists shun working with patients who are aggressive or self-destructive. Some fear that patients who hurt themselves are by definition suicidal or will become suicidal eventually.

Certainly, the potential for suicide is an issue for many self-injurers at one point or another, although relatively few actually carry through on their thoughts. Nevertheless, self-destructiveness as an umbrella concept stirs concerns for many health care professionals in our day and age when litigation for negligence and malpractice is at an all-time high. Clinicians are concerned they will be held responsible for the behavior of their clients, so the therapist is in a constant dilemma of whether to take swift action to hospitalize a client who self-injures— or even one who has urges to do so. The therapist may wonder, "What would be the consequences to me if I chose not to hospitalize this patient and something happened to her?" Some therapists elect not to take this risk at all, but for those who do, this chapter outlines our suggestions for managing these patients and the risks they pose through the careful structuring of the treatment relationship.

Given the growing population of people who exhibit this behavior, it is increasingly likely that a psychotherapist will encounter someone with the problem during her career. Private clinicians from around the country report they are seeing more clients who self-injure. At university health services, where most of the patients are in their adolescent and post-adolescent years, staff doctors and therapists describe the problem as epidemic.

While a therapist may find herself forced to confront a patient who self-injures, she probably has had no formal training or preparation for it. Self-injury is not an easily characterized diagnostic syndrome, and yet it is distinct enough from other impulse-control issues to warrant unique intervention techniques. The stakes may seem higher because the risk of severe harm to the patient is right up front. A therapist will certainly draw on her experience in treating other compulsions, but additional questions are likely to come up, which we attempt to answer here.

That said, not all therapists are ideally suited for working with this population. Some may find the behavior too upsetting or frightening to deal with, and a therapist who is repulsed by a patient's behavior can only do more harm by continuing the sessions. We constantly hear from our patients that prior doctors made remarks—such as "How could you do that?"—which naturally exacerbated their existing feelings of isolation and misunderstanding.

We acknowledge that treating self-injurers takes a certain type of fortitude and tolerance. It also takes great technical finesse since self-injurers tend to be good at making other people feel responsible for their behavior. They may draw the well-meaning therapist into a dance of distraction in which self-injury keeps the atmosphere charged with tension and worry, and the underlying emotions are continually kept at bay. The therapist finds that his or her capacity for empathy is challenged relentlessly. It's a delicate balancing act to keep professional boundaries, avoid the rescue trap, and simultaneously offer comfort and solace.

The following are answers to some of the most common questions that therapists ask us.

Q. How do I decide whether to take on a self-injurious person for outpatient therapy? What kind of commitment will be involved?

A. We believe that working with a self-injurer requires a long-term commitment. Short-term intervention has not proven to have lasting success with people whose underlying issues are this severe.

If you are considering entering an outpatient relationship with someone who self-injures, you should take into account that it is likely to involve several years of sustained work. Since fears of abandonment run high in this population, the patient must believe she can rely on you, that you will be there for her.

You must also consider whether or not you can be available to the patient in times of crisis. Some patients may not need to rely on you extensively in the off-hours, but many patients, particularly at the beginning of therapy, feel the need to have the therapist available by telephone or on call at all times for crisis intervention. Sometimes patients use this as a test of the therapist's commitment. In these cases the need for constant access diminishes as the alliance is forged.

Sometimes, simply knowing that the therapist can be reached between sessions is enough to alleviate the patient's anxiety, and she does not need to contact the therapist frequently. Other times—particularly with patients who have been recently hospitalized or in a partial hospitalization program—the need for contact is greater. The patient has grown accustomed to structured support and questions her ability to control herself without it. As time goes on, the patient's need for constant support can be discussed and placed in the context of her psychological issues.

A therapist preparing to work with a self-injurer should plan for periods of crisis intervention. If she cannot be available personally on short notice between sessions, she needs to make crisis intervention available through partner clinicians or health agencies. In a group practice this can be easy to work out. Sole practitioners can sometimes make similar arrangements with crisis hotline workers or other practitioners.

A therapist considering taking on a self-injurer as a patient may also need to examine her willingness to use adjunct supports, like medication, group therapy, or Twelve Step programs. Often, especially at the beginning stages of outpatient work, patients need these extra supports because they struggle with intense urges to self-harm, or because they are too fearful of depending on the new therapist for help. In either case, practitioners who are skeptical or opposed to these supports, or who are uncomfortable with the extension of therapeutic boundaries to other disciplines or organizations, might find working with self-injurers difficult.

Another topic to address at the beginning of a relationship is the therapist's compensation. If the patient is using health insurance to pay for therapy, this may complicate treatment planning, because most managed care plans do not cover long-term psychotherapy.

It's very important to discuss these issues up front, with the message to the patient that she needs to plan with you how therapy will be funded when the policy benefits are terminated. The patient may be able to find alternative resources, or the therapist may assist by negotiating her fee. Discussing this issue may serve as a valuable staging ground for talks about personal responsibility.

Q. Is it a good idea to set up a "treatment participation agreement" with a patient right away?

A. Yes. We recommend that the therapist start out by setting up all the tools in the S.A.F.E. Toolbox with the patient. This includes the treatment participation agreement (which at S.A.F.E. we call the No-Harm Contract), the list of alternatives, the writing assignments, and the Impulse Control Log, all of which are described in Part Two.

The treatment participation agreement organizes the goals and terms of the treatment relationship and provides the structure of the recovery plan. In the treatment participation agreement, which both the therapist and patient should sign, the client can agree when she will abstain from self-injurious behavior, and it should specify the procedure the client should follow if she feels the urge to self-injure.

The plan is devised by assessing your client's strengths and abilities, and what she is willing and able to do in a crisis. For example, it could stipulate that she should first try one—or several—of her alternatives, and if that doesn't work, then she should contact the therapist or an emergency crisis resource.

One thing we have found helpful for therapists is to spell out the boundaries and limits on their personal availablility in the treatment participation agreement signed with the patient at the beginning of her treatment. The contract should also require that the patient attend sessions regularly, with minimal cancellations; certainly, it would be unreasonable for a patient to cancel sessions frequently, then rely on the therapist to make time for crisis calls.

The contract should also state the mutual understanding that the patient is an active agent in her treatment, not a passive "victim." It should include reasonable goals. A sample goal might be that the patient aims to feel a greater sense of self-control and empowerment, as evidenced by consistent use of the Impulse Control Log and a decrease in self-injurious behavior. Setting forth these expectations early in the work will help the therapist avoid burnout and check the patient's tendency to regress excessively or damage the treatment relationship.

The treatment participation agreement can and should be reevaluated on a regular basis so that it is current with the patient's change in status. Not only will this maximize the helpfulness of the document, but it can also be an excellent way to address any concerns about your liability that may arise during therapy.

Therapists report variable results with the use of contracts. Some patients say the contract acts as a motivator and a mechanism for delay, allowing them to think through the conditions surrounding their urges and the consequences of their actions. The contract can have an organizing effect, in which the patient processes her panic and confusion and forms an orderly plan for coping with a crisis. Other patients, for whom a contract has not proven useful, view it as part of a power struggle between them and the therapist. They may interpret the terms of the contract as aggressive or controlling, or as proof that the therapist's affection and attention is conditional. Preliminary therapeutic work about these perceptions may be needed before the patient comes to view the contract as a recovery aid.

To be effective, the contract must be a collaboration between therapist and patient, one that specifies the exact consequences of failing to abide by the terms. The contract is useful only if the consequences are followed reliably and consistently. Consequences may include loss of a session, an extra writing assignment, a probation period in which the continuation of treatment is called into question, or the ultimate consequence, the actual termination of the therapeutic relationship. It goes without saying that termination should be a last resort.

Q. What is the optimal theoretical orientation for the therapist who wants to work with self-injurers?
A. No single orientation is recommended. We have found that therapeutic intervention from a variety of theoretical vantage points has proven useful. Patients report that they have made progress with therapists who are cognitive-behavioral in orientation, psychoanalytically

oriented, and humanistic. From anecdotal evidence, the specific orientation appears to matter less than the fit between the therapist and patient. This fit is something personal and subjective that both parties can probably sense.

The therapist's flexibility of technique and personality style can have some bearing on the patient's commitment and progress. For example, a psychoanalytic therapist should be willing to teach and rehearse new coping strategies and otherwise attune herself to the patient's needs at various stages of the work. She need not abandon her overall investigative and interpretive approach, but she might add on some slightly different techniques that are geared to the practicalities of daily life.

The main ingredients for success with self-injurers are stability, constancy, reliability, and the formation of a positive therapeutic bond.

Q. Does the gender of the therapist matter?

A. Some patients who have been traumatized or abused by someone of one gender or another may prefer not to select a therapist of that gender. This should be up to the client, and the therapist should not challenge the choice.

We believe patients can work well with an empathic, caring, and committed therapist of either gender. At some point in the treatment it may be helpful for the client to have adjunct sessions with a therapist of the feared sex, especially if the patient has rigid views about the impossibility of trusting such a person. This can be a good vehicle for challenging poisonous generalizations, like "all men are dangerous" or "women can't be trusted."

Q. How often should sessions take place with a self-injurer?

A. Patients vary considerably in how often they need to have contact. Some feel safe and supported with only one session a week, but many need two or three. Some patients find that frequent contact actually increases their anxiety or tendency to regress, and more sporadic sessions may improve her capacity to make progress.

The decision should not be made arbitrarily at the beginning of treatment. It can be negotiated over a trial period and may be renegotiated from time to time. If a patient can maintain her equilibrium between sessions and can leave the sessions without feeling disorganized, frightened, or symptomatic, then the right frequency has been found.

If therapist and patient cannot find a good stride, or the patient cannot control herself between sessions, the therapist may have to proceed to the next level of care—partial hospitalization, for example—until the patient feels comfortable in the outpatient contract.

Therapists should not use the absence of self-injurious behavior as the sole criterion for reducing the frequency of sessions. Self-control may signify the patient's readiness to work more intensively on underlying issues. Patients may also need the ongoing, unchanging nature of the psychotherapy schedule to maintain these gains. Changes in the frequency of sessions should be motivated and controlled primarily by the patient in accordance with her view of her status.

Q. When is the patient cured?

A. There is no consistent formula for how long it takes for a person who self-injures to cease needing therapy. Therapists themselves differ in their views about what constitutes a cure. For some the chief goal is abstinence from self-injury, and everything else is icing on the cake. For others (like us) treating the patient involves not only curing her symptoms, but helping her expand her self-awareness, improve her social skills and job performance, and heighten her quality of life.

Self-injurers may be in psychotherapy long after they have stopped the behavior. The decision rests on many factors, including the severity of the problem and the patient's underlying psychopathology. Either way, the therapist must be comfortable with the potential for a long relationship.

Q. What should I tell my patient about my view of self-injury?

A. You must convey your understanding that self-injury has been a vital coping strategy for her, one that may have helped her survive under unmanageable circumstances. You know it has been useful to her and do not consider it a crazy behavior.

However, you should also point out self-injury is ultimately a futile behavior. It has not been helpful in resolving her problems or managing her feelings in anything but a temporary way.

You should share your belief that self-injury can be treated and stopped, and that the patient can live happily and successfully without it.

Q. What other limits should I set at the beginning of therapy?

A. The patient should be told that she will not be permitted to come to sessions intoxicated or under the influence of nonprescription drugs. But the most important limit to set is that the patient should not be permitted to engage in any self-injurious or abusive behavior during the sessions themselves.

Tell the patient that if she is struggling with an urge to harm herself, she should contact you or someone else in her support system *before* she acts on the urge, not after.

If a patient contacts you directly after she has injured herself, limit this contact to an emergency assessment of the patient's need for medical attention or hospitalization. Exploring the underlying issues or reasons for acting out must be delayed until the next session, lest the patient link her self-destructive act to the feeling of being comforted.

Similarly, if a patient injures herself directly before a session and shows up bearing her wounds, the therapist should stop any discussion of therapeutic issues and assess the patient's physical condition. Even if she does not need to be immediately hospitalized, the therapist should help her seek medical attention immediately, and the patient forfeits the therapy session (if stated in the treatment agreement).

These interventions prevent the patient from feeling excessive gratification for harmful behavior. The goal is to discourage her from engaging the therapist solely around self-destructiveness, which interferes with work on underlying issues.

Q. What methods can I use to help a patient stop self-injuring?

A. The first step is to collaborate with the patient on making a list of alternative coping strategies—there can be five or more. These should be activities the patient can use to soothe herself or manage anxiety and tension. If she cannot identify alternatives or has a limited repertoire, you can help fill in the blanks.

Some patients benefit from writing in a journal to focus energy and contain diffuse emotions. Some enjoy painting or listening to music. Patients can be taught to use deep-breathing exercises and progressive relaxation. By exploring the patient's reservoir of talents and interests during sessions, you can identify other positive distractions. For example, if a patient is at work when she begins to panic, she may not be able to get out her journal and start writing. But she may be able instead to duck into the rest room for a quick deep-breathing exercise.

The strategies you pick must be ones that the patient is capable of using in moderation. For instance, if someone has a history of exercising to excess and causing bodily harm that way, then exercise would not be an appropriate alternative for her.

Second, you can help the patient learn to identify the warning signs of escalation: a racing heartbeat, rapid respiration, muscular tension in the limbs and torso, and other signs of distress. Or you can help her learn to recognize when she is shutting down, or becoming emotionally numb, which is another sign of distress—one less obvious to outsiders.

Another helpful tool is for the patient to make a list of typical stressors and emotional triggers, which she can draw on if she is finding it difficult to identify the cause of an urge to self-injure.

The patient should also make use of her Impulse Control Log, which you should explain to her and should ask her to bring to every session. The logs can be discussed frequently or at appropriate intervals.

Q. Why do some patients' symptoms worsen during therapy?

A. There are several reasons. One is the perceived—or actual—loss of stability in the patient's environment, and another is a disruption in the therapeutic relationship.

Therapist absences, intense transference reactions, or other impasses can trigger patients' urges to self-injure. Overstimulation during therapy sessions can produce the same result. Common clinical sense tells us that when the patient's defenses are overwhelmed, impulses to act out can erupt in the erroneous belief that she needs to get her feelings out.

We often find that our patients at S.A.F.E. have been subjected to probing, intense investigation of painful subjects and memories, without adequate preparation in the early stages of treatment. Because self-injurers are likely to appear highly functional in many areas of their lives—and because they are likely to hide their vulnerabilities from a therapist—they are often inadvertently ushered into deep self-exploration too quickly, exacerbating their symptoms. If this happens, the therapist should slow down to manage the affect that has arisen and not open up new areas of painful reflection.

Q. Which strategies have not been helpful to the self-injurer in treatment?

A. One we particularly discourage is the display of scars or wounds, or lurid descriptions of self-injuring episodes. When patients focus on the graphic details of their behavior, they glorify it and divert attention from the underlying issues. Talking about self-destructive actions may become a substitute for the actions themselves.

Another strategy we frown on is prescribing substitute behaviors—like snapping a rubber band attached to the wrist, submerging a limb in ice water, or writing on the skin with Magic Markers instead of razor blades. Some hospitals even have patients break eggs on their skin so it feels like blood oozing down. These strategies keep the patient focused on releasing tension through actions. This way the patient avoids reflecting on—and managing—her underlying feelings. They also send the message to the patient that every time she feels something, she must act—if not destructively, then in a way that mimics the destructive behavior.

A third strategy we find counterproductive is the use of cathartic methods, like punching a pillow or throwing a soft object. These methods tend to reinforce the erroneous belief that feelings of anger must inevitably bring about an expression of violence, that the patient is a pressure cooker who must blow off steam to function properly. This is not how human beings work.

Our approach stresses containment and the verbal expression of emotion. This is the way of the fully functioning, healthy adult. Maturity and psychological health involve learning to modulate and integrate feelings into everyday life rather than ridding oneself of feeling in an explosive fashion.

Self-injurers often report feeling hyper-aroused, agitated on a physical level as well as an emotional one. For such people physical catharsis can be disastrous. Engaging in deliberate physical activity to cope makes them feel even more revved up and less in control of their feelings and behavior.

Hypnotherapy should also be avoided at all costs with self-injurers, whose inability to regulate their internal states applies to the cognitive as well as the physical sphere. Patients who have undergone hypnosis by overeager therapists find themselves unable to resume their emotional balance after they are brought out of the hypnotic state. They experience confusion, psychological disintegration, and a dramatic increase in self-injurious behavior. The hypnotherapist may mistakenly see this as an emotional response to the material uncovered by the hypnosis rather than a side effect of the procedure itself.

The last category of intervention that has not been useful for this population might be referred to as hyper-nurturing, or "rescue behaviors." These include infantilizing the patient by taking away dangerous objects or asking the patient to purge her home of ordinary objects like kitchen knives. A related intervention is the holding, by the therapist or someone else, of such objects for safekeeping, as a second-grade teacher might with a troublesome student's water gun. We have already mentioned that virtually any object in the self-injurer's environment can be converted into an implement for self-injury, which makes this sanitizing strategy a futile one at best.

Other "heroic" types of rescue behavior include prescribing that a support worker sit with the self-injurer for unrealistic lengths of time or spending inordinate hours on the phone with the patient after she injures. These techniques amount to baby-sitting and imply that it takes an outside person to keep the patient safe. Healthy adults do not want to mother other adults or be mothered by them.

Q. Is it appropriate to ask if the patient has new injuries or scars?

A. We hold that it is better to place the responsibility of disclosure in the patient's hands. When this responsibility is in the hands of the therapist, she becomes an authority figure rather than an ally, and this is counterproductive.

Q. Should a therapist look at the patient's scars or wounds if she requests it?

A. That decision is up to the therapist. However, we believe the best therapeutic stance is to explore with the patient why she wants to show the scars to you. Her motives may stem from exhibitionism, or she may have an underlying concern that you will be so disgusted that you will abandon treatment. The patient may also believe such demonstrations are the only way to communicate her inner pain. Pinpointing the need for such graphic displays can often lead you to issues central to the patient's healing process.

Q. How should I respond if a patient tells me she has been injuring since I last saw her?

A. Without raising your voice in alarm or anger, you should ask calmly if she needs medical attention for the injury. You should talk to her about how dangerous she now is to herself, and if she requires hospitalization. If her danger level is low or moderate, she may be able to make an oral "safety contract" with you. If her danger level is high, she may not be able to agree to this, and you should send her to the hospital. Also, you should make sure that the episode of self-injury was not made with suicidal intent, and if it was, you should make arrangements for her to be seen in an emergency medical facility.

At that point, if the contract states that a session will be terminated as a consequence of injuring, you should enforce it. If not, the therapist and patient should proceed to explore what feelings and fantasies underlay the act of self-injuring. It is very important to talk about why the patient jeopardized her safety. Working through such an episode may take considerable time and should help the patient become more aware that the rifts in trust created by self-destructive behavior do not mend easily. The therapist, in the course of this work, could wonder aloud with the patient, "Is there something that we are having difficulty facing together?" This reinforces that two people are involved in the relationship, and both have suffered consequences from the self-injury.

Q. If a patient calls me between sessions and says she has an urge to self-injure, what should I do?

A. First, tell the patient how proud and pleased you are that she made the active choice to pick up the telephone instead of to injure herself.

Second, ask the patient to talk about her internal state. When did she recognize the urge? What are her thoughts and feelings? Is she alone or with other people? If a patient cannot identify her feelings or triggers, ask her questions that are guided by your knowledge of her typical stressors. "Are you feeling especially lonely tonight?" "Have you gotten any disturbing phone calls from anyone?" After identifying some likely causes, you might suggest the patient use one of her five alternatives. You might also suggest an extra therapy session that week.

Generally, we have found that patients are responsive to verbal intervention when the urge to self-injure strikes. The fact that she has that urge does not automatically mean she needs to be hospitalized. You must distinguish—along with the patient—between the *urge* to self-injure and the *act* of self-injury. You need to convey to the patient that there is a difference between thought and action, and that just because they have the urge doesn't mean they necessarily have to act on it.

In the crisis telephone call, your active interest in the patient and her state of mind, plus your calm, soothing voice, tend to diminish the urge to self-injure. Before ending the call, ask the patient if she feels safe enough to get through the evening or span of time until the next session, and make a contingency plan if she does not.

Q. What if the patient acts out during the therapy session?

A. You need to make clear at the outset what your expectations are for the office environment: that it is not acceptable for the patient to throw objects, break things, or strike out physically at herself or you. These limits should be included in the treatment contract and enforced without exception.

You should, however, encourage the appropriate verbal ventilation of these intense feelings. Each therapist should develop a consistent set of relaxing, calming responses that the patient recognizes as the routine and that serve as cues for lowering her intensity of response. For example, you could make a characteristic set of comments about the usefulness of the feeling the patient is having. You could convey that the intensity of the feeling will not last forever, or you could encourage the patient to breathe regularly, to pay attention to what is happening to her body, and to concentrate on your presence and available support.

On top of these techniques, you should convey empathically that you understand how difficult the direct confrontation of emotion is for the patient. You should reward the patient for attempting to face her feelings directly rather than avoiding them through self-destructive actions.

You must also be mindful of the time parameters of the session. If there are fifteen minutes left and the patient is highly agitated and emotional, it's a good idea to start calming her down. Sometimes the patient's escalation can have a particular meaning if it happens repeatedly toward the end of the session—she may wish to prolong the encounter and may fear the session's end. You should observe if such a pattern develops and comment on it to the patient.

Q. How do I know when to make the decision to hospitalize the self-injurer?

A. This is the single most difficult question that we are posed, primarily because therapists vary widely in their capacity to accept or tolerate self-injurious actions in an outpatient relationship. Some feel that one incident of self-injury is too many; others may wait and work for a longer period of time before hospitalizing.

In general, if the injuring behavior escalates to the point of preventing any progress in therapy, and if the therapist determines that the atmosphere of safety and serenity cannot be maintained in the therapy relationship, hospitalization is indicated. It is also called for when the behavior seems to jeopardize the health and safety of the patient, or when the patient can no longer agree to attempt alternatives to self-harm.

Obviously, these criteria give some latitude for interpretation, so we advise strongly that you confer with colleagues to reach a position in each individual case.

Q. Should a patient's family be involved in outpatient treatment?

A. Sometimes. In either case, the decision is one that the therapist and patient should consider carefully. It should never be a decision that is foisted on the patient.

For adult patients, involving the family can be complicated. It can be counterproductive in some cases, for instance, if the patient is struggling to define her roles and boundaries with other people, or if she needs to separate herself from intrusive, controlling, or abusive family members.

For some patients the desire to exclude a family member from the therapy—to keep a spouse away, for example—may be part of a therapeutic issue that is at the root of the injuring problem. She may feel unable to communicate distressing feelings in an intimate relationship. In this case, moving toward the inclusion of this family member may be part of the healing process.

For adolescents, it is probably wise to discuss family participation early on—particularly if the patient lives with her family, or if they are her main source of support. The family system of the adolescent may be a catalyst, something that reinforces and maintains the self-injurious behavior, and this is best investigated through family-oriented treatment.

Q. What is the role of group therapy in treating the self-injurer?

A. Group therapy can be a vital tool in the recovery process. When self-injurers are hospitalized, group therapy is often the first place they find other people who share their urges to self-injure. Communicating with peers offers support and decreases isolation. Group discussions can support healthy behaviors and challenge unhealthy ones.

Self-injurers can benefit from both structured and unstructured groups. In a structured group, the patient is encouraged to proceed through a series of assignments and exercises that challenge their belief systems and encourage them to practice new coping strategies. The patients use the group process to share what happens as they attempt new choices and learn new options from one another. In unstructured groups, the session may help patients learn about their relationship patterns and how they may use maladaptive defenses or avoid facing issues directly with the people in their lives, which opens the door for destructive coping.

Whatever the nature of the group, the general philosophy should be that it is an arena for growth and change. Group members may at first see the group as a place to share war stories, to compare wounds and count stitches. This behavior should be banned at the outset, and members should be helped to see that this is one of many ways they have learned to avoid facing their feelings.

Q. Is it okay for self-injurers to be in group therapy with people who don't injure?

A. It certainly happens often enough. Self-injurers are frequently lumped into groups with people who are depressed or with survivors of sexual abuse. Seldom does any one therapist or hospital find enough patients at one time to form a dedicated self-injury group.

While we believe these arrangements are better for the self-injurious patient than no therapy at all, they are not the most effective form of treatment. One of the reasons S.A.F.E. is so successful is that group members are able to mirror one another during therapy sessions, picking up coping skills and adaptive techniques from one another. Also, because everyone is there for the same problem, individual patients are less likely to feel alienated or estranged from the group.

Q. When should I seek consultation with other professionals?

A. Seek consultation with colleagues at *any point* in the patient's treatment. We believe it is wise to respond to your own inner discomfort or tension, no matter how minor, because it will help you avoid, or minimize, the intensity of a treatment crisis or impasse. Just as self-injurers can draw comfort from the company of people with the same predicament, so can therapists of self-injurers benefit from solidarity.

For therapists with little or no experience with this population, treating self-injurers probably looks like a formidable task. These patients constantly challenge the atmosphere of safety and serenity that we all consider crucial to our work. They deliberately provoke us, rousing feelings of frustration, despair, alarm, fear, and anger.

On the other hand, it's hard to describe the deep satisfaction that comes from watching such a person recover and knowing you played a central role. When a self-injurer begins to shed her behavior and live a safer and more gratifying life, her world opens up, and you see her revelations through her eyes. Few professional rewards can compare.

Chapter Fourteen

CLASSIFYING SELF-INJURY
AND PAYING FOR TREATMENT

D espite evidence that self-injury is reaching epidemic proportions, it is still considered a "rare" and "unusual" syndrome in
the health care community, much the way anorexia and bulimia
were twenty years ago.

One of our goals is to help bring self-injury out of the closet. That
means chipping away at the shame that surrounds the problem and
encouraging sufferers to seek help. It also involves educating the mental health community with the hope that health care providers and
insurers can find ways to provide the best treatment and coverage. Self-
injury is not a weird aberration among contemporary young people, but
a growing phenomenon that began more than sixty years ago.

A BIT OF HISTORY

The early pioneer in self-injury research was Karl Menninger, a
Harvard-trained psychiatrist who founded the Menninger Institute of
Topeka, Kansas, and who also served as president of the American
Psychoanalytic Association. In a 1935 paper and later in a 1938 book,
Man Against Himself, Menninger attempted to describe self-injury and

categorize sufferers. He coined the term *focal suicide*, suggesting that the act of injuring was a kind of compromise for people who had a desire to kill themselves.

Unfortunately, this led to a great deal of confusion and misunderstanding. As we have noted, most self-injurers are not actively suicidal when they are harming themselves; their behavior is a self-soothing mechanism that is not meant to be lethal. However, writers and psychologists who built on Menninger's work continued intermittently to conflate self-injury with suicidal tendencies. Most of the recent writing in the field makes the distinction clear.

Menninger should be credited, however, with launching the study of self-injurious behavior as a unique clinical problem. He had many interesting and astute observations about it. In describing the "localized self-destruction" he had observed in patients, he included "self-mutilation, malingering, compulsive polysurgery, [and] certain unconsciously purposive accidents resulting in local injury." He was already seeing a range of behaviors similar to those we see today.

Menninger was also aware of the continuum of behavior—from normal to self-injurious—with which we have concerned ourselves in this book. He understood that seemingly innocent behaviors could develop into troublesome ones. He wrote: "Biting the fingernails, for example, is a degree short of biting the fingers, and some individuals have a compulsion to bite themselves more or less severely in various other parts of the body. . . . Others stratch and dig at their flesh incessantly, pluck out their hair, or rub their skin to the point of inflammation." How different is this from our S.A.F.E. patients who began innocently scratching themselves, then progressed to a coarse and dangerous pattern of razor cutting?

When Menninger was not inferring an unconscious wish to commit suicide, he regarded self-injury as a strategy, like a compulsion, that kept the patient's anxiety at a manageable level and prevented painful memories from surfacing. He saw the behavior as symptomatic of a number of other possible underlying issues and took a rather broad view of its origins.

THE CLASSIFICATION ISSUE

Menninger tended to view self-injury as an indicator of other, more clearly identified disorders, and subsequent writers made the same point. Some scholars called the behavior one of many symptoms associated with borderline personality disorder, and others defined it as an addiction, which implied that it was disease-like in nature.

A breakthrough came in the 1970s, when certain theorists in Great Britain—later supported by American scholars like Armando Favazza—advocated strongly that self-injury deserved an identity all its own. They suggested that self-injury was a distinctive syndrome that merited its own diagnostic category, one which Favazza labeled *Deliberate Self-Harm Syndrome*. We understood Favazza's concern and believe that the proper description and categorization of self-injury is important, because it has an impact on the sufferer's quest for treatment.

While it was a step in the right direction when self-injury became conceptually separated from suicide, the drawback was that some insurers and clinicians began taking self-injury too lightly. Once self-injurers were no longer considered suicidal, their symptoms were viewed as less dangerous, "nonlethal," and less indicative of a psychiatric emergency. We believe these views—which still prevail among many clinicians and insurers—are absolutely false. We have detailed in many ways throughout this book the danger and intensity of self-injury, and the omnipresent threat that it will take a lethal turn. We have also described how self-injurers lose their abilities to function normally, grow less productive, and watch their relationships with other people disintegrate. The seriousness of self-injury as a psychological pathology cannot be in dispute. Sufferers and enlightened health care providers need to assert themselves against a powerful, profit-driven health care system that often seeks to contain costs at the expense of the patient who needs help.

The legacy of self-injury as part of a "borderline psychopathology" includes similar perils. The borderline personality disorder diagnosis has proven to be an albatross around the necks of its sufferers, who have gained a reputation as society's most profuse consumers of costly psychiatric and medical health care services. The long-standing nature of their difficulties has led them to myriad doctors, hospitals, and treatment programs. Because of this, many health care providers—and managed care entities—are reluctant to offer services, arguing that these patients are, in their words, "chronic and untreatable." For a time borderlines were considered "the patients who don't get better" in traditional therapy. They were considered suitable only for medication and a vague amount of psychiatric support. Self-injurers and their care providers still confront this prejudice today, particularly in their interactions with agencies and funding sources.

We consider this reputation undeserved and unfair. We have found that self-injurers who have borderline personalities most definitely benefit from treatment, just like anyone else. Their treatment must be reliable, stable, consistent, intensive, and respectful of them; it must imbue a sense of personal responsibility and appropriate limits. A large majority of patients who come to S.A.F.E. Alternatives may be described as suffering from borderline issues, and a recent survey of our program's graduates found that 94 percent had adopted more successful coping strategies, and 92 percent were very satisfied with the treatment regimen. Many reported that we had saved their lives from the brink. Like anyone else, self-injurers with borderline personality disorder do not benefit from inconsistency, infantilizing treatments, neglect, or revolving-door hospitalizations. It is as simple as that.

As we have stated before, there are conceptual difficulties with describing self-injury as a disease or addiction. While there is some social utility to these monickers—since people tend to adopt a more benevolent attitude toward sufferers who are sick or can't help themselves—the problem arises when the self-injurer begins to view herself this way. A self-injurer can become quite entrenched in being a victim, and can be loath to surrender this identity. Another problem lies in the backlash that seems to have taken place against the addicted population, one that the addictions movement did not intend. The drain on social and financial resources created by various types of addicts has fostered a type of discriminating mistrust, and many health care insurers in the 1970s and 1980s dropped *chemical dependency* treatment from their policy benefit provisions, unless the dependency was accompanied by a secondary, "legitimate" psychiatric diagnosis.

At the same time, we do not believe that self-injury should be identified as a distinct diagnostic category. Lumping self-injurers into one category would lend credence to the view that the behavior is a homogeneous, monolithic problem or disorder that can be understood in isolation. In turn, this would make it more difficult for self-injurers to get the holistic, individualized treatment they need. The risk is that people would try to develop one-size-fits-all medical recommendations for the population, ones that would overlook the context in which the behavior developed.

Generally, we continue to believe that the best way for the care provider to view self-injury is as a dangerous, ultimately futile, *action symptom* that disrupts lives and diverts energy that should be devoted to relationships, career, and creativity.

Financial Issues in Seeking Treatment

Paying for treatment is a complex topic. Many of the self-injurers we have worked with find themselves so disabled by their problem that they lose their jobs or are unable to work, and thus lose their health care benefits. Others are denied mental health care insurance because of policy clauses that cover preexisting conditions. Many insurers will not pay claims for a previously diagnosed or treated condition for a certain amount of time, often six months or a year into the policy holder's contract.

Some patients find that they quickly exhaust their mental health care benefits, which are typically set separately—at a lower amount—than the benefit amounts available to them for medical or surgical care. It is not unusual for someone to have a benefits cap, or maximum payment, of $10,000 per calendar year for mental health treatment, but a larger cap, or none at all, for other medical treatment. The good news is that parity laws, which require insurers to bring these two sets of benefits into parity with each other, have been passed in several states and are under consideration in numerous others.

For people who are fortunate enough to carry commercial health care insurance of some kind, there are other limitations, most of them brought about by the advent of managed care. Traditionally, health care insurance adhered to a simple fee-for-service model: the provider would submit his or her itemized charges, and the insurer would remit a reasonable fee for services provided. But the skyrocketing cost of health care in the United States led certain political and economic forces to generate the concept of managed care, with the originally laudable goal of containing the excesses and abuses of the fee-for-service system.

The American Medical Association's definition of managed care is "the control of access to and limitation on physician and patient utilization of services by public or private payors or their agents." In other words, health insurance companies began to turn health care into a commodity regulated by market forces. An insidious and hidden motive emerged as this took place: not only was management of benefits geared to contain costs, but also, unbeknownst to the American public, it was designed to generate and maximize profit for the managed care entity and insurance company. Because of this, managed care has an inherently adversarial relationship to the client seeking treatment; there is a motive that competes with the interest of the client requesting funds.

So how does this system work? Many insurance companies hire outside corporations, the "managed care companies," to serve as intermediaries between the insured person, her doctor, and the insurance carrier. Some managed care companies hire case workers—who are usually not therapists, but may have expertise in related fields—to review patients' records and assess the medical necessity of the treatment proposed. Essentially, the case manager acts as the "gatekeeper" to your health care benefits. They make decisions based on the information that you, your doctors, and your therapists provide—and do not talk to you, meet you, or examine you during the process. The managed care company has the privilege of approving or denying the reimbursement of any service rendered to you, whether it is surgery, cancer chemotherapy, or psychotherapy.

There are three types of review. *Precertification* is approval given for services about to be rendered, prior to their actual rendering. *Concurrent review* is an ongoing assessment during the course of treatment, which may be discontinued if deemed no longer medically necessary. *Retrospective review* is an after-the-fact evaluation. Charges are submitted, and the case manager decides whether or not to reimburse them.

Even if your policy stipulates a $10,000 allocation for mental health benefits, you may receive much less, depending on the results of the case worker's review. The figure is a potential amount, not an actual one. In one real-life example, the mother of a patient of ours named

Lucy told us that her insurance company covered only 50 percent of expenses related to the syndrome, with a lifetime maximum of $15,000. The family is now $10,000 in debt with Lucy's medical expenses.

This system is a particularly treacherous one for self-injurers. The concept of medical necessity is a slippery one when it comes to any mental health problem, but it is especially so for self-injurers, whose behavior can range widely in severity. Unlike the patient whose bursting appendix clearly makes the emergency appendectomy medically necessary, the patient whose premeditated act of self-harm poses a challenge to evaluators. The issues are more ambiguous and less easily categorized.

A federal law known as the Mental Health Code states that hospitalization is indicated (or medically necessary) when someone is either at imminent risk of harm to self or others, or when the person is so ill as to be unable to care for basic needs. For self-injurers, the concept of imminence grows murky. How much self-harm is enough to warrant hospitalization? Managed care entities have used various interpretations.

Some have argued that since the self-injurer's self-harm is generally not lethal in intent, hospitalization is not warranted. These companies use the most stringent reading of the law's harm-to-self criterion, interpreting it to mean that the patient must show imminence of suicidal or homicidal behavior, which is not the law's intent. As a result, many of our self-injurers have found themselves denied admission to hospitals, even though they were covered with wounds and completely unable to function. To guard against this heinous practice, we believe it is essential that all health care providers become familiar with the terms of the Mental Health Code and insist that insurance carriers and managed care companies adhere to them.

Unfortunately, denials of insurance reimbursement and restricted access to care are commonplace for self-injurers in our day and age. The insurance industry has suggested it is not cost-effective to hospitalize self-injurers. These companies argue that hospitalization will inevitably sap their resources enormously and only lead to recidivism for the patient.

We call these arguments fallacious. Our experience has shown us that inappropriately short hospital stays—or the denial of them—leads to more frequent relapses and more contact with the medical system.

Band-Aid treatments cannot patch severe problems. Patients who are denied the care they need will inevitably get worse, experience revolving-door hospitalizations, and cost insurance companies more than if the proper treatment had been provided in the first place.

Some health maintenance organizations have adopted three-to-five-day hospital stays as a recommended option for self-injurers. This so-called "crisis stabilization" model uses the hospital as a last resort. The only goals are to protect the patient from immediate harm and raise her to the questionable level of stability she had prior to admission. Indeed, there is no stability: the self-injurer's life has become a vicious cycle of destructive behavior and despair.

Our program has always been thirty days, and we want to thank those who have recognized the need for intensive therapeutic work. Thorough treatment is more cost-effective and humanitarian than con-tinuous crisis stabilization, which carries high financial costs—emer-gency rooms, burn units, ambulances, surgery—and takes a high toll on the human spirit.

PRIVACY

To secure reimbursement, managed care companies require that a psy-chotherapist divulge extensive details about the client's problems and the progress of therapy. Some therapists are even asked to turn over their notes from sessions to a managed care reviewer. The patient's right to privacy and confidentiality is essentially made null and void.

Many self-injurers are people whose privacy and boundaries have been violated; therefore the actions of the managed care companies can serve as an additional trauma, one that has a lasting and detri-mental impact on the therapy process.

Therapists can help minimize this phenomenon by talking to their patients about it up front. They should explain these painful realities so that the self-injurer does not feel ambushed by intrusions into the therapeutic space. In the best scenario, the discussion could provide a real-life context for working through painful boundary issues. We also advise therapists and counselors to take a minimalist approach when forced to interact with a managed care company: provide only the information necessary to ensure the continuation of treatment, make the barest notations in a client's official records about her symptoms and the need for service. Reserve your observation about the private content of the sessions for a separate record, your personal notes, which are not considered available to legal summons.

These issues may make it sound like getting help for a self-injurer is a potentially hopeless task. However, we at S.A.F.E. don't feel hopeless at all. Sweeping legislative reforms on the horizon are taking aim at the potential abuses of managed care. Preexisting condition clauses are under fire and are slowly being eradicated.

One legislative effort underway would make insurers and managed care entities legally liable for negative results of the decisions they hand down. Until now these corporate entities have shifted the liability burden to the care provider, arguing that the managed care company is not denying *care*, just *reimbursement*. In an ideal world, we would like to see everyone concerned with the problem of self-injury lobby Washington for reforms like these.

There are also many small and more personal ways that patients and their support team may become advocates for their own interests. Therapists and their clients should be informed about all the issues involved in the help-seeking process. They must be ready to describe in detail the profound impact self-injury has had on the sufferer's life and health. They must be prepared to argue that this is not a quality-of-life issue—that the ability to work, care for one's children, and carry on relationships without self-injury are necessities of life, not luxuries. One helpful resource for care providers and their clients is the National Coalition for Mental Health Consumers and Providers, headquartered in New York. Its goal is to advocate mental health reform and the right to decent mental health treatment.

THE UNINSURED

Self-injurers who lack conventional funding options for mental health treatment must begin by educating themselves about local community mental health resources. Often, you can find free or low-cost mental health clinics affiliated with universities, research institutions, or non-profit hospitals.

Although it's likely to be a difficult decision, applying for public assistance—welfare—is a way to gain access to the health care system. On the plus side, many publicly funded hospitals are major teaching institutions, where patients can benefit from state-of-the-art training given to psychiatric residents, student psychologists, and others. Remember, there is no shame in taking any and all steps on your own behalf to get the help you need.

If self-injury has interfered with your ability to work productively, you may also want to consult your doctor or therapist about applying for disability benefits through the Department of Social Security. Other options include inquiring with state or county government offices about special sources of private or community funding. One patient at S.A.F.E. applied for a special needs grant through her home community government and was able to secure enough money to finance her stay with us. There are always solutions to be found, but the person seeking help must take the initiative and do the research. She cannot sit passively and wait to be rescued.

The managed health care system may seem bewildering. But we know hundreds of self-injurers who have cobbled together ways to fund their treatment, despite bureaucracy, paperwork, and headaches. As anyone who has recovered from self-injury will gladly tell you, the results are truly worth it!

Part Two

THE S.A.F.E. ALTERNATIVES™ PROGRAM

Chapter Fifteen

WHY OLD CURES DON'T WORK, AND WHY OURS DOES

U ntil recently self-injurers were considered an oddity by the medical community, an untreatable population whose symptoms baffled even their own therapists. Mankind's instinctive aversion to physical pain is strong; the innate human instinct toward self-preservation made self-injury seem inexplicable and even terrifying. Therefore, those doctors who have even attempted to work with the problem have taken the view that it is an intractable disease like alcoholism.

Most treatments that do exist focus on the act of self-injury itself: how dangerous it is to harm one's body, what a toll it takes on the patient and the people around her, how aberrant or bad it is to take arms against one's skin.

In the standard hospital milieu, self-injurious patients are locked in a psychiatric ward where "sharps" are forbidden. Admission is seldom voluntary, and a doctor sets the patient's release date, which is often contingent on her showing good behavior. If a judge or other authority determines that the patient's behavior is dangerous to herself or others, the patient may be confined to the facility for many months. Some of our patients have been in state hospitals for a year at a stretch.

Nurses and doctors in hospital garb take the patients through their paces. It's unlikely that anyone on the medical staff has any professional expertise in treating self-injurers, so usually they just do the best they can, using group and individual therapy sessions to try to impress on the patient society's majority viewpoint that mutilating one's body is not a smart idea. Some psychiatric milieus become so exasperated that they become punitive with patients' self-destructiveness, despite their best intentions not to be. Not suprisingly, the use of rational, even Socratic, reasoning falls flat with self-injurers: if this clearly distasteful strategy did not make sense for them, why would they bother with it?

Because most doctors cannot fathom self-injury, they hold numerous misconceptions. They tend to view it as a random or chaotic type of behavioral expression, not as one with complex and hidden meanings that can be elicited during psychotherapy. Because of this lack of understanding, doctors routinely order that self-mutilators be placed in four-point restraints, a practice that may prevent their behavior, but that humiliates and infantilizes them, interfering with treatment.

Seldom do self-injurers' symptoms abate in any way in programs like this. Indeed, our patients say they tend to regress and worsen in hospitals, where they get caught up in a vicious cycle. They begin injuring more frequently and intensely, which lengthens their hospital stay— which in turn causes more severe injuring. This phenomenon only fuels doctors' beliefs that self-injury is intractable and uncurable.

To be sure, not all programs are the same. In traditional hospital psychiatry, treatment for the self-injurer varies considerably, depending on the theoretical leanings of the facility. Some clinics focus on the underlying depression and the suicidal thoughts that are presumed to be at the core of self-injury. Some clinics with an emphasis on biological psychiatry attempt to control the behavior through drugs. According to Karen Latza, former assistant director of S.A.F.E.:

> Our patients arrive having tried every medication known to the field. Some come in with prescriptions for twelve or thirteen psychotropic drugs to be taken simultaneously. Our patients have experienced everything from electroshock treatment to aversive conditioning and hypnosis, with varying levels of success.
>
> One constant theme, however, is that their past experiences in hospitals have unwittingly contributed to their behavior escalation and deterioration. They report atmospheres of contagion, in which patients share gory war stories about episodes of injuring, compare

scars as badges of honor, and wind up competing for the staff's attention by staging dramatic acting-out episodes. One patient told us she was forced to sit in a dayroom and exhibit her scars, so other patients could view them and give her feedback.

Though we disagree strongly with such tactics, we do have sympathy for the clinicians who tried them. When it comes to self-injurers, the entire hospital team can wind up feeling helpless and rageful. By wounding themselves, these patients also wound our professional egos and frustrate our attempts to forge engaging relationships with them.

Regardless of theoretical orientation, the common thread to the programs for self-injurers we have heard about—inpatient or outpatient—is the frantic, heroic effort on the part of the professionals to keep the patients safe. In inpatient settings, all potentially dangerous implements are confiscated from the start. Patients are humiliatingly strip-searched for "contraband." The patients are supervised morning, noon, and night. Those who are deemed to pose a particular danger to themselves are sometimes tied to their beds as a "precautionary measure." In outpatient settings, people may be assigned home health aides to watch them around the clock. The message is that the patient cannot be held responsible for herself or her actions, and it is up to others to guard her from her impulses.

These "heroic measures" are far from helpful. Indeed, we argue that they are counterproductive in the extreme. For one thing, they play directly into the "rescue fantasy" that all self-injurers harbor: that someone will constantly be available—and will love them enough—to maintain constant vigilance on their behalf. This may seem true in a hospital setting, but it is unworkable as a strategy for independent living.

Patients and their therapists must acknowledge to themselves that there will never be an omnipresent, all-powerful, all-loving "other" who will keep the patient safe. No therapist, no hospital, no doctor can do this, no matter how hard they try. The heroics—which backfire tragically in hospitals and outpatient programs—may stem from the therapists' empathic collusion with the patient's hopeful fantasy.

Our experience has shown us that an effective inpatient milieu for the self-injurer focuses on the expectation that patients will take responsibility for their actions, to learn to *keep themselves safe*. This contrasts with a more "authoritarian" treatment model, where the expectation is that the *helpers keep the patient safe*. We believe the

authoritarian model results in longer hospital stays and limited progress. Since patients often have the unrealistic and childlike wish to
be protected and "kept safe," they are gratified by an authoritarian
environment and unlikely to surrender their regressed behavior and
substitute a more autonomous way of life. Often, the resistance to
change stems from traumatic early losses and parenting deficits the
patient has experienced, which make her eager to take comfort from
an omnipotent, protective caretaker.

Techniques employed by the authoritarian hospitals—like seclusion
and restraint, giving patients teddy bears and dolls, and encouraging
them to imitate self-injury in nonharmful ways—reinforce the harmful
messages and encourage regression. Not only is an adult humiliated
when treated like a child, but it also does her no good when she must
return to her normal life.

Another common theme among other treatment programs is the
reliance on cathartic techniques—like throwing and punching pillows—
to help patients get it all out. Some programs recommend other substitute forms of action discharge, like snapping a rubber band against
the wrist, coloring on one's arms in red marker, or submerging body
parts in ice water.

We believe these types of activities keep patients who are already
overstimulated in high gear and reinforce their beliefs that feelings
must be responded to through physical action. Our program's philosophy is the opposite, that feelings must be responded to through words.
Our disagreement with the cathartic treatment model is one of the
S.A.F.E. program's most radical points of departure from standard industry practices, and we will discuss it further in this chapter.

THE S.A.F.E. ALTERNATIVES PROGRAM

The philosophical and structural tenets of the S.A.F.E. program are
fundamentally different from the prevailing approaches taken for this
population. Our major emphases are on treating clients with respect
and empathy and placing the responsibility for recovery squarely on
their shoulders. We do not view self-injurers as victims, we do not

think their behavior is an addiction, and we do believe they can get better.

S.A.F.E. accepts both inpatients and partial hospitalization (day hospital) patients, who do not need the safety of the twenty-four-hour setting but who can benefit from the structure of an all-day treatment experience. They are with us for about four to five weeks. Though they are obliged to comply with a daily schedule of meetings, meals, and therapy sessions, there is plenty of time for relaxation, reflection, and privacy. We keep tabs on our patients, but we do not police them; our dining room has regular silverware, and if patients wish to use scissors, knitting needles, headphones, and so forth, they are permitted to do so upon request. If the patient does not feel sufficiently in control of her impulses, then it is her responsibility to discuss the issue with the staff and make a choice not to use these objects. Nobody is baby-sitting the S.A.F.E. patient, since that is not our role; however, all the support they need is readily available for the asking.

Our patients must face up to the fact that they are the only ones who can keep themselves safe. The structure and philosophy of S.A.F.E. Alternatives is predicated on this assumption, that successful treatment of self-injurers involves a necessary shift of reponsibility from the therapist to the patient.

The first tool for engineering this shift is applied before the patient reaches S.A.F.E. In an initial screening interview the patient learns that this is a voluntary program. Admission is planned ahead of time and rarely takes place in the event of a crisis. Patients are admitted when their pattern of self-injuring has escalated so far that they cannot function well in daily life, or when the atmosphere of safety in the outpatient therapy is so damaged that progress is impossible.

In the initial screening the patient must demonstrate a heartfelt and *internal* motivation to stop injuring. We screen out anybody who does not sincerely, viscerally, want to get better and anyone who has arrived on our doorstep in response to an ultimatum from a relative, therapist, colleague, or friend. While the patient may struggle with profound ambivalence toward giving up self-injury, she must come to the program with a strong desire to seek healthier coping strategies. This desire is another way to empower the patient, since she is making an informed decision about whether the program is appropriate. We also interview her outpatient therapist to see if we're all on the same page. While it may sound as though screen out the most difficult or hard-to-treat cases, the opposite turns out to be true. Many of our patients have been hospitalized between fifty and a hundred times, with long and severe histories of self-injury.

A further note on the voluntary nature of the program: patients may end their involvement in S.A.F.E. whenever they want. They need only to ask, and after processing the decision with the treatment team— and with considered reflection—they may elect to leave, perhaps to return another time. In other words, they do not need to act out in order to be released or to have their anxieties responded to. This policy minimizes the power struggle between the patient and the support team and makes treatement a matter of the patient's choice—not the doctor's.

Our program is time-limited, and the length of stay is determined before the patient arrives. Thirty days is ideal, though these days it is more difficult to obtain funding for this length of stay because of insurance companies and managed care companies.

Upon admission, patients are asked to sign a "No-Harm Contract" (see page 297) in which they agree not to injure themselves while they are in the program. The contract is discussed during the patient's initial screening so that nobody is surprised when asked to sign it. Injuring during the program is grounds for probation or discharge, whether the patient does it at home (as an outpatient) or at the treatment facility.

The No-Harm Contract is designed to send a strong message from the beginning that self-control *is* possible, and that she must immediately challenge herself to find an alternative way of mananging her emotions and urges. Because the contract is in place and patients are not self-injuring, contagion and competitive swagger are kept to a minimum at S.A.F.E..

Our patients occasionally violate the contract. Depending on the circumstances, patients may be offered a probation option, which involves answering a written set of questions and exploring their commitment to the program. Subsequent violations can lead to discharge. About 10 percent of patients are asked to leave the program because of contract violations.

The staff is ready to help the patients around the clock. They teach patients about self-injury, train them to manage their moods, and help them rehearse and practice coping mechanisms and relaxation strategies. They offer comfort and guidance and dispense medications. Our adamant position is that the staff will *not* spend program time "keeping the patient safe" through regressive methods involving extreme precautions, like restraints. Patients are not restricted from the use of "sharps," like writing implements, scissors, hair dryers, or even shaving utensils. We do expect, however, that the choice to use these items—and the risks involved—will be discussed with program staff.

The No-Harm Contract tends to shake up the terms under which relationships between the self-injurer and her therapist—and loved ones—have been operating. Patients are accustomed to *more* attention, more hovering, more supervision, and longer hospital stays, which reinforce their childlike status and dependence on others. At S.A.F.E. Alternatives we are trying to create a culture of safety in which the continuation of the relationship with fellow patients and staff members is contingent on the patient's remaining injury-free.

Instead of getting attention for injuring themselves, our patients get attention for *not* injuring themselves. The message is that "self-destruction brings about the end of relationships," which we believe is a mirror of what has been occurring in real life. Injuring has been a way for the patient to reinforce her own isolation and loneliness.

The patient's decision to accept and abide by the contract is often her most difficult one. Since self-injury has been such a vital tool for her psychic survival—it may have been the only way she averted even more deterioration and madness—the request that she suspend this coping mechanism even temporarily needs to be weighed carefully. We remind patients that even though they may begin this time-limited undertaking with us, all their choices are available to them when they leave. We do hope, however, that they will come to see and feel the rewards of life without self-injury.

While in the program patients are discouraged from showing scars, discussing their methods of injuring, or describing the mechanics of self-injuring. We do not let anybody dwell on her methodology or harming routines—even in private conversations that take place outside of formal appointments—nor do we pass judgment on the behavior. In individual therapy we try to discourage people from talking about the origins of their scars, lest the gory description serve as a substitute for the violent act. We believe that talking in this way is a disguised form of action-discharge, which replaces self-injury. Though it is less dangerous, it keeps the patient at the surface world of action, precluding deeper understanding and reflection and more effective coping. This is not to say that we do not explore with the patient, in individual sessions, the potential meanings of their choice of self-injuring meth-ods. We are simply vigilant of the ways that patients may use graphic descriptions of their behavior not to understand themselves, but to shock or distract their helpers.

Another strict ground rule at S.A.F.E.—one that many patients gripe about but most appreciate—is the requirement that everyone refer to the behavior as "self-injury," not "cutting" or "burning" or anything else. Again, we don't want people to substitute the description of the action for the action itself. Also, given that we see self-injurers of all degrees of severity, we do not want people competing for the best self-injury method or learning new methods from one another. When everyone is a self-injurer, everyone has the same label: you're not sitting in a room where she's a cutter, and he's a self-castrator, and she's a wall puncher. As Colleen S., one of our program graduates, explained succinctly to a S.A.F.E. visitor, "We don't refer to specific injuries—we just say self-injury. It puts us all on the same level and takes away some of the uniqueness of it."

We have other guidelines that have evolved through our work with this population. For example, because so many self-injurers feel di-vorced from their own experiences, we encourage patients at S.A.F.E. Alternatives to speak in the first person. Newcomers inevitably fall into the trap of expressing themselves by saying, "You know when you start to feel like . . ." and we correct them so they say, "Whenever *I* feel like . . ." In our lingo, it's important for patients to "own their own experiences."

In addition to the No-Harm Contract, we use several other inno-vative techniques. These include copious writing assignments that help patients identify, express, and tolerate their conflicted feelings on paper instead of at knife point. We require patients to maintain an Impulse Control Log in which they record each urge to self-injure and what triggered it. Patients must consider what the outcome would be if they went ahead and harmed themselves (e.g., scars, shame, guilt) and what the consequence would be of staying injury-free.

Our approach is to look at the underlying dynamics driving the be-havior. We get patients to start thinking about what is going on in their heads that could be compelling them to do this. We try to avoid making simplistic links—"Oh, you were abused as a child, therefore you are abusing yourself as an adult"—but we do delve deeply into people's backgrounds and childhoods to pick up clues about what is going on with them. The point is not to find the victimized, helpless child within, but rather the empowered adult.

Another difference between our program and others is that we don't view the behavior as crazy. We impress on our patients our understanding that self-injury is a very meaningful and vital course of action for them, one that has served them well in many ways. While our goal is to show patients that *other* courses of action can serve the same caretaking purpose, we also know that self-injury is a sign they are managing their problems as best they can.

Our patients are pleasantly surprised by the neutral attitude staff members take when they conduct introductory interviews. Many patients say that at other programs the staff would gasp in horror when they described what they did to themselves. To us, regardless of the intensity of their symptoms, we see their underlying terror. These people would never have developed this behavior if they didn't need to work overtime to avoid feared feelings.

So we actively recognize and acknowledge the extent of their internal terror. But simultaneously we try to speak to the healthy and intact part of the person. Every self-injurer who wants to get better has a part of her that knows she is engaging in a hard-to-win struggle.

Dr. Latza said in a speech to fellow psychologists: "Once the patient feels understood, she can begin to take the necessary steps   and risks—toward change. When patients find the words to express the inexpressible, their agony is lessened. When the self-injurer's world becomes a less chaotic morass, and becomes governed by logical and rational explanations, her suffering is more manageable."

At S.A.F.E. Alternatives we strive to help patients internalize a sense of orderliness. The rules and procedures are an external way of guiding patients to the mental organization they need for recovery. As a patient progresses through the S.A.F.E. program, we go out of our way to explain everything that we are asking her to do, and the rationale behind it. This way she feels there is logic to the program, and that she is a collaborator in its success. Other programs do not take this approach, as our patients have often described.

Patients Speak Out

Colleen S. had been in myriad psychiatric hospitals before she came to S.A.F.E., and none of them did her any good, she says. Indeed, her attitude during her first inpatient stay at S.A.F.E. was so hostile and skeptical that she opted to leave and continue self-injuring. Once Colleen found the internal motivation to cease her habit, she returned to S.A.F.E. and completed the program with flying colors. Colleen now attends relapse group meetings, which she combines with graduate school work and other activities.

"Unlike everywhere else I've been, we could have sharps and shoelaces," Colleen says. "There's a quiet room, but it's not to lock someone in. They have more trust in you—you're supposed to be more responsible for yourself. I felt more respected here because they did trust us. I could borrow the scissors. I think it sent an important message that helped me get better."

Colleen perceived our intention behind the availability of the quiet room to be helpful, a place for chilling out and gaining control rather than a place of punishment for bad behavior.

"All the groups were really good. I hadn't met anyone from my hospitalizations before who self-injured except one girl in a hospital in another suburb. Actually, it was kind of a bad situation because we kind of spurred each other on and stole stuff from the cafeteria to self-injure with."

Many patients say S.A.F.E. is very different from other programs. "I liked the way the staff supported and didn't make everything better," Susan L. says. "They guided me to do my own work. They put me in control instead of taking control away. The things they said made sense. They said things that I didn't necessarily want to hear, but they helped me grow."

Donna W. says S.A.F.E. Alternatives taught her that "there is a distinction between anger and rage. I always equated the two. I have learned that anger is a feeling, and whether I have just cause or not, it doesn't stop me from feeling it. But it does give me a starting point to work from with respect to identifying the source of the anger and thinking it through rather than acting out on it."

All our patients have strong opinions about what aspect of our program helped them the most. Some praise the No-Harm Contract for offering a form of "tough love," while others are devoted to Impulse Control Logs, using them long after graduating from the program. For Jared T., the fifteen writing topics we assign to every patient were the most helpful.

"This is where I found out for myself what my real issues are, and the emotions carefully concealed within them," he told us. "I learned a lot about myself, and I'm proud to say that I figured out more completely who I am, and what my plan of action should be. The writing assignments are the most valuable because *I* do the work and make the decisions and dig for the answers. Nobody has outright told me, 'This is your problem and this is what you should do.' "

THE PRESSURE COOKER THEORY AND THE FALLACY OF CATHARSIS

Many of our patients come from homes in which anger—a feeling—merged with violence—an action. Thus, our patients fear that if they feel angry, they have to discharge that anger in a physical way. They believe that people have to "get their feelings out" or they will burst. This is the idea of catharsis, that you somehow have to release the unwanted tension into the environment. While catharsis may serve a purpose in the context of a satisfying movie or a good cry, it is not a good mechanism for day-to-day emotional release. Have you ever seen anyone literally burst from their feelings?

At S.A.F.E. we directly challenge the belief that every emotion must lead to a physical action of some kind. Self-injurers tend to believe this deeply and often have indoctrinated their therapists with this false assumption. Many of our patients arrive at S.A.F.E. armed with substitute "strategies" which—although safer than the act of self-harm—mimic or caricature self-injury in some way. They have been instructed by well-meaning helpers to color on their arms with a red Magic Marker, or snap a rubber band against their wrist whenever they feel an urge. One well-known therapist suggested to a patient that she break eggs over her thighs to approximate the sensation of warm blood flowing over her skin. Another suggested the self-injurer submerge her arm in ice water to obtain the "focusing" effect she so craved.

Many self-injurers have been indoctrinated with a variety of cathartic techniques that are intended to allow the release of tension through physical activity of some kind—a kind which, presumably, is less harmful and healthier than self-injury. They have been encouraged to run, take karate class, punch or throw pillows or stuffed dolls, or go into a quiet room and "give in to their urge" to scream if they really need to. It all sounds harmless enough, so what's the problem?

The problem is evident from these scenarios: a woman who adopted a strategy of plunging her limb into ice water soon showed up in an emergency room with a treatment-resistant case of frostbite. She explained placidly to the emergency room physician that her therapist had taught her a new way to injure herself. Another patient found herself getting repeatedly hurt, bruised, and sprained in her martial arts classes and soon acknowledged to her therapist that she had been allowing herself to be in the path of her opponents' blows as a means to continue self-injuring.

One woman at S.A.F.E., a kindergarten teacher in Kansas, had been told by her therapist at home to use red markers on her arm to simulate gashes, and the strategy had proven soothing for her. At our program she was surprised and angry to find that this seemingly innocuous activity got her placed on probation. We asked her: What would your five-year-old students think if you suddenly started drawing on your arms in school in the middle of the day? We gradually came to show her that this strategy does nothing to challenge her unhealthy model of emotional self-regulation.

Many self-injurers believe their minds work like a pressure cooker, which can only handle so much heat—the heat of emotions—before the lid blows off. According to this theory, when a human being reaches the boiling point, she must let off steam in some way.

Self-injurers often believe that emotions are like poisons or waste that must be expelled from the body. A corollary to this idea is that letting off steam must involve some kind of physical activity. "Every time I feel, I have to act" is the way some self-injurers put it; every time they feel "too angry," they are convinced they must become aggressive in some way.

The S.A.F.E. program has a big piece of news for people who view life this way: *there is absolutely no evidence in the field of psychology to support the Pressure Cooker Theory.* In fact, there appears to be no finite amount of emotion that the human mind can handle. Using these cathartic techniques reinforces this inaccurate idea about how the mind works—the self-injurer continues to feel that every time she feels something, she must find a physical or behavioral way to expel it. That, in our opinion, is the recipe for making almost any human activity into a potential method for self-harm.

Cathartic methods also have another side effect for many self-injurers. We have heard from our patients frequently that they continually feel overstimulated, revved up, and that this contributes to their escalating panic and agitation. Recommending physical activity to people who feel this way is like throwing gasoline on a fire: it makes them more out of control rather than less.

Another problem with cathartic strategies is that many of them are simply not realistic, mature, or age-appropriate ways to handle tension. A woman executive who has the urge to self-injure during a board meeting is not going to be able to whip out her punching bag for a quick fix. The real issue is that *there is no quick fix.* Self-injurers simply must learn more productive and realistically usable means for regulating their emotional temperature.

In contrast to the catharsis model, the S.A.F.E. program helps patients learn to articulate thoughts and feelings and begin to have tolerance for their mood swings. This lays the groundwork for them to begin a longer course of therapy, in which they can resolve their underlying conflicts. They learn to break down the absolute-thinking pattern, in which everything seems black or white, wrong or right, bad or good, and in which feelings are either all-consuming and destructive or completely absent, numb. They learn the difference between feeling and action, slowly recognizing that it is not the feeling that does the damage, but the choice of a harmful action. The goal is not to expel feelings, but to contain, manage, and integrate them.

At first our patients mourn the loss of their trusted—and loved—coping strategy. Soon they come to celebrate the alternative, to feel empowered with the knowledge that they can keep themselves safe from harm. They learn that this safety brings the reward of greater closeness to other people, and that the self-destructive habits they clung to only bring more shame and alienation. In learning what we call a "new language of feeling," they find they do not need to rely on the coded, indecipherable action language of self-mutilation to get a response.

S . A . F . E . 'S   VIEW   OF   RECOVERY   VERSUS THE   TWELVE   STEP   MODEL

Another important point is that our program is not a Twelve Step program like Alcoholics Anonymous or Narcotics Anonymous. We think the Twelve Step approach is helpful to many people with addictions—many of our patients are simultaneously enrolled in Twelve Step programs—but consider it the wrong treatment messages for self-injury. We believe the Twelve Step model conveys too much of a message of powerlessness to the addict. The philosophy of acceptance encourages people to believe that the behavior they are trying to gain control over is necessarily a permanent part of their identity. We know for a fact that people can give up self-injury, shedding the label as well as the behavior.

Most people know someone who has recovered or is recovering from some kind of physical or emotional condition. To be recovered means the person is free of symptoms, the disease or condition is no longer detectable, and the person is cured. To be recovering is to say the person's condition is in the process of mending, on the way to being cured.

In mental health, the distinction between *recovery* and *cure* is somewhat slippery. In the traditional addictions and Twelve Step model, the person who is in recovery will always be on the mend and will never be cured. The Twelve Step model has a particular slant on the concepts of healing and cure. AA members often say, "Once an alcoholic, always an alcoholic," and reinforce this idea every time a person introduces himself at a meeting: "Hi, my name is so-and-so and I'm an alcoholic." The importance of maintaining this label is so that the alcoholic—whether or not he or she is still drinking—will not forget "where they have been."

Because of these kinds of models, we are often asked if the person who self-injures can ever be cured. It's easy to understand why people would ask this question. Most professionals who have dealt with a self-injurer know how difficult it is to treat them, how stubborn their conditions seem. Many patients we see at S.A.F.E. previously had numerous therapists, years of hospitalizations, and have made limited or no progress.

Unlike the Twelve Step philosophy, S.A.F.E. maintains that it is possible to be cured of self-injury forever. We have found that when a self-injuring person has learned to tolerate her feelings and thoughts and to communicate in an age-appropriate manner, that person doesn't engage in self-destructive behavior. This can be said for alcoholics as well; however, the danger with an alcoholic's feeling better is that it can fool her into thinking that she can drink socially. Since self-injuring has never been socially acceptable, the recovered self-injurer doesn't face the same social or peer pressures.

Also, during a Twelve Step meeting, sharing how bad things were or how bad things can get is typical. These object lessons constantly remind the addicts of where they've been. Since, as the philosophy goes, the addict can't be cured, this constant reminder can be a matter of life or death for many. However, the sharing of war stories goes unchallenged and puts the focus on the behavior or activity rather than the underlying issues that drive the behavior. The behavior *is* the person, her whole identity; on or off the wagon, she is a drunk, an alcoholic, now and forever. Maintaining sobriety by keeping the dreaded disease behavior at bay is a primary focus. Drinking behavior is the enemy that must be battled continuously, abstained from completely, and any relapse from sobriety is failure in recovery, even if a temporary failure. At S.A.F.E. we minimize the sharing of war stories because in addition to reminding the self-injurer where she has been, it runs the risk of *keeping* her there through relentless focus on the behavior and nothing else.

The application of the Twelve Steps for all manner of so-called "dysfunctional/addictive" behaviors has spawned a belief that any potentially destructive behavior is to be seen as having an incurable disease at its roots. Unfortunately, this belief in the disease concept for almost any behavior potentially can set people up for relapse, because they are trapped in the mind-set of being powerless.

For many addictive-like behaviors—including self-injury—the underlying drive is psychologically rooted. There is no clearly established physiological cause, no known disease. The shift in thinking becomes one of being empowered over the behavior versus being powerless.

When someone is empowered, she loses the rationale needed to engage in the destructive behavior. Many people who have relapsed claim that the "disease" had gotten the better of them and was making them engage in the behavior. With self-injurers, we know this not to be true.

However, the addictions movement and S.A.F.E. have one thing in common. Like the Twelve Step program, one of the main components of S.A.F.E. is the group meeting, which gives sufferers the opportunity to share experiences, strength, and hope. In the late 1930s a man named Bill Wilson was:

> . . . overcome by the desire to drink. Several important events oc-curred. He picked up the telephone instead of a drink. Through that phone call he offered to help another. The drunken plea, "Can you help me?" was changed to "Can I help you?" For the first time, a drunk, the traditional taker, found the ability to give. Bill contacted Dr. Bob Smith, a suffering alcoholic, shared the experience of his sobriety after years of drunkenness, and together they founded the AA fellowship.

Bill discovered a vital truth about what is needed to get well. He found that by using verbal communication—as opposed to substances or destructive behavior—it opened a window of opportunity for him to get help. The addict in a Twelve Step program is soothed by talking and being listened to by others who share the same struggle for sobri-ety. For many addicts, this may be the first time that anybody took the time out to listen to what they had to say instead of just judging and criticizing. At S.A.F.E. Alternatives we share this notion that talking, sharing, and communicating are integral to recovery.

GOALS

Our goal for the self-injurer is to get her thinking and behaving in a developmentally age-appropriate way. We do this through therapy, ed-ucation, setting limits and boundaries, enforcing consequences, offer-ing encouragement and praise, and holding patients responsible for their actions. For patients who have grown up in damaged or dysfunc-tional households, our program can serve as a crash course in realism, a rare exposure to a life in which people are not constantly subjected to abuse and denigration, and where their thoughts and opinions matter.

Self-injurers see themselves as victims of external circumstances, powerless children at the hands of forces they cannot control. Self-injury becomes the sole way they interact with the world, and their only way to gain any sense of power, even if it is transient and fleeting. The most important goal of S.A.F.E. Alternatives is to show the person that this form of power is illusory, then to shift their thinking into finding true power over their circumstances.

The program tries to show each patient that she has the means at her disposal to stop injuring and control how she reacts to events in her life, but that these means must be *cultivated*. Once the self-injurer embraces the idea that she has responsibilities to herself and others, the stage is set for discovering new ways to cope with pain and distress. At first this responsibility seems like a burden to the patient, who wants to keep believing that self-injury is necessary to her. She *wants* to believe it is the only way for her to get anyone to listen or to respond to her. We try hard to show her the distortions involved in this thinking, pointing out that even small children are not allowed to be rampantly violent to obtain caring responses from others. Taking control of her behavior is an adult prerogative which actually does bring about responsiveness in others and also helps the person stop thinking like a victim.

The next goal, once this shift in attitude begins, is for the self-injurer to learn that *not every feeling has to be responded to with a physical action*. Once someone has developed an ingrained pattern of self-injury, she becomes accustomed to plunging into the behavior at the least sign of distress. She has lost the capacity to slow down, delay acting upon the urge, to think, reflect, and problem-solve. The person sees herself on automatic pilot, and there is little or no margin of time between the powerful desire to self-harm and the execution of the cut or burn. The first thing she needs to do is to begin expanding this valuable time frame, the period in which she might actually be able to interrupt the impulse to act. At S.A.F.E. we call this the *window of opportunity* between the urge to self-injure and the actual behavior of injury. People can learn many ways to create and cultivate their "window," and we will attempt to describe them in the next chapter of the book.

We don't view abstinence from self-injury as a cure in itself. Rather, we view self-injury as a form of self-medication: patients medicate their feelings (or suppress them) instead of dealing with the pain of emotional turmoil. Once the patient agrees to abstain from self-injury, we can begin to help her identify triggers, including feared memories, feelings, thoughts, and events. At that point, in an atmosphere of safety, where the therapeutic relationship is no longer in danger, the injurer can begin to face the things that have brought her pain.

Patients who have grown up in unstable environments may find S.A.F.E. to be a tranformational experience. It may be the first time they have ever had a glimpse of a life in which people are not constantly abused and denigrated, and where their thoughts and opinions matter. This joyous discovery also comes with the attendant revelation that other people's thoughts, feelings, and opinions matter also. The patient learns that she is not really free to do whatever she wants with her body, because that action might have a consequence for somebody else.

When we began our program, it lasted for thirty days. At the time, thirty days was considered a "short-term" hospital stay; most patients with this symptom were hospitalized for six months at the minimum— and often for years—at state institutions. Most professionals were skeptical that we could make inroads in such a limited time, and many people criticized us for "forcing" patients to give up their coping method of self-injury as a condition of admission. Given that we were working with ingrained behaviors and issues of character structure, the skepticism seemed reasonable.

The criticism has subsided as hundreds of patients have come through our program, many of them never to injure again. Thousands of other people have called us for advice or visited our web site. Our message over the years has remained consistent: self-injury can become a choice, and you can choose otherwise.

Chapter Sixteen

HOW AND WHY SHOULD I RISK CHANGING?

Is giving up a coping strategy and facing your fears worth it? Only you can say for sure.

If you have answered our questionnaire and learned that self-injury is indeed a problem for you—or you know it already—this chapter will describe how you might feel as the treatment and recovery process runs its course.

Among the things you need to know as you gather the courage to seek therapy is that you cannot approach treatment with the attitude: "I'm here—fix me!" Nobody, no program, no doctor, no friend, can keep you safe from self-injury or fix your problem for you. People can help you, people will help you, but it is your problem and your responsibility. And you have the power to overcome it. We can show you how.

Not every reader will be ready to stop self-injuring, but even those who are not ready yet may benefit from knowing what type of emotional readiness to be striving toward.

This chapter is meant to help you, the self-injurer, get motivated. Anybody who is having second thoughts about the value of recovery or her ability to get there should take heart in knowing that all recovered self-injurers have been in your shoes. We've heard a lot of justifications from self-injurers about why they need to hold on to the behavior, and we would like to debunk the most common arguments.

ARGUMENT #1: "SELF-INJURY DOESN'T HURT ANYONE."

The feelings of comfort that self-injury can stimulate may make it difficult for you to comprehend how severe the harm is to you and the people who care about you. Many of our patients don't even consider themselves in the equation—that is, they don't see themselves as *anybody*.

While the behavior might make you feel better temporarily, in the long run it is not a coping strategy you can sustain. Self-injury destroys relationships with others, and it wounds your relationship with your own self, or psyche. Your mind and body become increasingly disconnected, as self-injury takes the place of genuine emotion and direct communication with other people.

What we find the most telling, however, is the contention that *no one* gets hurt. What about you, the self-injurer? *You* are important, and *you* are clearly getting hurt—emotionally as well as physically. It matters that you are getting hurt. We hope that you will come to understand this during your treatment.

ARGUMENT #2: "I DON'T UNDERSTAND WHY IT UPSETS OTHERS."

Self-injurers truly have a difficult time understanding the effects of their behavior on the people around them. It's critical for them to learn to put themselves in other people's shoes. Since you are essentially seeking empathy from others for your pain, you must be able to feel empathy for others who must confront your self-injury all the time.

One way to practice empathy is to try to imagine yourself in the situation of one of your parents or friends. For example, one of the first questions we often ask self-injurers is: "If you had a child, would you think it was okay for your son or daughter to self-injure?" The resounding answer is always "No!" Then we ask the patient to reconcile why it's okay behavior for her, but wouldn't be good for her children.

It's natural for all living organisms—even one-celled amoeba—to recoil from pain. If you touched a hot stove as a child, you probably learned not to do it again. Self-preservation is a basic instinct. Abandoning that instinct seems frightening, crazy, or at the very least counterintuitive to people who don't self-injure.

Was there ever a time in your life—before you started self-injuring—when the concept would have seemed weird to you? When you first started doing it—whether it felt good or not—did you marvel at yourself for even considering such an option?

ARGUMENT #3: "IT'S MY BODY AND I CAN DO WHATEVER I WANT."

Aside from laws that apply to people who are deemed dangerous to themselves or others, this is largely true. No one can stop a self-injurer from harming herself in the long run.

We see this more as an issue of control. Rather than getting steeped in a power struggle with a self-injurer, we prefer to acknowledge that we can't stop her from hurting herself, if that's what she is truly determined to do. However, we pose questions back to her: "Yes, you can do this, but is it truly what you want to do? Do you honestly understand why you want to do it? Do you appreciate the ramifications of the behavior?"

ARGUMENT #4: "GIVING UP SELF-INJURY WILL ONLY MAKE ME HURT MORE."

Let's make an analogy. Suppose you are diagnosed with a cancerous tumor, and your doctor recommends chemotherapy. You don't feel too sick—you're still functioning—but the symptoms of the tumor are interfering with daily routines. Then you undergo chemotherapy, and you feel worse than you did on the first day you entered the doctor's office.

At some point in the treatment you may begin to feel like the treatment process is not worth the discomfort, and you may want to give it up.

At that point you have to recognize that you're in the middle of an unfortunate process in which you're going to feel worse before you get better. Doctors expect that you will get better and won't have to live with intense discomfort forever. After the treatment defeats the disease, you feel healthier and more productive than you did when you first sought help.

Another analogy goes as follows: you have a phobia of dogs, so you move to a high-rise apartment building where dogs are forbidden, and you feel safe inside. You have the illusion that you are in control of the phobia. But eventually you must go outside, where you will have to confront dogs on the street. You can cross the street to avoid the dogs, but the fear of them—the phobia—will be controlling your actions. You will never feel truly free until you can confront the phobia—see and touch a dog without fear.

When a self-injurer comes across a feared emotion, she rushes to her high-rise of self-injury. While this may work temporarily, she will never be truly comfortable until she can experience that emotion without fear.

ARGUMENT #5: "THE SCARS REMIND ME OF THE BATTLE."

Many self-injurers see their scars as constant reminders of the emotional turmoil they experience. We ask you to question why you want to hold on to such painful memories in such a graphic way. What is the need to show yourself and others what you've been through—especially when a more successful alternative would be to work through the pain and move on with your life?

ARGUMENT #6: "IT'S THE BEST WAY FOR OTHERS TO SEE HOW MUCH EMOTIONAL PAIN I'M IN."

Many self-injurers tell us that their scars stand testimony to the validity of their emotional pain. But most outsiders don't view the scars the same way, which defeats the purpose of the self-injurer's pride. In fact, the others to whom you are trying to prove yourself are more likely to see the scars as evidence of your craziness than of your pain.

All of us feel pain, which we experience as immediate and difficult. We don't tend to put our pain in relative perspective to that of other people. Thus, while you may feel that your scars show that your pain is particularly acute, the people you are trying to impress are likely to feel revulsion rather than empathy. They probably dismiss your emotional experience as too far out of their realm for sympathy—the opposite reaction from what you desire.

ARGUMENT #7: "NO ONE KNOWS THAT I INJURE, ANYWAY."

Many self-injurers can and do keep their behavior private—in the beginning. As the injuries escalate, people who see the self-injurer regularly—family members, teachers, colleagues, buddies—recognize that something is wrong. Often, medical professionals must be called in to help stitch the wounds, stave off infections, or set the bones.

While the most discreet of self-injurers can keep their activities private, this does not justify or reinforce the behavior. Self-injury does *not* occur in emotionally happy people. In general, an entire constellation of emotional difficulties accompanies self-injury. Thus, others know that *something* is wrong, even if they don't know the specifics or how to broach the subject. Sometimes the other people may be in denial themselves.

Many self-injurers harbor the fear that they're invisible. On some level, most of them want to be discovered so that others may see their "real" selves and their "true" pain. Thus, the better the secret is kept, the more depressed the self-injurer might become.

Keeping the behavior secret also serves to prevent intimacy. It's frightening to let somebody close if there's a secret to guard. Thus, secrecy usually carries a high emotional cost.

ARGUMENT #8: "IT KEEPS PEOPLE AWAY."

Some self-injurers use their behavior as a conscious or unconscious way to repulse people, to stave off intimacy. Usually, these are people who are afraid to say no, for fear they will be ignored or rebuffed if they try to set boundaries in a verbal manner.

These sufferers feel vulnerable, unable to protect themselves from rejection and possible abuse. Thus, self-injury becomes a method of self-protection from the scrutiny and potential criticism of others.

One interesting paradox here: the more you self-injure, the more likely that other people will intrude on your life and take control: therapists, hospitals, law enforcement.

Most self-injurers we've worked with fear closeness but simultaneously crave it. As treatment progresses, these people gradually confront this paradox and become more comfortable with other people as friends and intimates.

Unfortunately, physical scars are permanent and may scare away healthier companions.

ARGUMENT #9: "IT'S THE ONLY WAY TO KNOW IF PEOPLE REALLY CARE ABOUT ME."

Most self-injurers confuse being cared *about* with being taken care *of*.

If other people aren't engaged in dramatic rescuing or caretaking behaviors, the self-injurer has a difficult time believing that they *care*. The paradox is that this is an extremely narcissistic position, since the self-injurer shows a lack of caring about the other person and his or her emotions.

Unfortunately, this type of relationship is doomed: the rescuer ultimately feels used, coerced into taking a caretaker role—often with another adult—and usually severs the relationship with the self-injurer to preserve his or her sanity. When that happens, the self-injurer feels as though her worst fears have been proven true. Now she *knows* that the person doesn't truly care, because the person has abandoned her. She doesn't see the motivating factors at work for the other person, or how that person might feel overwhelmed by her symptoms.

ARGUMENT #10: "NEGATIVE ATTENTION IS BETTER THAN NONE."

As we've said, it's very common for self-injurers to feel invisible. Their worst reported fears are that "no one cares" or "I have no impact on others." Creating some rise in others, even if it's anger, convinces the sufferer that she's *there*, she's *noticed*.

This motivation is shortsighted. Self-injury never builds a relationship—almost always it causes the loss of one. Significant others feel poked and prodded into reacting, and the self-injurer ups the ante until she achieves the desired intensity of response.

This whole cycle can be very confusing to friends and family. The behavior often seems purposely designed to make them angry and to leave them feeling hurt, manipulated, and uncaring. It is hardly the way to solicit the kind of genuine affection you are seeking.

ARGUMENT #11: "I NEED TO BE PUNISHED—I'M BAD."

Most, if not all, self-injurers harbor a grandiose negative sense of their own faulty character. They see themselves as fatally flawed. Our patients have described themselves as "the black spot on a cancerous lung," "poisoned," "evil," and worse.

When we ask what they've done to deserve such an opinion, they're often at a loss for a clear example of how horrid they are. Even when able to provide an example of something shameful, it's usually a minor infraction at best.

Many of our patients believe that one or both of their parents didn't love them. They infer that there must have been something terribly wrong with them to be rejected in such a basic and visceral way. We ask how old they were when they first felt unloved. The answer is usually "as far back as I can remember." We have them visualize an infant or young child and ask if they would label that child evil or unlovable. Almost all our injurers can agree that there would be something wrong with a parent who would reject their young child in such a fashion.

The fact that shame and remorse are actually present is a testament to the individual's positive character traits. Our prisons are full of people who commit heinous crimes without any remorse, who receive far lesser sentences than self-injurers exact on themselves.

Most self-injurers agree that physical punishment is not the best way to teach children—or adults—how to learn from their mistakes. Yet they are often able to separate those beliefs from the conviction that they uniquely qualify for corporal punishment because of the wrongs they have committed. This is a warped outlook that others can help correct.

Putting yourself down—before someone else puts you down—can also be a defensive maneuver. It can protect you from the anger of others, particularly other people who feel they are walking on egg shells, worrying that criticizing you might spark a bout of violence.

ARGUMENT #12: "IT'S NOT MY FAULT— IT JUST HAPPENS."

This is often exactly what many self-injurers believe about their behavior. As we mentioned earlier, self-injurers are generally unable to identify feeling states, or events that are related to those feeling states. As a result, self-injurers can go through a day with numerous emotional stimuli—a harrowing phone call from mother, news of a friend's illness, disagreement with a coworker—yet be surprised when an intense urge to injure surfaces.

The S.A.F.E. tools, which will be described in the next chapter of the book, are designed to help you gather information about yourself and the patterns that usually surround self-injury, so you can begin to experience your feelings emotionally rather than having to reenact them through physical outbursts.

ARGUMENT #13: ''I'M STRONGER THAN OTHERS. I CAN TOLERATE PAIN.''

It's true that self-injurers can inflict bodily harm on themselves in a way that few can—or want to. However, the seemingly high pain threshold turns into a smoke-and-mirrors game. The self-injurer is ignoring what she is afraid to tolerate, which are her uncomfortable feelings or emotional pain. In addition, most self-injurers experience an analgesic affect. They are numb to the pain, and thus don't feel anything at all when they're self-injuring. Pain often comes later, however, when the wounds set in or begin to heal.

Some self-injurers become so numb they may feel as though they're not real people, but plastic or invisible in some way. In these cases the injurer seeks a sensation of pain to validate her existence—or, in psychological terms, to bring her out of a dissociative episode.

ARGUMENT #14: ''IF I DON'T SELF-INJURE, I'LL END UP KILLING MYSELF.''

Self-injury is designed to provide some temporary relief from intolerable anxiety and depression. Suicide represents a permanent escape. Most self-injurers don't want to die, but do want to live without the intensity of emotional pain. We feel this is a worthy goal and attainable without resorting to either self-injury or suicide.

The tools we will describe in the next chapter have helped hundreds of self-injurers live healthier and more productive lives. It is possible! The key to change is being open to new ideas and receptive to taking some risks.

· · ·

Most of our patients are highly dubious at first that change is even desirable, let alone possible. They fear they will be giving up as much— or more—than they are gaining. Gradually, after much hard work, they begin to open their eyes to all that self-injury has sapped from their lives. They begin to see a life of stability and comfort that can replace one of chaos and crisis. In the following chapter we will describe how this transformation takes place.

Chapter Seventeen

GETTING S.A.F.E.: THE TRANSFORMATION

This chapter describes the S.A.F.E. Alternatives program for recovery from self-injury. Though the methods and strategies described are specifically tailored to self-injuring patients, they can also be useful for people with other problems that stem from poor impulse control, including overeating, undereating, binge eating, alcohol dependence, compulsive smoking, etc.

To get the most out of the S.A.F.E. Toolbox, we ask that you be consistently honest with yourself. We encourage you to have an open mind and to strive for the desire to learn as much about yourself as possible. There is nothing magical about getting better—it takes a lot of courage and hard work.

At the beginning of the recovery process, most patients believe they are in some sense out of the circle of the human race. This thought dissipates after several weeks of self-examination and companionship. Thousands of our patients have done this successfully, and you can too.

Naturally, no book can take the place of a therapy program. Ours is meant to complement an inpatient or outpatient therapy regimen, to get self-injurers and their therapists thinking about the best ways to combat the behavior.

This is the game plan of the recovery program:

The self-injurer begins the healing process with the idea that her behavior is *out* of her volitional control. She experiences it as a compulsion, something she is destined to repeat over and over.

The overriding goal in recovery is to transform this frame of reference. The tools, exercises, and therapy strategies described in the pages ahead are meant to bring about a shift in your view of self-injury from "uncontrollable compulsion" to "choice" to "unhealthy choice." The S.A.F.E. philosophy is that self-injury can become a chosen course of action, and that the patient can at the same time learn to choose *another* course of action.

This can happen only when you learn to interrupt the vicious cycle of automatically responding to discomfort with self-harm. We will discuss the window of opportunity that needs to be created, in which you can *delay* the impulse to hurt yourself, *reflect* on your situation, and— eventually—learn to *choose* an alternative solution.

INPATIENT VERSUS OUTPATIENT

Our view is that most self-injurers can be treated without hospitalization. While the most severe cases—including the kind we are likely to see at our program—can benefit from the structured environment of a clinical setting, most self-injurers—people who continue to function in their lives while engaging in this behavior—can learn to abstain from self-harm on an outpatient basis, working with a therapist and/or a support group. The treatment program described here can be used in either setting. We use it with both kinds of patients.

Nonetheless, it is useful to make some distinctions between inpatient and outpatient treatment goals.

By the time someone reaches the inpatient setting—a hospital or other residential facility—her self-injurious behavior has generally escalated so far that it has become highly disruptive to her life. She may not be able to function on the job or in school, and she may not be able to fulfull household responsibilities, or even to take care of her own grooming and personal needs. The problem has grown so overwhelming that her therapist feels the behavior has taken grip of the therapist/client relationship, and no more progress can be made in outpatient work.

The threshold at which a therapist or someone else will recommend hospitalization varies, depending on the clinician's willingness to tolerate potentially dangerous activity. Our general yardstick for inpatient admission is when the self-injurious behavior has gotten to a point that both therapist and patient feel it is disrupting their relationship and affecting all areas of the patient's life. By this point the behavior has usually become so frequent, dangerous, or potentially lethal that the patient's safety is severely jeopardized. The therapist is likely to feel held hostage by the patient's increasing self-harm, unable to focus on the patient's underlying issues because of the need to worry about her day-to-day well-being.

GROUND RULES

When prospective patients call us at S.A.F.E., we ask them a few questions to gauge how ready they are to make a commitment to recovery. We also tell them we require a few conditions and basic understandings of all patients, and which we ask readers to adhere to for maximum success of the S.A.F.E. Alternatives program:

1. The patient must truly want to get better. If the desire is half-hearted, insincere, or driven or imposed by others, recovery is probably a distant dream.
2. Having a therapist is extremely valuable. Recovering from self-injury requires the careful examination and analysis of difficult thoughts and feelings, many of which you may never before have put into words. It is crucial that you have the support and guidance of a therapist during this process.
3. Every patient is unique, and recovery times can be long or short. Though our program runs an average of four weeks (which can combine inpatient and partial hospitalization), many patients need more time and may petition for an extra week. Self-injurers are also expected to continue the work in an extended outpatient therapy. Recovering from self-injury is not a timed contest, but sufferers should know that the results they see are likely to be correlated to the efforts they put in.

After those ground rules are squared away, there are several steps, or stages, toward recovery that we pursue. First, we ask patients to reexamine their mind-sets, to make sure they are mentally prepared for the challenges ahead.

STEP 1: THE RIGHT FRAME OF MIND

As we've said, the self-injurer must *want* to get better if she is going to make any progress.

While it may seem obvious to outsiders that self-injurers should want to stop their behavior, often that is not the case. Patients self-injure for many reasons—the behavior serves a purpose for them; it is a comforting and ingrained habit—and many are in strong denial about the scope of the problem and the toll it takes.

At S.A.F.E. Alternatives we routinely reject applicants who do not show evidence that they want to get better. Many people who contact us express total comfort with their behavior and say they are calling only because of coercion by others. We know we can do little for such people. Sure, your mother—or spouse, or therapist—can probably force you to go through the motions of a program that you're told is for your own good, or at least in your best interests. You can be prodded into therapy sessions, forced to attend meetings or groups, coaxed into completing writing assignments. But you're probably not going to get any better. If you're resisting the recovery process, your mind is probably closed to it. You don't see any reason to try; you might think it's all silly or stupid or pointless. Someone with a closed mind won't be willing to challenge her thoughts or delve into her feelings. She is not likely to be someone we—or anyone—can particularly help.

Likewise, some patients come to us saying, "I'm feeling suicidal—I need *something* to make me feel better, or I'll kill myself." Though many of our patients have experienced suicidal impulses and attempts, our program is *not* oriented toward suicide prevention. Indeed, we tend to view suicide as a separate issue from self-injury, one that needs to be addressed before someone is ready to begin the S.A.F.E. program. People who are looking for the ultimate escape have, at least for the time being, given up hope for a better future and narrowed their options to one. Their thinking is inflexible, and they are unwilling to consider new ideas. They need psychiatric intervention to help them to see that they have options. Our treatment program is one of those options, but patients need to avail themselves to it mentally, or it won't work.

If you have a suicide plan, we urge you to get the help you need. Call a hotline in times of crisis; make sure you have a therapist who is aware of your condition. When you have this issue resolved and have decided to opt for life and possibility, S.A.F.E. is ready to help you transcend self-injury and make a better life for yourself. Sometimes patients come back to us after they have found that motivation within them, which we find very heartening.

Finally, a lot of self-injurers feel that they're on the fence. On one hand, the behavior *feels* helpful and relieving, and on the other hand, the sufferer knows it is interfering with her life in a severe and debilitating way. Summoning the desire to stop the behavior is difficult indeed and is compounded by many factors: denial, the desire to seem normal, fear of failure, fear of disapproval from family members and others. Most of our clients are ambivalent. However, if they are willing to give the program the benefit of the doubt, we accept them. Similarly, if you are willing to give our program a try despite a nagging skepticism, please read on.

STEP 2: THE RIGHT THERAPY

All patients who come to S.A.F.E. have an outpatient therapist, since this is a prerequisite for admission. We strongly believe that using a therapist to weather emotional storms and sort through confusing relationships is the best road to health.

How do you find a therapist in the first place? It's helpful to ask around. You might want to consult your family physician, your gynecologist, or anyone else you know and trust in the medical field. A personal referral from someone you know is usually the best method, though this person might not necessarily be right for you. If you don't have a trustworthy source for a direct referral, you can always look in the telephone book under "mental health," where you will find names of clinics, hospitals, and individual therapists.

You might want to consider a few issues before you start interviewing candidates. Do you want an older therapist, someone your age, or someone younger? A man or a woman? How important are location, distance, surroundings? How much can you afford to pay? You will need to find out up front whether your therapist is willing to bill insurance or if she expects you to be responsible.

Teaching hospitals and some clinics offer low-cost/sliding-scale treatments. There, you may be assigned to a professional in training, such as an intern or psychiatric resident who is supervised by a senior physician. If you choose this option, know that you may have to terminate with that person once his or her training requirements are met, but that the two of you can still have a productive and rewarding relationship, and he or she will most certainly arrange for you to continue working with someone else.

Psychiatrists are medical doctors who are trained to diagnose any illness and prescribe medication. They have specific training in the treatment of emotional disorders and have graduated from a traditional medical school. Some psychiatrists are doctors of osteopathy, fully licensed physicians trained in osteopathic medicine. This is a holistic field based on the interrelationships between various body systems.

Psychologists are also trained to conduct psychotherapy, though they are not medical doctors and cannot prescribe drugs (the latter may change in the near future, for there is a movement to allow certain psychiatric professionals to prescribe limited types of pharmaceuticals). If you want to work with a psychologist, whose rates are usually less expensive than a psychiatrist's, try to find someone with a minimum of a master's degree in social work or in clinical or counseling psychology. Those with doctoral-level degrees (Ph.D. or Psy.D.) have even more experience and training. Some registered nurses who have had master's level training with supervision also offer psychotherapy or counseling. Some states offer counseling credentials to people with other types of training in mental health fields. Be sure to ask what a therapist's background is.

Additionally, there are several theoretical orientations in psychotherapy, and all of them can be helpful to the self-injurer. When interviewing therapists, ask which of the following they adhere to:

- *Insight-oriented*, or *psychodynamic, therapy* focuses primarily on understanding the motives for a patient's behavior. The patient's choices are seen as complex outcomes of wishes, fears, memories, unresolved feelings, and conflicts. The patient may or may not be aware of some of these motives that drive her behavior. The premise of the therapy is that the more someone learns about her unknown inner world, the less she will feel compelled to engage in maladaptive strategies to cope with life.

- *Cognitive-behavioral therapy* starts from the premise that the way a person thinks strongly influences the way she behaves and feels. Therapy focuses on helping clients recognize and change their *automatic thoughts* (their internal dialogues and statements about themselves), *underlying assumptions* (the beliefs they hold about what people are like and the way the world works), and *cognitive distortions* (errors in logic that lead people to draw faulty conclusions). The behavioral aspect of cognitive-behavioral therapy combines work on faulty thinking patterns with teaching, training, and guided rehearsal of new coping strategies. Patient and therapist work back and forth between stepwise practice of new behaviors (often in the form of homework assignments) and the examination of belief patterns.

- *Supportive therapy* focuses on helping patients manage the day-to-day practicalities of their lives. Rather than treating underlying or past issues, the supportive therapist offers advice and support for daily living problems. While therapy is usually limited to once a week, contact between sessions is often encouraged. The overall goal is to increase the patient's stability and self-esteem.

The boundaries between these orientations are not rigid, and while most therapists profess to emphasize one approach, there is a great deal of overlap. Think of them as different denominations of the same basic religion, each of which may play up certain rituals or beliefs. For example, a cognitive-behavioral therapist will focus her efforts on exploring the causes and motives behind a self-injurer's actions, even though this will not be the primary target of intervention. Similarly, the psychodynamic therapist might challenge a patient's thought patterns, and at times help her devise more effective strategies.

Whatever the therapist's orientation, a self-injurer usually benefits the most from treatment that regards her behavior as an expression of her underlying issues. In other words, it is more helpful for the therapist *not* to view self-injury as the sole problem, but rather as the obstacle that keeps the patient from facing her issues and anxieties directly.

This is not to say that all therapies or therapists or forms of treatment are equally beneficial. Many of our clients have had numerous therapy experiences, often bouncing from one therapist to another for years. Sometimes the change is the client's choice, and sometimes it is the therapist's. Part of the reason has to do with the nature of the syndrome: self-injurers tend to have stormy relationships with people, and this turbulence can carry over into therapy. But such difficulties may also reflect problems with the therapist, who may recoil from self-injurers for a variety of reasons, from emotional aversion to legal liability.

Other therapists may suggest the use of hypnotherapy and cathartic methods, which may be counterproductive for self-injurers. Many self-injurers are tempted to try hypnosis to modify their behavior or forcibly remember painful feelings and memories, with the hopes it will speed recovery and help them control themselves. Our experience has been that many self-injurers who try hypnotherapy find it to be a very disorganizing and overwhelming experience, one that brings about regression, hospitalization, and more self-injury. We strongly caution you to consider this before trying the technique with your therapist.

There is no specific credential, or certificate of specialty, in treating self-injurers. Psychotherapists of all types and orientations vary widely in the amount of experience they have with the problem. It may be helpful to ask the prospective therapist how familiar she is with the issue, and how many patients she has seen who have the problem. While you may feel more comfortable with someone who has broad experience with self-injurious patients, keep in mind that this quantitative criterion is no guarantee that the therapist is skilled or successful. Some therapists with little experience may do well with self-injurers because they are inherently good at what they do and can sense instinctively what their patients need.

Finding the right fit between therapist and patient is a highly subjective process. When meeting a prospective therapist for the first time, go in prepared with ideas about your needs and goals, as well as what you *don't* want from your therapy. You might want to jot down in advance a list of questions to ask.

When you meet a therapist, be aware of how you *feel*. Does this person seem like someone you can trust, confide in, feel safe with? Do you find yourself wanting to come back for a second meeting? Trust your intuition about these issues, but realize that you don't need to make a long-term commitment to anyone after one meeting. It's perfectly acceptable to schedule a second and third trial session, or a trial period, to test your initial impressions and decide whether the fit is right.

We have found a few ingredients that help make the relationship a positive one:

1. A therapist whose demeanor is calm and serene usually works best with self-injurers. Someone who grows alarmed and fearful by the patient's injurious urges is unlikely to be of much help. While the therapist must acknowledge that the behavior is damaging and dangerous, she must express her alarm and concern in ways that benefit the patient.

   In one case of a therapist/client mismatch, a patient told us of a therapist whom she used to call routinely when she felt the urge to injure. Each time the doctor felt obliged to call paramedics and have the patient hospitalized (doctors can be legally liable or stripped of their licenses if they know a violent act or a crime is about to occur and do not intervene). While the doctor's reaction was understandable, the patient believed she could have regained control and avoided injuring if she had been able to talk to the doctor about the feelings connected to her urges. The doctor, who did not feel comfortable enough with the risk involved to delay the emergency intervention, ultimately decided that the fit was wrong. She helped the patient make a transition to another therapist, someone who promised to try intervening in a way that would avoid hospitalization.

2. The ideal therapist should be open-minded and empathetic yet firm. A nonjudgmental attitude toward the self-injurer and her behavior is essential to a successful relationship. A therapist who sees self-injury as manipulative or morally wrong is not going to fit the bill. Your therapist needs to see self-injury as a sign of desperate struggle, a symptom that needs to be understood.

   At the same time, no psychotherapy relationship can progress or succeed if the self-injurer does not curtail her behavior. You must demonstrate ongoing motivation to change. It's unreasonable to expect your therapist to permit unlimited self-destruction. You owe it to her to work diligently as a partner in the restoration of your health and safety.

3. The therapist must have a reasonable degree of availability and must manage well in times of crisis. When you are interviewing, ask about the therapist's understanding of your problem and the potential it raises for crisis intervention. Make sure the therapist understands the difference between any suicidal thoughts you might have and your nonsuicidal self-injurious behavior. Disclose any suicide attempts.

   Talk in advance with the therapist about your expectations in times of crisis, and how she might best help you. Ask what a reasonable crisis plan might be, and if she would be available for emergency phone calls. When and how often? How are holidays, vacations, and weekends handled? Would she work with you to devise a contract, with consequences for self-destructive behavior? Is her schedule flexible enough to work in all the sessions you think you will need, or to increase sessions if necessary?

4. The therapist must respect the patient's autonomy as an adult. Self-injurers say their most successful experiences have been with therapists who do not infantilize them or try to rescue them from themselves. From the therapist's perspective, it is very tempting to become parental, to tell the patient what to do, to advocate round-the-clock supervision, or to take away dangerous objects. In general, this will not help the self-injurer reorient herself to assume personal responsibility for her behavior and its repercussions. Look for a therapist who wants to enlist your active participation in recovery, one who tells you straightaway that her goal is to *help* you become autonomous and self-disciplined.

Finally, if you are relying on insurance benefits to help pay for treatment, learn as much about your policy limitations as you can. Know what your deductible is (the amount of charges you must accrue at the beginning of the calendar year before the insurance will begin to reimburse you), and if there is any co-payment (an amount you are expected to contribute toward each session's fee). Ask the therapist whether she expects payment up front, or if she is willing to wait for insurance reimbursement. Find out if you will be expected to pay for missed appointments. Knowing as much as possible about the practical arrangements will help prepare you to make a commitment to the therapy and your recovery.

Ideally, your therapist should not be the only person on your recovery support team. We suggest you take an active role in enlisting others—friends, family members, trusted clergy—to set aside time for you on a regular basis. This time could be spent just talking out issues, or it could involve discussing your work from the S.A.F.E. Toolbox.

STEP 3: THE S.A.F.E. TOOLBOX

In addition to therapy sessions, the S.A.F.E. Toolbox consists of four key implements, all of which should be used simultaneously during treatment. They are as follows:

- No-Harm Contract
- Impulse Control Log
- Five Alternatives
- Writing Assignments

All components of the Toolbox may be useful for people with a variety of problems and in different situations and stages of recovery. The Toolbox contains many strategies that our clients at S.A.F.E. have used successfully to create and cultivate their windows of opportunity, the time in which they could find another way to cope without resorting to self-harm. Collectively, these can be seen as strategies that help people slow down the runaway train of the impulse to injure and jump-start the ability to think their way through a bad moment, or to understand what is going on in a self-injury crisis. These tools help mobilize *thoughts* and *words*, which are a person's best ammunition in the battle for self-control.

TOOL ONE: THE NO-HARM CONTRACT

At the very beginning of therapy, you should develop an agreement with your therapist which may take the form of a formal contract, or a less formal verbal agreement. The agreement should spell out the expectations and responsibilities both you and your therapist have with regard to the process of therapy, and how behaviors that threaten the treatment process will be handled.

A written contract is useful for many self-injurers because it lessens the likelihood that the terms or expectations within the treatment will be misunderstood. In a hospital-based program like ours, where support resources are readily available, we think it is reasonable to expect patients to use these resources to keep themselves safe. Because of this, the consequence for self-injurious behavior can ultimately be the termination of the treatment relationship.

In an outpatient relationship, abiding by a contract helps the patient stay focused on her goal, not on self-injuring. Written parameters help encourage the recovery process. Enforcing the consequences is of utmost importance—otherwise the contract has minimal significance. Attributing responsibility to the self-injurer decreases her ability to hold others accountable for her behavior.

We encourage the self-injurer to participate in the development of the contract, thus taking an immediate and active role in her recovery. She should come up with a list of fair and attainable goals—and consequences—and should sign it, along with her therapist.

Some patients bristle at the word contract, which can remind them of various contracts they may have failed to fulfill in the past. For these people we recommend calling it a "treatment participation agreement."

In order for the contract or agreement to be a successful part of your Toolbox, it must be free of any overtones that it is an instrument of control or punishment by an authority, meaning your therapist. This is not what we intend. The therapist cannot be perceived as your adversary, someone who is making you do things against your will. Many of the traps people fall into at the beginning of the therapy relationship involve creating unrealistic contracts with rules that the patient cannot possibly adhere to at the beginning of the work. We view a treatment participation agreement as a *collaboration*, with the therapist and the client making decisions *together* over what is reasonable behavior and what the consequences will be of stepping out of bounds. We see it as a democratic process taking place between two responsible parties.

The therapeutic participation agreement might involve a no-harm clause, in which the therapist and client come up wtih a reasonable span of time, or specific circumstances, in which the client will refrain from self-injuring. For example, some therapists would prefer that the patient refrain from self-injury on the days of their sessions. The argument goes that injuring before therapy is like slugging back a six-pack on the way to the office or just before an AA meeting. If the client arrives for treatment already having "calmed" her anxiety, it could be hard to find that anxiety to work on during the session.

Some patients prefer to try short term no-harm agreements, day by day or week by week, finding that the success in adhering to them inspires them to continue. Others feel more comfortable with more general agreements, in which they commit to a motivation to work on remaining safe. Even in these contracts specific responsibilities are laid out for the patient during the regular course of therapy and in event of crisis.

Whatever the format or level of specificity, many former self-injurers have told us that the presence of a contract or agreement helped them to stop and think, "Hey, wait a minute, I have a responsibility to a relationship which I value a great deal." This moment of delay and reflection was sometimes enough for them to open a window of opportunity, put down the injury tool, and find another way to cope. It's not really the contract so much as the *idea* of the contract that helped them arrest the impulse and make another choice.

Copies of the actual contracts we use at S.A.F.E.—one for inpatients and one for outpatients—are included in the appendix of this book. We have not reproduced them here because they are fairly specific to our treatment program and clientele. Instead, we thought it would be more helpful here to supply a sample of the type of contract you and your therapist might want to use or adapt to your own circumstances.

My No-Harm Contract

I recognize that self-injury interferes with all aspects of my life, and I am committed to treatment of my problem and to stopping all self-injurious behavior. I am aware of and agree to the following guidelines for my treatment:

1. I agree to abstain from self-injury twenty-four hours before my therapy session. I understand that if I injure prior to the session I must seek medical attention, and I understand that I will forfeit the session for that day.
2. During the therapy session I will not engage in violent or

property-damaging behaviors. If I do, I understand that the session will end, and the need for hospitalization will be assessed.

3. I will set a regular schedule of therapy sessions and arrive on time to each session. If I need to be late or miss an appointment, I will call in advance with a valid reason. I understand that my therapist reserves the right to charge the fee for the missed session, pending discussion of the cause.

4. I understand all the components of the S.A.F.E. Toolbox and have worked out with my therapist how I will use them. I will fill out Impulse Control Logs whenever I identify an urge to take action against myself. I will use my alternatives instead of self-injury. I will complete all writing assignments and share them with my therapist.

5. If I have a concurrent eating disorder, I agree to follow my therapist's recommendations for this problem. If I have a concurrent drinking or drug problem, I will seek help through Alcoholics Anonymous, Narcotics Anonymous, or another treatment method that my therapist and I agree on.

6. If I think I am suicidal, I will call a crisis hotline or my therapist (or whatever plan my therapist and I have agreed upon).

7. If I think that I am about to self-injure, I will _____ (fill in the specific terms of the plan for management of self-injurious crises that you and your therapist have worked out).

8. If I need contact with my therapist between regularly scheduled sessions, I understand that _____ (fill in the parameters for such availability).

9. I understand that violating the terms of this agreement will result in certain consequences. Those consequences are _____. (These should be spelled out specifically for each issue: the occurence of self-injurious behavior, excessive absences from therapy sessions, noncompliance with the crisis plans.)

(signatures of patient and therapist)

Think of the contract as you would any other contract that gives you privileges and opportunities. If you want to own a home or rent an apartment, you'll have to sign a contract. If you want to drive a car, you have to abide by certain rules. You have to stay away from thinking of a contract as something that gets you into trouble—regard it instead as a benefit that gives you the chance to participate in a positive change process.

When constructing your own contract, think of consequences that are therapeutic rather than punishing. If you are in a Twelve Step program and attend sporadically, you may want to include extra meetings as one of your consequences. Writing assignments can also be used as a consequence.

Losing the treatment relationship with your therapist for a period of time is not an unrealistic consequence. This consequence in particular gives you the chance to reflect on how your behavior sabotages meaningful aspects of your life.

Many professionals in our field have questioned—and criticized—our policy of discharging patients who continue to self-injure during their hospital stays or inpatient treatment. We still maintain that this is one of the most important features of our program, though we don't necessarily hold the same standard in an outpatient setting. Our reasons are several:

1. Discharging patients who self-injure during treatment sends a powerful message to them and their peers to think about the consequences of actions *before* they act.
2. Someone who self-injures is medicating her symptoms by herself and therefore has less motivation to deal with underlying problems.
3. If one person starts injuring, others will follow suit. In psychology, this phenomenon is called *contagion*.
4. Discharge reinforces the notion that self-injury brings about loss and helps dispel the rescue fantasy.
5. Drug and alcohol programs have similar policies, and most people don't question them. If we did not enforce a discharge policy for self-destructive behavior, we would send patients the message that we don't believe they can survive without self-injury. We know they can.

We aren't so harsh that we dismiss patients right away after the first time they violate the contract. Usually, we'll put someone on probation first. The probation period is designed to allow the patient to take a good look at self-injury as a *choice*. She may not have ever before viewed it as something optional or volitional. During probation we ask her to focus on what led up to the incident, what she could have done differently, and if she truly wants to stay in the program. If yes, what would she like to do differently in the future? These exercises help her reevaluate what broke down in her attempt to manage the impulses without resorting to physical action. She also reflects upon and re-evaluates her motivation and commitment to treatment.

If a patient violates a contract term and gets put on probation, we ask her to answer this set of written probation questions.

1. What precipitated the behavior?
2. What was the feeling?
3. Why did you choose destructive behavior?
4. What could you have done differently?
5. What can you do differently in the future?
6. Do you want to continue with a recovery program? Why?

Similarly, when a patient misses a therapy session or group meeting, we ask her to write about it. Patients and their therapists who are simulating our program could use these techniques when the patient has a behavior lapse or misses an appointment without a good reason.

Again, the twenty-four-hour milieu of our inpatient program is different from the more sporadic support offered by an outpatient program, ours or any other. As residents, our inpatients have staff members and peers available constantly for crisis intervention, so excuses for self-injury are more difficult to come by. The No-Harm Contract is meant to make injury the less attractive choice and to force people to take the less comfortable route of asking for help directly.

TOOL TWO: THE IMPULSE CONTROL LOG

Self-injurers often say the urge to harm themselves comes out of no-where. They cannot fathom the reason, but the sensation feels overwhelming and uncontrollable.

We tell patients that the impulse to self-mutilate does *not* come from nowhere—it is driven by something deep-seated: a feeling, thought, or memory that perhaps is so submerged the patient herself may not be aware of it. One way to start creating this awareness is to try to describe the impulse, to analyze it, and to postulate what it might be communicating.

To help patients become more aware of their self-harm urges, we ask them to keep a running diary of them. We call this the Impulse Control Log, and our patients routinely report that it is the most helpful tool we give them at S.A.F.E.

The log format we have developed is geared specifically for our population, but people with other types of compulsions—binge eating, drug abuse—can use it successfully as well. The concept of controlling a compulsive behavior by monitoring it closely is not unique to S.A.F.E.

Anyone who has ever gone on a weight-loss diet through a formal program like Weight Watchers knows that keeping track of what you eat is a centerpiece of the regimen. Dieters are asked to keep a daily record of every meal and snack not just as a way of counting calories, but also as a visible record of the person's eating habits and hunger patterns. These food logs help dieters feel that they have control over their pangs and cravings.

Controlling self-injury is not exactly like dieting, but there are points in common. Both overeating and the urge to commit bodily harm are compulsions, and compulsions are easiest to control when the sufferer understands them and can break them down into more manageable units. The Impulse Control Log is designed to do just that.

The Impulse Control Log requires that a person write down every thought and feeling associated with a particular urge to self-injure, whether or not she actually goes through with the act. The goal at first is that the writing will become a substitute for—and diversion from— the act itself. The ultimate goal, however, is to understand the connection between your thoughts, feelings, and behaviors. The hope is that after the self-injurer fills in her log and perhaps relies on some other alternatives, she will no longer be driven to act out.

You should begin keeping an Impulse Control Log as soon as you embark on your treatment program and should use it in conjunction with the other treatment steps described here. The log should be maintained as long as you feel urges to self-injure. You can either copy out the sample log here into a journal of your own or make photocopies of the one included in the appendix.

To create a log from scratch, you should make a grid on a blank piece of paper, with nine categories running across the top:

1. Acting out/self-injury thoughts
2. Time and date
3. Location
4. Situation
5. Feeling
6. What would be the result of self-injury?
7. What would I be trying to communicate with my self-injury?
8. Action taken
9. Outcome

Every time you have an urge, be sure to make an entry in each category. For example, one of Ashley P.'s Impulse Control Log entries read this way:

Self-injury thoughts: Burning, cutting, punching
Time and date: 7/23/98, 2:15 p.m.
Location: S.A.F.E. group room
Situation: In group therapy, talking of people whose urges have gone away, imagining mine always there.
Feeling: Scared, helpless, lonely, angry
What would self-injury accomplish? Scars, discharge
What would I be trying to communicate with my self-injury? I was angry and lonely. I don't want my self-injurious thoughts to be gone, but sometimes I do. I see no end to my thoughts, though.
Outcome: I challenged my thoughts. If others can do it, so can I. I'm not so different from the people who have succeeded in getting healthy.
Comments: My desire to act out decreased.

To get the most from the Impulse Control Log, you need to understand that the wish to self-injure is a *thought*, not a *feeling*. Once you internalize that, you can begin to understand that self-injury is a behavior, and behavior can be changed. This behavior has been distracting you from difficult feelings, serving as a disguised way of expressing unacceptable feelings or thoughts. The desire to self-injure is a signal that you are experiencing a feeling—anger, sadness, embarrassment—and the log attempts to make that connection clear. Ultimately, we hope you can dispense with the signal and attend to both the feeling and the thought.

Self-injurers become so absorbed with the fix of self-injury that they are usually unaware it is connected to anything. The obsession to engage in the fixing behavior serves as a distraction. Some people believe that when alcohol or drug abuse disappears, that is the end of the problem, and the person is cured. Not so with self-injury. The symptom is only a clue to the deeper problems. We ask patients to ask themselves anytime they have an urge to injure, "What are you feeling?" and "What are you trying to fix?" The urge may be related to trying to erase a feeling, the desire to return to a numb or dissociative state, or the urge to alleviate loneliness by getting someone to take care of them.

Impulse Control Logs "have really made a difference," according to Susan L., who learned the technique as an inpatient at S.A.F.E. "They slow me down and make me think. They make me focus on the consequences—guilt, shame, hopelessness, and anger—that I don't want anymore. I've learned that I'm in control, that I'm the one who makes the choices."

Ashley P.'s Impulse Control Log (as S.A.F.E. outpatient)

Self-injury thoughts: Cutting, burning
Time and date: 7/20/98, 5:30 p.m.
Location: Living room of my friend and her family.
Situation: I was watching my friend's family get along so well.
Feeling: Disappointed, alone, upset, angry
What would self-injury accomplish? Scars, ending a wonderful pattern of not self-injuring.
What would I be trying to communicate with my self-injury? That I wish my family was close, and that I felt alone.
Outcome: Started talking to people, challenged thoughts.
Comments: I noticed a decrease in my desire to act out.

Self-injury thoughts: Cutting, punching, burning, scraping
Time and date: 7/21/98, 2 p.m.
Location: Group room at S.A.F.E.
Situation: Talking about my loneliness and suicidality.
Feeling: Lonely, scared
What would self-injury accomplish? Discharge, go back to adolescent inpatient ward.

What would I be trying to communicate with my self-injury? I am
alone and very scared. I think of suicide and am afraid of relapsing.

Outcome: Talked to group, used alternatives.

Comments: Desire to act out decreased.

Self-injury thoughts: Cutting, burning, starving

Time and date: 7/24/98, 12:08 p.m.

Location: School cafeteria

Situation: I was with a group of peers but on the outside.

Feeling: Sad, lonely

What would self-injury accomplish? Scars, discharge

What would I be trying to communicate with my self-injury? That
I am lonely and wish I fit in better.

Outcome: I thought through the issue more, and realized that my
therapy might be able to help me learn how to get closer to
people and not to feel so alienated. Being on the outside of things
might be temporary.

Comments: Desire to act out is still with me, but I'm handling it
better.

TOOL THREE: THE FIVE ALTERNATIVES

Before working in the Impulse Control Log, you should have some
coping strategies in place. We call these "safe alternatives" to self-
injury. Each patient picks her own list of comforting activities or temporary distractions. There can be five or more—many patients choose
to identify as many as ten so they know there is a wide variety of
calming activities to choose from.

A few guidelines: several of the alternatives should be activities that
can be done anytime or anyplace, so that you are always prepared when
the impulse to injure strikes. The goal is that instead of moving directly
from impulse to injury, you will remember your alternatives and can
interrupt the crisis long enough to think rationally. This period of clar-
ity is what we call the window of opportunity, and it plays a key role
in recovery.

Another advantage to the Five Alternatives plan is that it weans people from the type of all-or-nothing thinking that prompts them to behave in extreme ways, rarely aware that there could possibly be other courses of action.

Some of the most common and useful safe alternatives include:

1. Filling out an Impulse Control Log
2. Writing in a journal
3. Talking and listening to a trusted person
4. Challenging distorted thinking
5. Just sitting with—and allowing yourself to experience—feelings
6. Taking a walk
7. Listening to music
8. Working on an arts or crafts project, like needlepoint, painting, knitting, ceramics
9. Playing an instrument, like guitar or piano
10. Cooking a meal

A warning: when you begin using the alternatives, you will *not* experience the same quick relief that self-harm provided. What you will begin to experience, however, are genuine emotions and feelings, which you must learn to live with if you are to work through your problem. You will also begin to trust in the healing value of human relationships. This will start with your relationship with yourself.

You have been using self-injury to deny human emotions and combat your sense of being physically alive. The wounding assault severs the spiritual connection that a healthy person has between mind and body. You have been driving a tangible wedge between your body and your self. Once you begin to forge a connection to your self by halting the attacks on your body, the next relationship you experience will be with another person. In time the goal is that there will be many trusted "others" in whom you will want to confide. Many self-injurers engage in self-harm with the hope of bringing about relationships and fail to accept that self-harm brings about the true loss of relationships.

To feel comfortable with other people, you have to feel comfortable with yourself. That's why we think that the alternative listed as #5 on our list—just sitting with and allowing yourself to experience feelings—is such an important one.

This alternative will be the hardest one to tolerate in the beginning.

Most self-injurers say that in order to "get it out"—meaning their feelings—they need to harm their bodies. They may describe their feelings as poisonous, bad, or evil, which would explain why they need to get rid of them.

Most injurers believe their acts of self-harm release the bad or evil or poison from the body. This belief can be sustained because the self-injurer experiences temporary relief through her action, or because she has come to injure herself as a habit. Until you learn to tolerate feelings—uneasy ones as well as comfortable ones—your behavior will continue.

Here are some suggestions for "just sitting with yourself and allowing yourself to experience feelings":

Start by telling yourself that feelings won't kill you. Then tell yourself that it's okay not to like how you're feeling. Remind yourself that feelings are not bad or good, just comfortable or uncomfortable. Remember that it is your global, all-or-nothing thinking that scares you, so stay with the thoughts that are soothing.

Find a location where you can experience your feelings in privacy and comfort. You may want that to be a special zone you designate where all feelings are okay. It could be your bedroom, living room, or kitchen table—but try not to make it your closet, bathroom, or a place where you might have once gone to retreat and engage in self-mutilation. Optimally, it will be a place that you don't associate with the behavior, a place that you can come to associate with the process of healing and recovery.

Once you are there, try crying, writing, reflecting, and having empathic thoughts for yourself. If you are angry, write about what is triggering your anger.

Get in the habit of taking time out for yourself on a daily basis to think about your feelings before they feel out of control. Start with a set amount of time and add more time as you feel more comfortable with it.

Our patients' lists of alternatives

Donna W.

1. Call a family member
2. Call my primary therapist
3. Write in my journal
4. Take a shower
5. Write a letter to a former S.A.F.E. peer
6. Go to an AA meeting
7. Clean my apartment
8. Draw
9. Go to a grocery store or restaurant
10. Fill out an Impulse Control Log

Jared T.

1. Call upon the Lord
2. Read the Bible
3. Tell someone about it, talk it out
4. Exercise
5. Impulse Control Log
6. Coloring, drawing, artwork
7. Aggressively challenge irrational thoughts
8. Play/learn to play the piano or other instrument
9. Put together a jigsaw puzzle
10. Pet the cat

TOOL FOUR: THE WRITING ASSIGNMENTS

Writing tasks are extremely useful to the self-injurer. They help you organize your thoughts and focus your energy in a safe and constructive manner.

The S.A.F.E. program relies on fifteen writing assignments, given in sequential order. The first one asks the self-injurer to write her autobiography; later assignments grow increasingly challenging and analytical. The assignments focus on self-awareness, identification of feelings, family/relationship issues, and gender/body image issues. We encourage patients to get creative and work with their support team to develop additional assignments relevant to them.

The rule of thumb is that any tool that helps you slow down, redirect your thinking, channel your energies, and articulate thoughts and feelings will help you navigate emotional distress more effectively. Thus, these writing assignments—which can begin once the self-injurer has a working understanding of all the components of the Toolbox—serve a dual purpose. On one hand, they might give someone who has the urge to harm herself an alternative outlet for exploring her feelings. On the other, they might give someone who does not feel in crisis mode a chance to delve into underlying issues, to make better sense of her emotional life.

The assignments can be as long or short as you like, but in general, we believe it takes at least two or three pages of writing to complete them thoroughly and thoughtfully.

We usually assign them progressively at S.A.F.E., at the rate of four or five a week, but readers and their support team may decide that a different rate—or different order—makes better sense. You can also design your own assignments to address particular issues that might shed light on your situation or pattern of self-injuring.

Here are fifteen sample writing assignments and the rationale behind each:

Assignment One: Your autobiography

Rationale: Writing a chronology of your life's events helps you synthesize them and place them in perspective. Putting difficult memories on paper can not only vent anger, but also lead to realizations or discoveries you may not have made before. Recalling happy times can give hope and solace and can lend promise of joy in the future. This first assignment is typically the longest—responses tend to run five to ten pages—and serves as a helpful foundation for subsequent assignments.

Questions:
   Describe what has happened to you in your life, starting with your childhood and earliest memories and continuing, as thoroughly and in as much detail as possible, up to the present. Among the specific topics to address are:

1. What was the family composition and emotional climate when you were growing up? Describe your relationships with your mother and father, or the people who raised you. Also include relationships with any siblings. Who were the people you felt close to? Who couldn't you get along with?

2. Describe any special hardships or losses you experienced while growing up: divorce, death, abandonment, assault, abuse, etc. How did you react to these as a child?

3. What were the strengths and positive aspects of your childhood?

4. Describe your medical history, including operations, pregnancies, deliveries, and abortions. Also include information about your eating patterns and any problems you have had with your weight: overweight, underweight, bingeing, purging, food refusal.

5. Write about your alcohol and drug history. When did you start? What have you used? How much and how often have you used? What has been your usage over the past year?

6. Describe your school history. Did/do you like school? What was the last grade you completed? What were your interests and activities? How were your grades?

7. Describe the friends you have had as a child, adolescent, and adult. Have you had a best friend? What has this person been like? What has your dating experience been like? What kind of people have interested you romantically?

8. If you are married or have a live-in relationship, describe the situation. Tell about your children.

9. Describe your job history. What jobs have you had, and which ones have you especially liked?

10. How do you spend your free time? Describe any special hobbies, talents, or interests that you have. Describe which of these makes you particularly proud.

11. Describe the history of your self-injury. When did it start? What sort of self-injury has occurred? How often and how severe has the injury been? What seems to prompt the urge to self-injure?

12. What have been the happiest moments in your life so far? What have been the unhappiest?

13. Include any other information you feel will help others—your

therapist and any other people on your recovery team—get to know and understand you.

Assignment Two: "How do I see myself?"

Rationale: The purpose of this assignment is for you to identify your strengths and weaknesses. It is important that you acknowledge both positive and negative traits and decide which ones enhance your ability to cope and which ones cause difficulties. By sharing this assignment with others, you can get feedback about whether your perceptions seem accurate.

You may also use this assignment to prioritize your good and bad points and to size up how your personality traits help or hinder your goal of stopping self-injury.

Questions:

1. What am I like as a person—emotionally, intellectually, in manner and behavior?
2. What roles do I play, and how do I feel about them? For instance, as an adult man/woman, a student, employee, wife/husband, lover, mother/father, daughter/son, sister/brother, etc.
3. What are my particular strengths and weaknesses as a person? Which characteristics do I want to change for sure, and which ones would I never change?
4. Identify the patterns that are repeated in the roles you play.

Assignment Three: The female most influential to me

Rationale: This assignment is meant to identify the woman who has figured most prominently in your life—whether it is your mother, another caregiver, or someone else entirely—and to identify ways in which this woman has influenced the development of your character. The assignment should be used to explore ways that this relationship could be used to overcome self-injurious behavior. Alternatively, if the relationship is one that undermines your recovery progress, you can use the writing task and the thought behind it to explore the best ways of negotiating the relationship.

Questions:

1. Describe this woman.
2. What about her is most significant to you?
3. Has her influence on you been mostly positive or negative?
4. How does she react to your problem of self-injury?

Assignment Four: The male most influential to me

Rationale: The purpose of this assignment is to identify ways in which this man influenced the development of your character. How can you enlist this person to help you solve your problems? Or, if you do not believe he can be helpful to you, how can you handle the relationship in a way that will not thwart recovery?
Questions:

1. Describe this man
2. What about him is most significant to you?
3. Has his influence on you been mostly positive or negative?
4. How does he react to your problem of self-injury?

Assignment Five: The emotions surrounding self-injury

Rationale: This assignment is meant to help you become more aware of the emotional dynamics involved in your self-injurious behavior. The ability to identify the feelings or thoughts that lead up to an episode of self-harm can help you conquer the behavior by placing its origins in the proper context. This type of self-awareness will help lead you to begin thinking and analyzing yourself and your motives before taking action against your body.
Questions:

1. What feelings and fantasies do I typically have prior to, during, and after an episode of self-injury?
2. What feelings have I wanted to create in others through this?
3. What feelings do I elicit from others, even if I don't intend to?

Assignment Six: The anger inside me

Rationale: The purpose of this assignment is to better understand your anger so that you can develop the ability to manage and tolerate

it effectively. Viewing your angry feelings with sympathy and accep
tance—e.g., "It's okay to get angry, everybody does"—can help contribute to your self-esteem and your control over impulses.
Questions:

1. What situations seem to evoke my anger most frequently?
2. What does becoming angry feel like? What kinds of thoughts
   arise once I'm aware that I'm angry? Am I afraid of others seeing
   my anger?
3. What do I need to learn about handling my anger?

Assignment Seven: "What I can't stand about the people in my life"

Rationale: Difficult, conflicted relationships—and the sustained anger they generate—contribute greatly toward self-injurious behavior. By
making these conflicts and the anger or resentment they cause more
explicit, you can begin to take steps toward facing these feelings in a
more constructive way.
Questions:

1. Identify the person or people.
2. Describe in detail the conflicts and disliked behaviors.
3. When do you feel more satisfied with this person or these people?
4. What are some possible strategies for improving these relationships or dealing with the conflict more directly?

Assignment Eight: Compensation for life's injuries

Rationale: Unrecognized hurt, abuse, and victimization may foster
self-injurious behavior. Identifying these sorrows is the first step toward
having empathy for oneself and toward developing strategies that will
help you feel empowered. This is a particularly popular assignment
among our patients, many of whom have had troubled childhoods and
feel the pain they experienced has never been properly acknowledged,
and that the perpetrators have gone unpunished.
Questions:

1. Identify ways in which you have been hurt, abused, or victimized.
2. In what ways has this harm been acknowledged or recognized by others?
3. What compensation or recognition do you *imagine* would really make up for those injuries? Include punishments and revenge you imagine.
4. What compensation or recognition that is *actually available* would make you feel at least a little repaid?

Assignment Nine: Nurturing myself

Rationale: The purpose of this assignment is to develop self-soothing behavior, which can divert you from self-injury and promote self-esteem. Many self-injurers say they have trouble nurturing themselves because they don't believe they "deserve" it. Thus, they have often failed to develop habits or strategies for consciously trying to alleviate grief.

Questions:

1. Describe the ways in which you take care of yourself and give yourself a lift—special ways to feel good.
2. What, if anything, keeps you from nurturing yourself more often?

Ways Our Patients Nurture Themselves

Susan L.

1. Hot baths
2. Listen to music (Elton John!)
3. Sing
4. Play with nieces and nephews
5. Talk to friends
6. Think about special people
7. Pray
8. Go to church
9. Hugs
10. Watch favorite TV sitcoms
11. Take a short nap

Rosa G.

1. Get a massage
2. Take a walk in the arboretum or go to a park
3. Take a bath
4. Call a friend
5. Go to t'ai ch'i class
6. Go to the movies
7. Give or get a hug
8. Go to church
9. Primp
10. Take time to prepare healthy meals
11. Use heating pad on lower back
12. Play my guitar
13. Do something creative or artistic
14. Hold my cats
15. Eat ice cream

Assignment Ten: A time I was comfortable in someone else's presence

Rationale: This assignment can help you identify the factors necessary to allow you to feel comfortable with another person, thus to build relationships. The ability to draw greater comfort from other people will enhance your self-esteem and decrease inner turmoil and loneliness.

Questions:

1. Describe in detail a time when you felt comfortable just being with another person.
2. Include as many details and specific memories about that time as you can, to highlight what the necessary ingredients are.

Assignment Eleven: The person I want to be

Rationale: The purpose of this assignment is to identify positive goals and personality characteristics that you want to achieve or enhance.

Setting goals for giving up self-injury involves adding new thoughts, behaviors, interests, and gratifications to replace the old symptoms.
Questions:

1. How do I want my life to be?
2. Identify attitudes, feelings, and behaviors that interfere with making progress toward this goal.

Assignment Twelve (for women): "How I feel about being a woman"

Rationale: Negative thoughts about gender and gender identity can contribute to self-hatred and self-destruction. On the other hand, making positive appraisals of gender identity can contribute to self-esteem. This assignment aims to help you analyze and break down any negative thoughts, preconceptions, or myths you may have about your gender and replace them with more helpful paradigms.
Questions:

1. What feelings and ideas do I have about being a woman? Include feelings about your body and size as well as your psychological attributes.
2. Do I attribute greater ability, competence, or adequacy to men?
3. What aspects of womanhood do I find discouraging or unappreciated? Which aspects do I find positive or rewarding?

Assignment Twelve (for men): "How I feel about being a man"

Questions:

1. What thoughts and feelings do I have about being a man? Include thoughts and feelings about body and size as well as psychological attributes.
2. What ideals of manhood do I find discouraging or hard to appreciate?
3. What ideals of manhood do I find discouraging or unappreciated? Which do I find positive and rewarding?

Assignment Thirteen: Saying good-bye to self-injury

Rationale: This assignment will help you understand that self-injurious behavior has become a way to define yourself—a negative way. Saying good-bye to this behavior as you give it up will make way for new and more positive definitions of yourself to evolve.
Questions:

1. How do I imagine my life will be without this behavior?
2. What will I miss about my old ways?
3. What new definitions do I want to apply to myself now?

Assignment Fourteen: What I have learned about myself through these assignments

Rationale: The purpose of this assignment is to accept that knowledge is the path that leads to change. Understanding your internal motivations will help you make more conscious and helpful choices.
Questions:

1. What is the most important thing I learned about myself from these writing assignments?
2. What is the most unpleasant discovery I made about myself?
3. What is the most surprising thing I learned?

Assignment Fifteen: Future plans

Rationale: Making plans for the future will give you a goal structure that directs your thoughts, productivity, and growth. By setting reasonable, attainable goals, you can channel your energy toward positive accomplishments and find ways to boost your self-esteem on a regular basis. Do make sure that the goals are modest, since setting unachievable hurdles will guarantee failure and self-recrimination.
Questions:

1. Make a list of concrete, specific goals you can accomplish monthly for the next six months. The goals can pertain to your

personal development, your professional or therapeutic development, or any other area you would like to work on.

2. Describe where you see yourself in five years.

One Patient's List of Goals

Donna W.

Month one: Contact consumer credit counseling to ask for help in managing medical bills.

Month two: Contact America Online about creating a message board for S.A.F.E. Alternatives.

Month three: Send Christmas cards and letters to everyone on my Christmas list.

Month four: Revise my resume and begin looking for a new job

Month five: Join a Christian singles group to make new friends

Month six: Celebrate six-month anniversary of being injury-free and one year anniversary of being sober.

KEEPING A JOURNAL

Depending on how you feel about writing—love it, hate it—you and your therapist may decide it makes sense for you to keep a daily (or regular) diary of your thoughts, feelings, and experiences along with the Impulse Control Logs and writing assignments you are already filling out.

A journal can be very helpful. It lets you chronicle your life, organize your thoughts, and vent your feelings and reactions to people and events. But we do have one warning about journals: they can be misused. Some self-injurers use "journaling" in punitive and self-destructive ways, writing over and over again that they're fat, ugly, stupid. In a heightened state of emotion a patient might use the journal to give in to her negative thoughts without any attempt to challenge them. Or she might give in to unbridled rage, in which she graphically depicts the violent fantasies of destruction swirling in her head.

If you find yourself using your journal as another weapon against yourself, put it aside. It would be far more productive to challenge your thoughts and try to understand why the reaction you're having seems so very big. You should view your journal as an educational aid, one that helps you document experiences and reach epiphanies. It is not a tool you should use to beat yourself up psychologically.

SPECIAL WRITING ASSIGNMENTS

Writing assignments that are specific to your situation or experiences can help you make sense of your psychological condition. There may be significant events from your past that don't fit the mold of our prescribed writing assignments and that might benefit from independent exploration. Or a special writing topic might be as seemingly mundane as something you did recently that was out of the ordinary.

For example, when a patient does something different on a weekend—goes on a trip, meets a new person, does something adventurous—we often encourage her to write about it, something along the lines of "Ten things I learned this weekend." If a patient has an encounter with someone who stirs difficult feelings—a parent, for instance, or a sibling—we might ask her to write about that experience too, parsing the emotions that transpired before, during, and after the encounter.

STEP 4: CREATING THE WINDOW OF OPPORTUNITY

Sometimes we surprise our patients by telling them that the act of self-injury itself is not their biggest problem. Everyone in the group gives us a quizzical look. We tell them that the real problems are the thoughts that come to mind before the act, thoughts that lead to the injury. These thoughts are often a mixture of the rational and irrational, healthy thoughts and distorted ones.

Self-injurers often have a sense of how their thoughts might be inaccurate or distorted. If someone thinks, "I'm a bad person because

I failed the math test," she might then have two supplemental thoughts. One would be: "I'm going to hurt myself to prove what a bad person I am and to show how terrible I feel about the failure." The other thought might be, "I'm having trouble in math class right now, so maybe I need some extra help from the teacher or some tutoring." Guess which thought is likely to sabotage the other?

The window of opportunity is the time in between the *impulse* to self-injure and the *act* of injury. For most self-injurers at the beginning of treatment, this is a very narrow strip of time indeed. They plunge headlong into the act, often without even being aware of what they are feeling or reacting to. Their thoughts and feelings often do not rise to the level of their conscious awareness, and this starts the downward spiral into injury. The point is to place a barrier between the difficult thought—"I'm bad for failing at math"—and the injury. Whether or not the sympathetic and healthy thought already exists in the injurer's mind—"I'm not a bad person, I just didn't understand this particular material"—the idea is to place the thought there and to get it listened to once it is there.

The self-injurer needs to understand that the wish to harm herself is not a feeling—it is a thought in response to a feeling. The statement "I feel like injuring myself" is an indicator, or signal, that you are experiencing an intolerable feeling: anger, misery, worthlessness, emptiness, loneliness. Being able to understand the difference between a feeling and a thought is important, as is the ability to understand the process that translates a feeling—for example, "I feel lonely"—into a thought—"I want to burn my skin"—into an action—burning. When you are caught in a repeating cycle of destructive thinking and behavior, there is no time to slow down, figure anything out, or cope. There is no room in this cycle for anyone to intervene or for any dialogue to take place.

Your goal throughout recovery is to increase the window of opportunity between the urge and the action that follows. In this space you can identify your feelings, find help, and cope in alternative ways. The first step is to begin viewing the urge to self-injure as a signal, something that points to something else, like painful feelings. Once the feelings are identified, you can begin to understand why they are there and talk them out with someone. You can also engage in an alternative behavior to alleviate the intensity of the feeling and the desire to self-harm.

The desired goal is to go from the noxious feeling (sad, lonely) to the tense thought ("I hate the way I look") to the urge to act ("I want to cut myself") to the coping strategy ("I think I'll take a walk instead; then I'll call my best friend on the telephone").

One thing to keep in mind as you are working to create this window is that you cannot lean on other people to open it for you. While you can and should seek help from the people you trust, you shouldn't expect them to keep you from harming yourself. If you do, you are falling into the rescue trap. You can't just call someone and expect her to fix it.

A typical fix-me conversation might go like this: The self-injurer calls up her best friend and says, "I feel like hurting myself." The friend says, "Why?" The self-injurer says, "I don't know." The person on the other line is left trying to decide what to do next. Your friend feels worried, guilty, scared, and helpless, and you feel that she had better do something to help you, or else she's not your real friend.

What if you called her instead and said, "I'm feeling overwhelmed, and I'm not sure what it's about or where it's coming from, but I know I want to hurt myself to make myself stop feeling it"? Now your friend has more information to work with—more avenues to explore. She could say, "Well, what was going on when you thought you wanted to hurt yourself? What were you doing?" You might remember that the thought occurred when you got some bad news in the mail or started thinking about the breakup with your boyfriend. Now you and your friend have a lot of material to work with, and there's a much better chance that you can have a meaningful conversation about your feelings and, hopefully, can hang up the phone feeling better.

REVIEWING PROGRESS AND MOVING FORWARD

Once you have set up your Toolbox, you are ready to take the steps that will lead to ceasing your self-destructive behavior.

First, you have prepared yourself by becoming truly convinced that self-injury is something you would like to get rid of. That does not necessarily mean you think you can live without it—you may still think it is something you need.

Next, you have signed a relevant contract and devised a list of appealing alternative activities. You have begun keeping an Impulse Control Log and have tackled the first writing assignment or two. You have a trusted therapist and/or a network of people to turn to in times of crisis.

With this structure and these supports in place, you are ready to grasp the most basic principle of recovering from self-injury—that in order to get better, one must stop injuring. Before one can stop injuring, one must create a barrier between the impulse to injure and the action itself. At first this barrier can simply be a pause.

Pausing between thought and action is one of the most critical skills a self-injurer can teach herself. The pause allows you to consider your alternatives and to reflect—however fleetingly—on the feelings that are driving your potential actions. If the S.A.F.E. tools give you as much as a moment's hesitation before wielding a weapon against yourself, then you have successfully opened a window of opportunity against self-injury. With time this window will grow wider, as you discover the reasons behind your behavior, the emotions driving you. One discovery leads to another, and gradually the window opens. As you continue your work, the likelihood exists that it will remain open, never to shut again. Refraining from self-injury feeds on itself much the way destructive behavior does, and people who learn to abstain are so proud of their achievement that they are motivated to continue.

By deciding against a single act of self-injury—even by pausing once to reconsider—you have begun your journey to recovery in a real and concrete way.

STEP 5: DEEPER ANALYSIS

After you have been adhering to the S.A.F.E. program for a short time—using all the tools in your kit and striving to create and prolong your windows of opportunity—you are ready for deeper analysis of the problems and feelings that have led to your behavior.

After a while without self-injury (even a week), you can look back on your journal entries and Impulse Control Logs and begin to see patterns. You and your therapist should work on identifying these patterns: when you feel most prone to self-injure, under what circumstances, what the thought processes are that lead to the impulse. Do you tend to feel more anxious at night? When you are alone? Before mealtimes?

Going over the log with a therapist can be particularly enlightening, helping you see patterns you may have overlooked, suggesting additional coping strategies, helping you prepare for difficult times. The therapist is also there to offer praise and encouragement for the hard work you have done. Now that you are no longer using self-injury to medicate your problems, you have a clearer head and are more receptive to exploring your psychological issues.

To keep track of what is working and what is not, your daily journal is particularly helpful. By reviewing log and journal entries, our patients often find that they do in fact see growth in their thinking and in managing their impulses. Recognizing this growth helps them retain the lessons they have learned so that challenging thoughts about self-injury becomes an intuitive process.

Once you have begun to grow in self-awareness, you should set aside a consistent time every day to review your writing and answer questions. For instance, in a daily journal you might:

1. Record feelings and thoughts over the course of the day.
2. Record reactions to people and events and activities, particularly your feelings about interactions with people.
3. Describe any intense, highly charged, or uncomfortable feelings in as much detail as possible.

At a designated time each evening you might then begin to ask yourself:

1. What did I learn about myself today?
2. What seemed useful to me?
3. Who or what stirred up conflict, or feelings of being misunderstood?
4. When did I feel most at ease and "myself" during the day?
5. What goals can I think of for tomorrow?

Once the self-examination process is under way, you must continuously try to hone your skill at something we call "challenging distorted thinking." Self-injurers tend to see their problems in global and cata-strophic ways—it's a style commonly referred to as black-or-white or all-or-nothing. The patient traps herself with terms like *always*, *never*, and *no one*. Thinking this way, she feels panicked—there seem to be no options, no solutions—and her fears escalate quickly into out-of-control behavior.

Your goal is to be cognizant of the statements you make to yourself, and to challenge why you are thinking that way. If you think, "I never do anything right," then you must challenge that sentence, because the word never is in it. If you think, "Nobody likes me—I am unlovable," then you must challenge that thought too.

One way is for you to first ask yourself, "Why am I thinking this way about myself right at this very moment?" By categorizing the thought as something you are thinking under a certain circumstance, you can analyze your emotions and try to clear away part of the distortion.

Here are some suggestions for breaking down absolute thinking:

- Ask yourself what you would say to your best friend if he or she gave voice to the same thought you're having, like "I'm so stupid" or "I never do anything right." If you're with a trusted person, run your thought by her to see if she considers it to be all-or-nothing. If she says yes, trust her, then discuss other ways of expressing the emotions behind the thought.
- If you are by yourself, write a list of objective appraisals of what you are thinking. For example: in a column called "Distorted thinking," you could write: "I'm a bad person for feeling angry." In a column called "Realistic alternative," you could write: "I'm not a bad person for feeling angry. I'm human." A good rule of thumb would be to remember that most unhealthy and unrealistic thoughts reside at extreme ends of the continuum. Healthier thoughts generally lie somewhere in the middle.
- Explore what you may be getting out of thinking in absolutes. Does this way of thinking hold you back or let you move forward?
- Ask yourself if someone you like and trust would want you to be thinking in absolutes. If your answer is yes, explain it, and if your answer is no, explain that. Show your answers to a trusted person and see if she agrees with you.

Once you become more aware of your reactions to daily events, you will grow more adept at intepreting them and less inclined to turn to self-injury as a reflexive response to stress or confusion. This new level of awareness will lay the groundwork for the next step of your recovery.

STEP 6: EXPERIENCING FEELINGS

Self-injury is a way of displacing the feelings in your head onto your body. Active self-injurers usually cannot tolerate being alone with their feelings and tend to act out instead of examining what is uncomfortable. The ability to just sit and let feelings wash over you is a strong sign of recovery.

Self-injurers say they need to harm themselves in order to "get it out"—meaning their feelings. Feelings don't have to be gotten rid of. In fact, they are valuable clues about things that need to be looked at, resolved, worked through. Without our strongest feelings available to us, we are clueless about how we need to respond and adapt.

Until you become more aware of the true issues underlying your behavior, you are likely to continue harming yourself. Once you feel capable of being alone with your feelings and holding onto them—no matter how upsetting they may be—you are recovering.

Try this sample lesson in learning to experience feeling injury-free:

Start by telling yourself that feelings won't kill you. Then tell yourself that it is okay not to like how you are feeling. Remind yourself that feelings are not good or bad, just comfortable or uncomfortable. Remember it is your global thinking that scares you, so stay with the feelings and thoughts that are manageable.

Find a place where you can experience your feelings. Try crying, writing, reflecting, and having sympathetic thoughts for yourself. If you are angry, write about what is evoking your anger.

LISTENING AND COMMUNICATING

Learning how to communicate what is going on—verbally and in writing—is a key skill for self-injurers. It allows you, often for the first time, to accept the support and help of other people. This type of help is far more meaningful and empowering than the type of self-medication you have been engaging in through self-harm.

Another aspect of the art of communication is the ability to listen to what another person is saying through a distortion-free lens. It is often extremely difficult for self-injurers to hear what is being said to them. When someone—a therapist, support person, friend, colleague—suggests she look at her behavior and what it is doing to her, this sounds like a criticism. She is feeling so defensive about her actions that she fails to hear the concern or caring that someone else might have. Empathy is a foreign experience to her, and she rules it out straightaway. Instead of responding in a way that could evoke sympathy or forge a human connection, the self-injurer is likely to brush aside the comment or counter with a hostile one. Like a lion with a thorn in his paw who roars at all around him, the self-injurer is unable to let anyone get close enough to help alleviate the pain.

Over and over again we have seen how a self-injurer's world opens up for her when she learns to listen and communicate. Self-injurers are notorious for deflecting questions and inquiries. "I don't know" or "It doesn't matter" is the automatic response to any query. When a self-injurer responds this way, she is sending herself tacit messages. The messages are, "I'm stupid. What I have to say doesn't matter. Nobody cares about me, and anybody I tell my true thoughts to will laugh and humiliate me."

Learning to challenge deeply held assumptions and thinking patterns is one of the most difficult requirements for recovery from self-injury. It takes a lot of reinforcement and a lot of talking and writing to brush away the stubbornly lingering damage of an abusive or unhappy childhood. But it can be done. Though you may have persistently been disappointed and hurt by people in the past, you *can* learn to trust and confide—it is vital to your health and happiness.

STEP 7: PLANNING FOR AN INJURY-FREE LIFE

Every day and week that you abstain from self-injury, you will become that much more confident and proud. The deeper you get into the

S.A.F.E. program, the more that living without self injury will seem like a tangible reality.

S.A.F.E. is designed with progress in mind. Writing assignments grow more intense and personal with time. The psychological exploration that patients are called on to do—on their own and with others—grows deeper and more sophisticated. The insights patients gain tend to be more valuable after they have completed the program's exercises and writing assignments.

It's hard to gauge when someone has "recovered" from self-injury, and often the patient herself can't be entirely sure. But if at least a month has gone by in which you have lived injury-free, complied with the terms of your contract, used all the tools in your S.A.F.E. Toolkit, and learned to turn to others for help, you are ready to begin planning for your new, injury-free life.

We are not suggesting that you should abandon any of the coping mechanisms you have learned through S.A.F.E.—you should hold on to them and continue for as long as they seem helpful. But we recommend specific exercises to get people mentally prepared for the next stage of life, in which combating self-injury will, with luck, be less of a challenge and no longer a central focus of attention. Here are the three Exit steps:

1. *Bid good-bye to self-injury.* When you and your therapist feel you are ready to move on with your life, it is time to find a way to say farewell to your former habit in some meaningful, symbolic way. Though the writing assignment that addresses this topic is a helpful start, often there are other ways that will make your new beginning seem more real and immediate. For instance, you can start by imagining what life will be like without this behavior, if there is anything you will miss about your old ways, and what "new definitions" you can apply to yourself now that you are no longer a self-injurer. Write down at least three thoughts in each category.

2. *Make a list of goals.* Since you no longer need to spend so much time and energy fighting self-injury, you need to identify other things that will help you move forward with your life. We ask patients to make a list of concrete goals they feel they can accomplish monthly for the next six months—career goals, thera-

peutic goals, personal goals. By making modest achievements on a regular basis, you can continue feeling the success you felt when every day was a struggle against self-injury. Make sure the goals are not too ambitious, so you don't set yourself up for failure.

3. *Identify trusted others.* To ensure you will have help in times of crisis, you must compile a list of people to turn to for help and advice. These may be the same people who helped during recovery, or they may be a wider group of people who may not necessarily have been appropriate as confidantes during the recovery period, but whose trust may now be enlisted.

R E L A P S E

We believe relapse is a process. Someone doesn't just impulsively injure after a period of wellness. In our experience, recidivism typically occurs when someone is under unusual stress, and usually there is a wide window of opportunity for intervention. A person probably won't injure until she has been distressed and upset about something for hours; she may begin to isolate herself and refuse to process what is really going on inside her. When asked how she is doing, she usually says, "Fine," even though she is aware that she is anything but fine and is struggling over whether to injure. The main theme in relapse prevention is to identify the struggles and make choices *before* the crisis has progressed to such an advanced level.

You must keep a handle on your tendency to fall into old traps or revert to negative patterns in relationships. The process of change and growth is difficult and not easily trusted at first. The recovered self-injurer may sabotage herself to express her anxiety. Frightened of change, she may cling to unhealthy coping mechanisms, which, ironically, feel the least dangerous. She may at first want to call someone who's healthy, but may wind up choosing someone who is hurtful to her. Other acts that set people up for relapse more directly include tampering with medication, refusing support that *is* offered, failing to take care of health and body to maintain stamina, or failing to comply with therapy recommendations.

Since the S.A.F.E. approach encourages you to abandon the idea that a disease is driving your actions, you are left to contend with your personal responsibility in maintaining control. During recovery, then, the task is to identify what choices you might make that would put you at risk for relapse.

Many people don't realize that they have set themselves up for relapse until the act of injury is done, but we believe that people can pick up on signals beforehand. Attentive use of S.A.F.E. tools will help self-injurers and their therapists attend to those signals.

Relapse circumstances generally fall into two categories:

1. The person may leave or complete a treatment program without having anticipated the stressors that lie ahead. She winds up feeling blindsided by events that she might have prepared for. At S.A.F.E. we always say that "the best ammunition is anticipation."
2. The person may put herself in a situation that inevitably will lead to relapse. She may seek out the company of people whom she knows are self-injuring. She may isolate herself when she knows that solitude is difficult for her to bear. She may take on unbelievable amounts of work or actively place herself in situations that she knows are stressful to her.

To avert relapse, we suggest several exercises. These include:

1. Anticipation and preparation are the best interventions against relapse. Anticipation begins with identifying experiences in your past that stimulated episodes of self-injuring. Think about situations, events, interactions, music, changes, feelings, thoughts, smells, voices, celebrations, etc. Write down all these situations. List the reasons you gave yourself permission to injure, and see how many of these reasons still seem valid to you. Try to think if there was something different you could have done instead of self-injure, listing as many scenarios as possible.

   This data gathering helps you grow in self-awareness, which in turn prepares you to feel less ambushed by trigger situations. Mapping out your coping options in advance makes you feel more in control, less victimized.
2. If you usually have little or no memory of injuring, try looking at your state of mind during the twenty-four hours prior to self-

injuring. Do you see any patterns, like being aware of feeling more stress, conflict, certain feelings/thoughts, etc.? Do you notice that you usually end up self-injuring when you are around certain people or in certain situations? If so, try to begin dealing with each of the conflicts at the time of your awareness of them. Don't wait until discomfort escalates to panic. Daily logs can help you identify patterns and defuse situations before they reach crisis proportions.

3. If you tend to get up to injure in the middle of the night or after you have fallen asleep, securing your home before bedtime can help. Try replacing the injuring objects at your night table with pen and paper, drawing materials, cups of water to drink, Impulse Control Logs, a list of your alternatives, or a handful of telephone numbers. Get in the habit of seeing and using all these alternatives throughout the day and night so that you can establish a new, healthier, and eventually familiar routine. Many patients at S.A.F.E. have said that one reason they self-injured was because the ritual became so familiar to them, and the familiarity was comforting.

At S.A.F.E. we run an outpatient relapse group for people who have graduated from our program. It is quite different from the regular S.A.F.E. sessions because the focus of attention is no longer on stopping the behavior. The central question becomes, "How should I handle such and such situation that has just come up in my life now that I'm trying to do it without self-injury?" In a relapse group it's assumed that self-injury is no longer the automatic response to all of life's challenges, even though members may continue to struggle with and talk about urges from time to time.

Recovered self-injurers are far less fragile than people who are still undergoing recovery. They can take a joke, talk easily with others, accept gestures of friendship. Victoria R., who attends S.A.F.E. relapse groups faithfully, describes the experience this way:

"We do a lot of working through of whatever is going on in our lives and get feedback, but you're dealing with different issues once you have gone through the program. A lot of us have cleaned up certain parts of our lives, so there's not as much focus on the basic abuse issues.

"People also are really accountable in that group. One girl was complaining about the same problem week after week, so I told her to 'grow up.' I said it was time for her to get rid of the problem and move on. She laughed—she took it the right way. People will say stuff like that, stuff they never would have said while we were still working to get rid of self-injury."

Chapter Eighteen

OUR PATIENTS' EXPERIENCES WITH S.A.F.E.

L iz C. is shaking her head with a wry smile. "I can spew off all the philosophy I learned at S.A.F.E.," she says with a light cackle. "The program works, but you have to work the program."

Liz went from being a constant self-injurer to someone who does not injure most of the time. A year out of the program, she continues to use the S.A.F.E. tools. "I'm the queen of Impulse Control Logs," she says. "I find them to be very useful because I really examine what it is that I'm trying to get out of it."

Like many patients, Liz said the No-Harm Contract was the toughest stipulation. "It was really hard to sign," she said. "I had to look really deep within myself to commit to the program, but I'm glad I did."

Amanda B., a thirty-three-year-old kindergarten teacher, said the No-Harm Contract wasn't a problem for her because she felt so motivated to shed the behavior. "It had gotten to the point where I was self-injuring so often and getting so depressed that I couldn't go to work, and I was feeling very guilty—which led to more injury. It was a vicious cycle."

Shortly after graduating from S.A.F.E., Amanda still kept a folder of Impulse Control Logs tucked in her bag wherever she went. "I anticipate after a few months I won't need to carry it everywhere. I will just know it's there if the urges get too intense."

Almost a year out of the program, recovered self-injurer Susan L. still uses Impulse Control Logs too. "They have really made a difference," Susan says. "They slow me down and make me think. When I think about the consequences of self-injury—guilt, shame, hopelessness, anger—I know I don't want that anymore."

For Yvonne K., filling out logs has led to psychological discoveries. "Through my Impulse Control Log I've learned that I want people to respond to me with attention," she says. "I never thought I needed attention, because I didn't have any when I was a child, so I figured I don't need it now. I was wrong, though. My self-injury forced people to respond to me with some type of attention—a nurse in the E.R., my friends, or a doctor stitching me up."

Some patients who are ending their journey at S.A.F.E. fear the loss of the support from the treatment team and may struggle harder with urges right before they leave. For Susan L., it was the perception that her two S.A.F.E. therapists had "abandoned" her by going home at the end of the workday. While she knew intellectually that everyone has to go home after work, she felt inside that they were leaving her in the lurch, as so many supposedly caring people had done in the past.

The day Susan nearly self-injured at S.A.F.E., she had attended a group session during which she talked about how her father had emotionally neglected her by ignoring her mother's abusive behavior and withholding affection and approval. By nightfall "I was in my room crying and wanted to cut," she recalls. "I went to the lamp and unscrewed the bulb and threw it at the bathroom wall. I was going to find the sharpest piece."

Then Susan's window of opportunity kicked in. Instead of cutting, she found a S.A.F.E. staff member to talk to and wrote in her journal. The urge finally passed. Susan felt immensely proud.

"I felt hopeless—I had such pain inside," she says. "I was lying in my bed and feeling like my heart had been ripped out. I chose to use my *old* behavior—I almost gave in. I realized I broke the bulb—but I didn't cut.

"The progress I've made since I've been here has amazed me," she wrote in her probation assignment. "Breaking the bulb but not cutting with it was the hardest choice I've ever made. If it had not been for the ounce of confidence I've gained or the staff's encouragement, I could never have made that choice.

"In the future," she concludes, "I will make different choices. Before I let the feelings overtake me, I will find someone, get a hug, talk to someone, write in my journal, or pray harder. I have learned that I can feel angry without self-abuse. I have never had this much confidence in myself."

Susan—a victim of severe child abuse who had self-injured almost every day for thirty-three years—is now living a productive and injury-free life. She is employed and has a boyfriend. "I have felt feelings that six months ago would have led to self-injury," she says. "My life is free of emergency rooms. No more scars. I have peace of mind. I can have a husband and a baby. No more psychiatric wards. I feel worthy of God's love."

As their recoveries proceed, our patients usually find themselves relying on the S.A.F.E. tools less and less. This takes place unconsciously. One day someone will wake up and realize she neglected to fill out an Impulse Control Log the day before, then momentarily feel guilty, then suddenly swell with pride realizing that she didn't fill out the log because she didn't feel the need to. Self-injury has receded to the back of her consciousness and continues to ebb as she carries on her successful new life.

Chapter Nineteen

SUCCESS

W̶e can never tell which of our patients are going to recover and which ones seem unable—or unwilling—to get better. We have seen people with the most egregious cases of self-injury make full recoveries, and we have seen people with comparatively mild cases linger with the behavior, unable to shed it.

Recovery from self-injury seems not to correlate directly to the severity or frequency of the symptoms. It seems to have a lot to do with willpower, determination, and faith in the treatment program. In that context, we have identified three factors that make significant contributions to recovery:

1. Motivation
2. A willingness to look at oneself openly and honestly
3. The presence of an ongoing context of support, which helps the patient continue to strive toward healthy behavior
4. Rigorous pursuit of after care, including following through with one's therapeutic plan, being willing to use all the tools of recovery one has learned, and diligently maintaining a relationship with one's therapist and other care providers

Some people do relapse, but the good news is that once someone has been able to contain her self-injurious behavior for a while and has begun an earnest struggle with the distorted thinking and emotional issues beneath it, the intensity and frequency of the urges to injure diminish. "It's not like alcoholism, where you have to get up every morning and say, 'Today's another day when I won't drink,' " says Nora A., a recovered self-injurer. "I haven't had an urge or impulse for five or six years now."

Among the categories of people with whom S.A.F.E. Alternatives has had the most success are young people, who have had less time to develop a fixed, intractable self-injury pattern and whose minds may be more open. We have also had considerable success with extremely severe self-injurers, possibly because their lives and relationships have become so profoundly damaged by the behavior that they are eager, willing, and at times desperate to embrace any hope for a better life.

Jane O.

Jane O. had the most frequent and severe case of self-injury that we had ever seen. She was thirty-nine when she arrived at S.A.F.E., and since age thirteen had not lived a day of her life without self-injury. Everything looked like a weapon to her.

We first met her when she flew to our treatment center from her home in New Mexico. She arrived with third-degree chemical burns on her arms, cigarette burns dotting her body, razor-blade slashes running mazelike over her limbs, and a blood-alcohol level four times over the legal limit of intoxication. During her airplane ride Jane had overdosed on alcohol and prescription medication. We brought her directly to the hospital emergency room, questioning if she would survive the drinking binge, let alone make it through our program.

Jane started hurting herself when she was four years old, when she would burn herself with matches and stab her thigh with scissors. The youngest daughter of a short-order cook and a telephone operator, Jane was close to her sister, who was two years older, but not to her brother, who was ten years older.

Jane describes her family as having a very strong work ethic. Her mother worked days in an office and nights as a waitress. Her father often came home exhausted from the long hours he would put in at an all-night diner. Jane routinely slept in the same bed with her father, whom she idolized. Jane called him Hercules because he was so strong, and she wanted to grow up to be just like him. Some of her fondest childhood memories were of helping him cook elaborate dinners on the weekends.

Jane remembers being left alone a lot as a child. From an early age she and her sister would fend for themselves—for meals, entertainment, and self-care—while their parents worked long hours. When their mother was home, she was often irascible and subjected the children to frequent beatings, for reasons seldom disclosed. By the time Jane was five—and continuing throughout adulthood—she began fantasizing about her mother's beatings and finding pleasure in the daydream. Jane explained this by saying, "Some attention is better than no attention at all."

Jane's family had a summer house in the mountains, and she and her brother were often left there alone for long periods of time. The children befriended a young family that lived nearby, and the family kept an eye on them when the parents were absent. Beginning in the summer of her fifth year, the father of this family began sexually molesting Jane. That same summer Jane's sister, who was seven, turned on the stove and accidentally started a fire. She was engulfed in flames and ultimately suffered third-degree burns; while her sister tried to flee the fire, Jane ran to get help, but was unable to locate her parents.

Home life began to grow even more difficult as Jane progressed through grade school. Her parents would argue loudly, and Jane was aware of her mother's adulterous relationship with a close friend of the family. The beatings continued, as did Jane's self-abuse. At age eight Jane began cutting herself with razor blades and other sharp implements. As she remembers, the overwhelming feeling during these early bouts was a yearning to be noticed and to gain her parents' attention.

When Jane was ten, she fell asleep with her parents in their bed. Her father sexually molested her while her mother lay asleep next to her. Jane pretended she was asleep and eventually left their room. She did not tell anyone what happened—indeed, it was only recently that she acquired the language necessary to express what happened. Until her treatment at S.A.F.E. she had been unable to talk about the abuse and to feel the emotions that accompanied the memories.

Even as a child who lacked the language to express her feelings,

Jane had a firm, visceral feeling that she was to blame for her father's actions, that it was her fault for having been in bed with him. Accepting that the abuse was not her fault would have meant blaming her father and losing her idol, and Jane was not willing to do that. Her self-injury escalated. When she was fifteen, her father was diagnosed with liver disease and began dying a slow death. Jane responded by supplementing self-injury with substance abuse. By age sixteen she was an alcoholic and a drug addict. Her father died when she was eighteen.

As the years passed, Jane's self-injury worsened and took on new forms: restricting food, purging, shoplifting, over-exercising, sexual promiscuity, prostitution. Cutting, burning, drinking, and drugs were her mainstays. Despite her behavior Jane managed to attend college and hold down a job, though she tells us she was unable to perform at school or at work without injuring or getting high. She earned a master's degree in business, tutored children at a local high school, and graduated with honors. After graduate school Jane joined a business consulting firm.

But Jane's problems did not subside and ultimately forced her to resign from her job. At age twenty-seven she entered her first treatment program for alcohol and drug abuse, marking the beginning of what was to be a long and anguished relationship with the mental health system.

Before coming to us, Jane had had more than forty hospitalizations. Her early treatments generally focused on her substance-abuse problems: she would spend several weeks in detox, going to Alcoholics Anonymous and Narcotics Anonymous meetings, then, right after discharge, would return to drinking, drugs, and self-injury. Each time she was going through the motions; the programs had little or no impact.

This is not to say that Jane didn't want to get better. She desperately wanted to recover, but lacked the tools, the ability, the language, the expression, and the treatment team to solve her manifold problems. As her difficulties worsened, Jane became severely depressed and suicidal.

At this point her doctors pursued a different treatment strategy. They tried to alleviate her depression through drugs and electric shock treatments. These measures did not seem to help, and her self-injury persisted inside and outside the hospital. The medical professionals assigned to help Jane seemed frightened of her, she told us. Their medications "turned me into a zombie," she said. She was supervised around the clock, but grew aggressive and resisted their help. After

Jane ran away from several hospitals, doctors in one mental health unit ordered that she be placed in four-point restraints—wrists and ankles cuffed to her bed—to manage her out-of-control self-destruction. Ultimately, she was committed to a state hospital for over a year.

Jane found out about S.A.F.E. through a magazine article; before then she and her therapist had not heard of a program specifically addressing the problem of self-injury. Like many of our patients, previous treatment programs had tackled only one problem—like substance abuse or an eating disorder—but not the entirety of the problems, or the emotional roots of them. In such programs the patient can often gain some mastery over the initial symptom, but finds that other forms of self-injury increase. In effect, they substitute one form of self-injury for another.

When Jane arrived in such terrible shape, we questioned if she would be able to handle the intensity of our treatment program. We were not sure, given how chronic her self-abuse was, if she would be able to follow the terms of the No-Harm Contract. But once Jane reached a stable condition, she told us that she was determined to follow our program to the letter. Like most patients, she told us we were her last hope. (What we did not know was that Jane had a suicide plan in place if our program failed her.)

To our surprise, Jane took very gravely her responsibility for signing and abiding by the No-Harm Contract. Unlike many patients, she did not joke around about our rules, which include a stipulation that patients cannot discuss the ways in which they injure themselves.

Even so, Jane took a while to come out of her shell. Her level of fear was extraordinary, her dependence on self-injury practically unparalleled. She had *always* used cutting and burning to regulate her feelings and distract herself from uncomfortable emotions. When she felt empty, she hurt herself to feel alive, and when she felt overwhelmed with emotions, she hurt herself to feel numb. She called self-injury her best friend and had no idea how to have relationships with people. Self-injury had always regulated her contact with others. When she injured, she was able to draw people close enough to help her, but she also kept them at a distance.

Some part of Jane wanted people to fear her. Before arriving at S.A.F.E, she cut her hair short and dyed it in a punk style to try to look tough, unapproachable, unfeminine. In reality, of course, Jane, like every other human being, wanted people to love and accept her. But unlike healthy people, Jane was completely unable to express this or find ways to bring it about.

At first Jane was afraid to leave her room and spent many hours tossing and turning on her bed. She was tormented by thoughts of suicide and self-injury. "My daily life is a battle—I am at war with myself," she wrote in her diary at the time.

Coupled with these problems, Jane had a hard time reaching out, both to peers and staff members. She felt profound guilt, self-hatred, and shame. She believed she had screwed up her life, and she was responsible both for taking the blame and for fixing it. She did not feel worthy of human contact. She did not open mail from friends and family and did not take time for herself in group therapy. Jane could not tolerate facing herself, her history, or her feelings. She felt continuously out of control and had voluntarily given up her security blanket for dealing with such emotions—self-injury.

Because she could not rely on her time-honored friend, she gradually realized she would have to reach out. Slowly, very slowly, she developed some trust with her treatment team and began talking about her life. For the first time Jane began facing her father's death, her childhood abuse, and the toll that so many years of substance abuse and self-injury had taken on her. It became clear that Jane had never addressed these underlying issues before, even though she had been in the mental health system for nearly ten years.

Heavy grief accompanied her memories, and Jane often felt immobilized by the intensity of her feelings. She had never spoken to her family about the abuse or about her own behavior and began experiencing the feelings that accompanied that realization. To Jane it was a profound revelation when we helped her understand the function of her self-injury in light of her background. To Jane it was initially inconceivable that she would learn to tolerate her feelings—particularly anger and sadness—without falling back on self-injury.

In an amazing and poignant turnaround, Jane grew to trust the people around her at S.A.F.E. and to claim responsibility for herself and her actions. She gradually began to put the events of her life in perspective and to synthesize early experiences that had gone unspoken for so many years. As hokey as it may sound, Jane was able to learn the "language of feeling," and she took to it like a child who has just learned to read. Jane's world opened up. The woman who had arrived on a gurney in a blood-soaked, alcoholic coma finally emerged from her cocoon as a successful graduate of S.A.F.E.

Miraculous to say, Jane has been injury-free, alcohol-free, and drug-free for over two years since her completion of the S.A.F.E. program. She hasn't had a single lapse. Jane attended a partial-day outpatient program for several months, then came to need a less intense level of care. She got a job as a consultant to a local business, opened her own checking account, and began socializing with friends outside the world of psychiatric hospitals.

Most recently Jane has moved back home to New Mexico, where she is working and taking care of two cats. She sends us letters and pictures of her kittens. When Jane arrived home, she told us she was surprised to find that people she had known used to be frightened of the purple-haired woman who lived so hard and seemed so unapproachable. "Isn't that what you wanted back then?" we reminded her. "Yes," Jane said reluctantly. "But I can't for the life of me remember why."

LESSONS

While the severity of Jane's case may seem extreme, in many ways she is typical of the patients we see at S.A.F.E. and of self-injurers in general. For example:

- Her self-injury began in response to neglect and abuse.
- She maintained the behavior as a way to regulate uncomfortable feelings.
- The mental health care system misunderstood her problems and was unable to offer effective treatment.

Jane's story and others show how self-injury is an adaptive response to trauma, and how a holistic approach to treatment—focusing on the underlying issues and self-responsibility—can prompt people who self-injure to recover.

Even more meaningful were the lessons Jane taught us about the resilience of the human spirit. She could have plodded methodically through our multi-step recovery plan, half convinced she would get better simply by playing the game by the rules. Instead, Jane poured her body and soul into the S.A.F.E. program, diving into the assignments because they were important to her and not because someone told her she had to do them. In the end, the last person we ever expected to graduate from S.A.F.E. became our model alumna.

We can't predict who will become a self-injurer; nor can we predict which self-injurers will make full recoveries. There seems to be a wild card in the healing process, one that galvanizes a person's soul and her survival instincts. Jane found the courage to pick up this card, and so have many others. You can do it too.

A CLOSING MESSAGE FOR SELF-INJURERS

E veryone who has ever self-injured and stopped is eager to pass the message along about how this soul-destroying behavior can be overcome. Our patients' message is that the road to recovery is bumpy indeed, but is the best journey they ever took.

There is nothing mystifying about the healing process—it is an attainable goal.

At S.A.F.E. Alternatives we maintain a large, ongoing diary that we call "the green book." Graduates of our program write letters in the book, and newcomers peruse the pages for hope and inspiration. The entries are comfortingly repetitive. People describe the unyielding agony they felt on arrival, the gradual warming process as they became more trusting, and the boundless feeling of relief when they finally sensed that controlling self-injury was within their grasp.

"There is hope, healing, and life after S.A.F.E.!" wrote Eileen, a formerly suicidal patient who arrived at the program full of hate and mistrust. The weeks she spent with us were "the best thing I ever did for my healing process.

"I learned how to express my anger appropriately," Eileen wrote. "I realized, with everyone's help, that my anger was a result of my fears and hurts, rooted in a life of abuse, and that the anger I had bottled up, stuffed, or took out on myself physically was a symptom and not the root.

"The biggest thing I learned was how to identify my 'cycle' and 'triggers.' It was toward the end of my stay at S.A.F.E. Alternatives that this identification even began to happen, and I couldn't even identify it at first."

Eileen wrote to us two months after leaving the S.A.F.E. program. "My first week home was horrible," she reported. "All my buttons got pushed, triggers triggered, and cycles all over the place. However, day eight got better, day eleven even better, and so on. All that I had learned and was applying from S.A.F.E. really worked!

"Sure, I've been up and down these past two months, but the ups are getting longer and better. I can even say now that I am happy and content for the first time in many years."

Alison, who is thirty and had been injuring herself for fourteen years, wrote a particularly inspiring essay for our green book. Alison had been hospitalized more than twenty times between ages twenty-five and thirty.

"Every time I went into the hospital, my plan was that somebody was going to take this hell away from me, and nobody ever did," she wrote. "Now I know what the problem was. No one took away my hell because no one could but me. So I come to S.A.F.E. and they say, 'You do it. I will help you, I will guide you, I will teach you, but you are the one who has to do the work if you are ever to get better. I did the work, and I *did* get better."

Alison had been home for only three days when she wrote her letter for the green book, and she still wasn't sure what the future held. "I cannot say that I will never drink or cut again—I don't know that to be true," she wrote. "What I can say is that I feel stronger, I feel more in control, and I feel better about myself. I worked damned hard to get where I am, and that is why I am as strong as I am. I am proud of that fact."

Alison included her address and phone number at the end of her essay and encouraged other patients to get in touch with her. "I don't wish you luck," she wrote. "I wish you the courage to heal."

Appendix

S.A.F.E. ALTERNATIVES
NO-HARM CONTRACT
FOR INPATIENTS

As a candidate for the S.A.F.E. Alternatives program, I recognize that self-injury interferes with all aspects of my life. I am committed to treatment of my problem and to stopping all self-injurious behavior. I am aware of and agree to the following guidelines for my treatment:

1. No self-damaging or property-damaging behavior throughout my hospital stay. Failure to comply may lead to dismissal from the S.A.F.E. Alternatives program.
2. If I have a concurrent eating disorder, I agree to follow treatment recommendations to address this problem. I understand that failing to comply may lead to dismissal from the S.A.F.E. Alternatives program.
3. Sexual contact with others, physical threats, assaultive behavior, stealing, use of nonprescribed drugs, or use of alcohol may lead to dismissal from the S.A.F.E. Alternatives program.
4. Elopement will automatically lead to discharge from the S.A.F.E. Alternatives program.

(Patient signature and date)
(Witness signature and date)

S.A.F.E. ALTERNATIVES NO-HARM
CONTRACT FOR OUTPATIENTS

1. Members will make a six-week commitment to attend S.A.F.E.
2. Group members must call another member if unable to attend a meeting.
3. If a member misses more than two groups (other than for an emergency), she will drop out until the next six-week period.
4. No member is to talk about specific acting-out incidents (for instance, "Last night I cut myself" or "I burned myself").
5. Each member shall have a strong desire to stop acting out.
6. No calling up members and saying, "I want to kill myself." If a member thinks she is suicidal, she should call her therapist or a crisis hotline.
7. No drinking or drugs before group. Any member who breaks this rule will leave the group immediately and shall not return until the next six-week period.
8. If any member has a drinking or drug problem, members are recommended to seek help through Alcoholics Anonymous, Narcotics Anonymous, or other appropriate treatment.
9. No member will physically harm herself during group time. If any member does so, she will drop out until the next six-week period.
10. No member will physically or verbally threaten anyone in the group. If any member does so, she will drop out until the next six-week period.
11. Members are responsible for their thoughts, actions, and feelings.
12. Members shall speak using "I" statements.
13. Group shall start and end on time. If any member is late more than twice, she will drop out until the next six-week period.
14. What is said in group and who is seen in group shall remain confidential. Members may share their experience and only their experience with other nonmembers (e.g., friends, family, and therapists).

I as a member of S.A.F.E. agree to follow these guidelines. I am also aware of the consequences of not adhering to these guidelines.

(Patient signature and date)

(Witness signature and date)

S.A.F.E. ALTERNATIVES
IMPULSE CONTROL LOG

Acting Out/Self-Injury: Thoughts e.g., cutting, running away	Time and Date e.g., 9:00 p.m. 6/3/96	Location e.g., bedroom	Situation e.g., I was by myself, thinking about getting better	Feeling e.g., scared	What Would Self-Injury Accomplish? e.g., more scars and discharge from program

S.A.F.E. ALTERNATIVES
IMPULSE CONTROL LOG

What Would I Be Trying to Communicate with My Self-Injury? e.g., I'm scared, and I need attention.	Outcome e.g., Used my five alternatives. Confronted my distorted thoughts. Challenged my thoughts.	Comments e.g., I noticed a decrease in my desire to act out.

RESOURCES

If you would like to contact the S.A.F.E. Alternatives Program for additional information,

call 1-800-DON'T CUT.
Or write to:
S.A.F.E. Alternatives L.L.C.
7115 West North Avenue, Suite 319
Oak Park, IL 60302

Or visit our web site at www.selfinjury.com.

You may also order our audiotape for professionals: *Understanding and Treating the Self-Injurious Patient: A Guide to Assessment and Intervention Strategies*, by Karen M. Latza, Ph.D., Karen Conterio, and Wendy Lader, Ph.D. The tapes are $29.95 and may be ordered by writing to the address above.

BIBLIOGRAPHY

Articles in Scholarly Publications

American Psychiatric Association. *Managed Care: A report of the council on medical service and the council on long-range planning and development,* December 1991.

Bleiberg, E. "Adolescence, sense of self, and narcissistic vulnerability." *Bulletin of the Menninger Clinic,* 52, 211–228, 1988.

Carroll, J., C. Schaffer, J. Spensley, and S. Abramowitz. "Family experiences of self-mutilating patients." *American Journal of Psychiatry,* 137(7), 852–853, 1991.

Chowanec, D., A. Josephson, C. Coleman, and H. Davis. "Self-harming behavior in incarcerated male delinquent adolescents." *Journal of the American Academy of Child and Adolescent Psychiatry,* 30, 2, 202–207, 1991.

Cross, L. "Body and self in feminine psychology: Implications for delicate self-mutilation and the eating disorders." *MSPP News* (The Newsletter of the Michigan Society for Psychoanalytic Psychology), February, vol. 6 (1), 1996.

Doctors, S. "The symptom of delicate self-cutting in adolescent females: A developmental view." *Adolescent Psychiatry,* 9, 443–460, 1981.

Favazza, A. and K. Conterio. "Female habitual self-mutilators." *Acta Psychiatrica Scandinavia*, 79, 3, 283–289, 1988.

———. "The plight of chronic self-mutilators." *Community Mental Health Journal*, 24, 22–30, 1988.

Favazza, A., L. DeRosear, and K. Conterio. "Self-mutilation and eating disorders." *Suicide and Life-threatening Behaviors*, 19, 352–361, 1989.

Gardner, D. and R. Cowdry. "Alprazolam-induced dyscontrol in borderline personality disorder." *American Journal of Psychiatry*. 142, 98–100, 1985.

Glover, H., W. Lader, J. W. O'Keefe, and P. Goodnick. "Numbing scores in female psychiatric inpatients diagnosed with self-injurious behavior, dissociative identity disorder, and major depression." *Psychiatry Research*, 70, 115–123, 1997.

Kaplan, S. and E. Fik. "Male wrist cutters: Coarse and delicate." *Military Medicine*, 142, 942–945, 1977.

Latza, K. "The Savage Embrace: Reflections on the Inner Life of the Self-Injurious Patient." Unpublished manuscript, 1996.

Menninger, K. "A psychoanalytic study of the significance of self-mutilation." *Psychoanalytic Quarterly*, 4, 408–466, 1935.

Pattison, E. M. and J. Kahan. "The deliberate self-harm syndrome." *American Journal of Psychiatry*, 140, 867–872, 1983.

Richardson, S. and W. Zaleski. "Endogenous opiates and self-mutilation." *American Journal of Psychiatry*, 743, 938–939, 1986.

van der Kolk, B. A. "The trauma spectrum: The interaction of biological and social events in the genesis of the trauma response. *Journal of Traumatic Stress*. 1, 273–290, 1988.

van der Kolk, B. A., M. S. Greenberg, S. P. Orr, and R. K. Pittman. "Endogenous opiods and stress induced analgesia in posttraumatic stress disorder." *Psychopharmacology Bulletin*, 25, 108–119, 1989.

van der Kolk, B. A., J. C. Perry, and J. L. Herman. "Childhood origins of self-destructive behavior. *American Journal of Psychiatry*, 148, 1665–1671, 1991.

Winchel, R. and M. Stanley. "A review of the behavior and biology of self-mutilation." *American Journal of Psychiatry*, 148, 306–317, 1991.

Articles in the Popular Press

Spragins, E. "Shortchanging the Psyche: Will Your HMO Be There If You Need Therapy?" *Newsweek*, August 25, 1997.

Schappell, E. "The Unkindest Cuts." *Allure*, August 1995.
Todd, A. "Razor's Edge." *Seventeen*, June 1996.
Pedersen, S. "Girls Who Hurt (Themselves)." *Sassy*, June 1996.
Egan, J. "Cutting." *New York Times Magazine*, July 27, 1997.

Books

Ackerman, T. *The Scarred Soul: Understanding and Ending Self-Inflicted Violence*. Oakland, CA.: New Harbinger, 1997.
American Psychiatric Association. *Diagnostic and Statistical Manual of Mental Disorders*, 4th ed. Washington, D.C.: 1994.
Brumberg, Joan Jacobs. *The Body Project: An Intimate History of American Girls*. New York: Random House, 1997.
Favazza, Armando. *Bodies Under Siege*, 2nd ed. Baltimore: Johns Hopkins Press, 1996.
Grosz, E. *Volatile Bodies*. Bloomington: Indiana University Press, 1994.
Kaplan, L. J. *Female Perversions*. New York: Doubleday, 1991.
Kroll, J. *The Challenge of the Borderline Patient: Competency in Diagnosis and Treatment*. New York: W.W. Norton, 1988.
Latza, K., K. Conterio, and W. Lader. *Understanding and Treating the Self-Injurious Patient: An Audiotape for Professionals* (110 minutes), 1996. Published by SAFE Alternatives, 7115 W. North Ave., Suite 319, Oak Park, IL 60302.
Menninger, Karl. *Man Against Himself*. New York: Harcourt Brace, 1938.
Miller, D. *Women Who Hurt Themselves: A Book of Hope and Understanding*. New York: Basic Books, 1994.
Pipher, M. *Reviving Ophelia: Saving the Selves of Adolescent Girls*. New York: Ballantine, 1994.
Shengold, L. *Soul Murder: The Effects of Childhood Abuse and Deprivation*. New York: Ballantine, 1989.
van der Kolk, B. A. *Psychological Trauma*. Washington, D.C.: American Psychiatric Press, 1987.
Wakefield, H. and R. Underwager. *Return of the Furies: An Investigation into Recovered Memory Therapy*. Chicago: Open Court, 1994.
Walsh, B. W. and P. M. Rosen. *Self-Mutilation: Theory, Research, and Treatment*. New York: Guilford Press, 1988.
Zimberg, Wallace and Blume. *Practical Approaches to Alcoholism Psychotherapy*. New York: Plenum, 1987.

ACKNOWLEDGMENTS

Just as the S.A.F.E. Alternatives program embodies a philosophy of teamwork aimed at healing, this book has been a team effort, involving many talented and generous individuals.

Our deep thanks are extended to Jennifer Kingson Bloom for her tireless efforts at compiling this manuscript, for bringing it to life with her stylistic and creative input, and for her astounding speed and efficiency in doing so. We are also grateful to Laurie Abkemeier, former senior editor of Hyperion, who provided the original impetus for the book, encouraging us to take on the project. Her editorial skill was superb, and in addition to her help, we had the enthusiastic and talented Hyperion staff—including Tracey George, Jennifer Landers, Martha K. Levin, Mary Ellen O'Neill, David Lott, Anne Cole, Kim Fine, Leslie Cohen, and Laurie Rippon—to promote the final work. We also owe our tremendous thanks to Elyse Cheney of Sanford J. Greenburger Associates, our agent, for her skilled management of the project, and her support and guidance through our relationship with her. And thanks to her assistant, Kyung Cho.

We are also enormously thankful to Dr. Karen Latza, former assistant director of S.A.F.E. and our longtime consultant, for her extensive contributions to the text, particularly in the chapters that focused on early life development, trauma issues, gender issues, and the dynamic meanings of self-injury. She was involved in every step of the writing, adding depth and dimension to our thoughts, and she kept us moving when inertia threatened to settle in.

We are also endlessly grateful to our staff at S.A.F.E. Alternatives, the professionals who form the backbone of the program and who have been patient, tolerant, and encouraging during the labor of writing this book, and who also contributed their ideas and gifts either directly or indirectly through their everyday work. Many thanks to Dr. Janelle Hart and Program Director Jerilyn Robinson for their contributions of case material and treatment experiences. The rest of the S.A.F.E. team includes Drs. Maleeha Ahsan, Maureen Ford, Ann Kaplan, Paula Machtinger, Dale Monroe-Cook and Niquie Dworkin; social worker Carrie Torgenson; Paulette Pasquale, R.N.; and Jean Kulander, who manages our office and our everyday lives.

We also thank Catherine Blount, who contributed an excerpt of her extraordinary poetry, for taking the time to dialogue early in the project and help develop the book's title. Also thanks to a friend of Karen Conterio's, Catherine O'Connell, herself a published author, who helped educate us in the ways of the publishing world, for which we are very appreciative. Another thanks for our friend and our professional photographer for the book, Kenji Kerins; without him we would have taken a chance in a photo booth.

We also owe a debt to the historical places and figures in S.A.F.E.'s genesis and development: to Hartgrove Hospital in Chicago and Dr. Alan Showalter for providing S.A.F.E. with its first home base from 1985 to 1995; Dr. Armando Favazza for the opportunity to publish collaborative research on self-injury, for his friendship, and for his ongoing commitment to helping self-injurers find quality treatment. Currently, we are grateful to the administration of MacNeal Hospital in Berwyn, Illinois, for providing S.A.F.E.'s flagship location in the Midwest.

Loving thanks are given to some of our personal allies in this journey: to Wendy Lader's husband, Michael, and to her parents, Jerome & Shirley Friedman, for their unconditional love and support. Loving thanks to Karen Conterio's mom, Virginia Johnson, for her enthusiasm throughout this project. Thanks also to Lolly Dominski, Deb Zwick, Lucy Freund, Mary Jo and Pete Jacobs, and the ladies of LeClaire. Jennifer Kingson Bloom would like to thank her family: Jack and Valerie Bloom and Nancy and Charles Kingson.

Finally, our thanks to the patients who courageously contributed their stories, providing encouragement and hope to the readers of the book.

INDEX

ABOUT THE AUTHORS

Karen Conterio is the Administrative Director of S.A.F.E. (Self-Abuse Finally Ends) Alternatives™. The program was founded by Conterio in 1984 as the first outpatient support group for those who engage in repetitive self-harm behavior. In 1985, Ms. Conterio teamed with Wendy Lader, Ph.D., to offer the first structured inpatient program for deliberate self-harm behavior. Ms. Conterio trained as an alcohol and addictions counselor and is a certified group facilitator. She lives in Chicago.

Wendy Lader, Ph.D., is Clinical Director of the S.A.F.E. Alternatives Program. Dr. Lader also serves as a consultant to the Women's Services at the Loop YWCA in Chicago. Previously, Dr. Lader was the Director of the Girls' Program at Mercy Hospital & Medical Center and the Women's Program at Hartgrove Hospital in Chicago. Wendy Lader earned her Ph.D. in Clinical Psychology and M.S. in Behavioral Sciences at Nova University in Florida and M.Ed. in Special Education at Lesley College in Massachusetts. She lives in Chicago.

Jennifer Kingson Bloom is a former reporter for *The New York Times* and *The Boston Globe*, and is currently an editor at *The American Banker*, a daily business newspaper.